Italian and Italian American Studies

Stanislao G. Pugliese
Hofstra University
Series Editor

This publishing initiative seeks to bring the latest scholarship in Italian and Italian American history, literature, cinema, and cultural studies to a large audience of specialists, general readers, and students. I&IAS will feature works on modern Italy (Renaissance to the present) and Italian American culture and society by established scholars as well as new voices in the academy. This endeavor will help to shape the evolving fields of Italian and Italian American Studies by re-emphasizing the connection between the two. The following esteemed senior scholars of the editorial board are advisors to the series editor.

D0173509

A New Guide to Italian Cinema

Carlo Celli
and
Marga Cottino-Jones

palgrave
macmillan

A NEW GUIDE TO ITALIAN CINEMA
© Carlo Celli and Marga Cottino-Jones, 2007.

First published in 2007 by
PALGRAVE MACMILLAN™
175 Fifth Avenue, New York, N.Y. 10010 and
Houndmills, Basingstoke, Hampshire, England RG21 6XS
Companies and representatives throughout the world.

PALGRAVE MACMILLAN is the global academic imprint of the Palgrave Macmillan division of St. Martin's Press, LLC and of Palgrave Macmillan Ltd. Macmillan® is a registered trademark in the United States, United Kingdom and other countries. Palgrave is a registered trademark in the European Union and other countries.

ISBN-13: 978–1–4039–7560–7 (hardcover)
ISBN-10: 1–4039–7560–4 (hardcover)
ISBN-13: 978–1–4039–7565–2 (paperback)
ISBN-10: 1–4039–7565–5 (paperback)

Library of Congress Cataloging-in-Publication Data

Celli, Carlo, 1963–
    A new guide to Italian cinema / Carlo Celli and Marga Cottino-Jones.
        p. cm.
    Includes bibliographical references and index.
    ISBN 1–4039–7560–4 (alk. paper)—ISBN 1–4039–7565–5 (alk. paper)
    1. Motion pictures—Italy—History. I. Cottino-Jones, Marga. II. Title.

PN1993.5.I88C45 2006
791.430945—dc22   2006044820

A catalogue record for this book is available from the British Library.

Design by Newgen Imaging Systems (P) Ltd., Chennai, India.

First edition: January 2007

10 9 8 7 6 5 4 3 2 1

Printed in the United States of America.

Transferred to digital printing in 2007.

"Lorenzo was a man; his humanity was pure and uncontaminated, he was outside this world of negation. Thanks to Lorenzo, I managed not to forget that I myself was a man."

—Primo Levi

Contents

Preface and Acknowledgements

The title of this book, *A New Guide to Italian Cinema*, refers to the earlier editions by Marga Cottino-Jones of *A Student's Guide to Italian Film* (1983, 1993) of which the present volume is a complete revision. The earlier editions focused on directors who gained international recognition during the years of the post–Wold War II Italian neorealist school and continued to bring the Italian cinema renown in later decades. This guide to the Italian cinema with Carlo Celli retains earlier editions' interest in renowned films and directors but is also attentive to popular cinema, the films that actually achieved box office success among the Italian public. In addition to contributions to art and avant garde cinema, the Italian cinema has been profoundly tied to the reaction and the support of its public. Like previous editions, this edition is based on the premise that film is an art form that is very closely related to everyday reality. Consequently, the appreciation of Italian film is greatly enhanced by a basic knowledge of Italy's political, economic, and cultural history. This volume introduces the Italian cinema not just as a twentieth-century phenomenon but as an expression of the deeper roots of Italy's historic, cultural, and literary past. Any study of Italy or Italian culture should also make an effort to include some introduction to the wealth of Italy's contribution to world artistic culture. Thus this guide begins with summary information on the period predating the cinema. Given the unparalleled Italian tradition in the visual arts and the breath of the Italian artistic tradition, it should come as no surprise that Italy has also contributed mightily to the cinema. Despite working within the constraints of cultural and political realities that have dominated Italian life in the twentieth century, the Italian cinema has provided a forum for expression in a manner that has not only reflected the times but even anticipated them. Chapters offer a historical timeline and commentary on political and cultural events and trends, followed by discussion of the state of the Italian cinema industry and presentations of key films. Appendices offer a short introduction to film study with a focus on Italy, statistical data of Italian box office history, and short biographies and selected filmographies of important Italian directors. The aim of the book is to provide the cinephile, student, teacher, or fan with a guide where points of interest may be intentified and studied with clarity. In each chapter the titles of films are given initially both in Italian and English and in most cases in English thereafter. In the text and director filmographies in the appendices, titles of films not distributed in English-speaking countries and without ready literal translations are given in Italian. Only Italian titles are given in box office lists in the appendices.

We should like to express our thanks to colleagues and students at Bowling Green State University and UCLA whose encouragement, criticism, and collaboration have helped us to bring this *New Guide* to completion. We hope that this guide will be useful and worthy of criticism and that our students and colleagues will share suggestions for improvements. For kind aid in the acquisition of photos and permissions and such we would like to thank Roberto Benigni, Giorgio Bertellini, Grace Bullaro, Andrea Ceccarelli, Giovanni Cobolli-Gigli and Fabbri Editore, Joseph Francese, Ben Lawton, Maurizio Nichetti, Franco Ricci, Stacey Salling of the University of Texas Press, Antonio Vitti, Monica Vitti. Further thanks to Silvio Alovisio at the library of the Museo Nazionale del Cinema at Turin, Stefano Losurdo at the Biblioteca AGIS in Milan, Gioacchino Balducci, Stanislao G. Pugliese, the editors of the Italian and Italian American Studies Series, Farideh Koohi-Kamali and Julia Cohen, Erin Ivy, Maran Elancheran at Palgrave MacMillan, and Howard Mandelbaum at Photofest.

Remote History*

1400 BC	First Greek incursions into Italian peninsula
800	Beginning of *Magna Grecia* (Greater Greece) settlement in southern Italy
753	Foundation of Rome
509	Roman Republic
264–241	First Punic War
218–202	Second Punic War
149–146	Destruction of Carthage
73–71	Spartacus slave revolt
50	Caesar crosses the Rubicon river
AD 285	Separation between western and eastern Roman empire
313	Contantine accepts Christianity
410	Sack of Rome by Visigoths
476	Last Roman emperor (in Rome) deposed
568–774	Lombard invasion and rule
800	Charlemagne (king of Franks) crowned emperor of Rome by Pope Leo III
827	Arab invasion of Sicily
	Early to late 1000s Beginning of Norman (Scandinavian) conquest of Sicily and southern Italy from Arabs
1190	Hohenstaufen (German) of the Holy Roman Empire gain control of southern Italy
late 1100s–1300s	Period of Independent Communes (city states) leading to conflict between Guelphs (supporters of the Pope) versus Ghibellines (imperial supporters)
1182–1226	St. Francis of Assisi
1265–1321	Dante Alighieri author of *The Divine Comedy*
1298	Marco Polo returns from Orient to Venice
1304–74	Francesco Petrarca, poet
1348	Bubonic plague
1313–75	Giovanni Boccaccio author of *Decameron*
1452–1519	Leonardo Da Vinci
1454	Peace of Lodi, Italian league of city states
1469–1527	Niccolò Machiavelli, author of *The Prince* (1513)
Late 1400s	Turkish incursions against Venice
1475–1564	Michelangelo Buonarroti

1494–1559	Italian Wars (1494–1559) between France (Valois monarchy) and Austria/Spain (Hapsburg monarchy) for control of Italy
1527	Sack of Rome by Charles V Hispanic/ Hapsburg Imperial forces
1564–1642	Galileo Galilei
1571	Battle of Lepanto, Venetian navy and Allies defeat fleet of Ottoman Empire (Turkey)
1618–48	Thirty Years War
1707–93	Carlo Goldoni, playwright
1720	Piedmontese monarchy (Turin) gains Sardinia
1785–1873	Alessandro Manzoni author of *The Betrothed*
1797	Peace of Campoformio—Venice ceded to Austria by Napoleon— end of Venetian Republic
1814–15	Fall of Napoleon, Congress of Vienna, Bourbon rule restored in southern Italy, Austrian rule in northeastern Italy
1848	Nationalist revolts in Italy and throughout Europe

The word Italia (Italy) is not identifiable with a single invader or ethnic group as is the case with most countries in Europe. In Italy such geographical identification is at the regional level such as Lombardy (the region of the Germanic Lombard tribe that invaded northern Italy in the Middle Ages), Tuscany (around the lands of Etruria—the ancient Etruscans), or Lazio (the lands of the ancient Latins around Rome). Italy's geographical position in the middle of the Mediterranean Sea has made the peninsula a cross roads for numerous invaders, who not only changed political realities, but also brought cultural, linguistic, and artistic influences. The first Italic peoples to inhabit the peninsula developed a local culture until the appearance of Greek traders, who eventually established southern Italy and Sicily as Magna Grecia (Greater Greece), an extension of the ancient Greek city states. In fact many of the classical figures such as Pythagoras or Archimedes lived in Greek settlements in Sicily. The arrival of the Greeks would be the first in a long series of foreign influences that formed Italian culture and history. At one time or another, parts of Italy were controlled by the Greeks, the mysterious Etruscans, Germanic tribes, Scandinavians (Vikings), Moslem Arabs, as well as consolidated monarchies of France, Spain, and Austria in the early modern era. The latest military invasion and establishment of foreign hegemony was by the United States and its allies, which defeated the Italian fascist regime and expelled Nazi German troops from the peninsula during World War II. The position of Italy as a cross roads of the Mediterranean has continued to the present day with the influx of North African and worldwide immigration.

To the question of why Italy has historically been overrun by foreign invaders since Roman times, the short answer is that the geographical and political makeup of the country did not facilitate the establishment of a central power base. No Italian city after Rome during its republican and imperial period was able to enforce language and rule over the regional centers, not even Rome itself, which was under sporadic Papal control during the early Middle Ages. Italy's political makeup consisted of a conglomeration of city states fighting for supremacy and calling in extra peninsular powers for aid, thus destroying any chance for a central peninsular government. Actually the lack of central power enhanced the vitality of Italy's regional centers such as Florence, Genoa, Milan, Naples, Turin, or Venice, fostering an artistic and cultural legacy unique in the world.

The Italian cinema has a curious relationship with Italy's more distant past. Stories set in Greek or Roman times have been afforded their own genre, the peplum, connoting a separation from the cultural identity of contemporary Italy. The Italian's cinema's relationship with its pre-nineteenth-century history has included relatively continuous biopics about subjects in Italian Renaissance and Medieval history such as the personal dramas of Beatrice Cenci, Lucrezia Borgia, the Medici dynasty, artists such as Caravaggio, military figures like Giuseppe Garibaldi and Giovanni dalle Bande Nere, figures important to the country's Catholic culture including St. Anthony or St. Francis and finally musical biopics about operatic composers such as Giuseppe Verdi. But given the abundance of figures in Italian artistic heritage it is noteworthy that the Italian cinema has not developed a wider tradition in the biopic genre. Films depicting the lives of Italian composers were a staple of Italian production from the late 1930s into the 1950s, but the life stories of many of the artists and writers listed below such as Machiavelli, Dante, or even Raphael have not been a frequent subject for Italian film directors.

The Realist Tradition

In broad terms, "realism" in the arts means an effort to precisely imitate external and historical experience, to make empirical observations, and to follow the laws of probability. This description applies as well to the Greek poet Homer as to the Italian film director Vittorio De Sica (1901–74). This trend in art is as ancient as Aristotle who wrote as early as 335 BC about how art imitates life. In the Medieval period, Dante Alighieri's (1265–1321) *Divine Comedy* represented human actions in actual historical situations. Giovanni Boccaccio's (1313–75) *Decameron* offered a multifaceted representation of real life in a comic mood. The Renaissance treatises by writers such as Niccolò Machiavelli (1469–1527) with *The Prince*, Baldassarre Castiglione (1478–1529) with *The Courtier*, and Francesco Guicciardini (1483–1540) with his *History of Italy* attempted to interpret and represent the nature of the reality they experienced. The scientific observations by Galileo Galilei (1564–1642) or the observations on human interaction by Cesare Beccaria (1738–94) also developed in this tradition.

The realist and mimetic tradition in Italian visual arts is among the strongest in the world. The Western tradition in realist painting developed from the frescoes of Giotto (1267–1337), Cimabue (1240–1302), or Piero della Francesca (1415–92) and culminated during the Renaissance in the paintings of Leonardo da Vinci (1452–1519), Michelangelo Buonarroti (1475–1564), Raffaello Sanzio (1483–1520), Tiziano Vecellio (Titian) (1485–1576), Tintoretto (1518–94), to name only a few. This rich tradition was continued by Baroque-era painters such as Antonio Merisi a.k.a. Caravaggio (1571–1610) and neoclassicists such as Tiepolo (1696–1770) and the sculptor Antonio Canova (1758–1822), among many, many others. In fact the Italian patrimony in the visual arts is so rich that many regions are often overlooked by historians who tend to concentrate on the *città d'arte* (the cities of art) Rome, Florence, and Venice.

Credit for the invention of perspective has often been attributed to the Florentine architect Filippo Brunelleschi (1377–1446). Precursors of photography, the *camera obscura* (dark chamber) and *camera ottica* (optical chamber), were used by the architect Leon Battista Alberti (1404–72) and later for the vistas of Venice painted by Canaletto (1697–1768). The stylistic frameworks for the division of subjects between portrait, still life, and landscape were explored in the Italian artistic schools of the Renaissance and Baroque are evident in the basic shot selection and visual codes of the cinema. The development of silver back mirrors at the Murano glasswork factories of the Venetian Republic allowed humans to examine themselves in a realistic, reflective manner.

Italian developments in architecture came in the rediscovery of classical forms through the work of Renaissance architects such as Alberti, Filippo Brunelleschi, Andrea Palladio (1508–80). Italian influence in music has also been immense including the nineteenth-century operatic tradition of librettists such as Lorenzo Da Ponte (1749–1838) who penned operas with Mozart and composers such as Gioacchino Rossini (1792–1868), Gaetano Donizetti (1797–1848), Giuseppe Verdi (1813–1901), and Giacomo Puccini (1858–1924) to the point that Italian became an international language of musical scoring.

Perhaps due to the realist, iconographic tradition of the Renaissance and the Baroque eras, the more abstract and expressionistic developments in modernism, existentialism, and surrealism never found fertile ground in Italy as they did in France, for example. Of course there have been Italian artists who have contributed to the modernist schools of visual arts, such as the surrealist Giorgio De Chirico (1888–1978), the futurist Umberto Boccioni (1882–1916), or the sculptor Amedeo Modigliani (1884–1920). But their contributions have not been as decisive or influential in world culture as were the centuries old Italian prominence in the realist style. This realist tradition would also be the high moment of the Italian cinema in the early postwar period with the style of Italian neorealism.

To study the cinema as an art form based on realism, which is reflective of the society and culture that produced it, is somewhat of a departure from current approaches in academic Film Study. The tradition of mimesis and realism, or reflectivity between art and culture, has been overshadowed by contemporary theoretical paradigms. For example, psychoanalytically based criticism concentrates on the manner in which conscious and unconscious mental processes appear in art. Marxist theories read art in terms of economic and class issues. Close textual readings/semiology seek to understand works by the way in which they transmit signs and codes of the culture from which they emanate. Feminist criticism seeks to read a work through the perspective of gender and societal hierarchical relationships.[1] Yet the realist tradition remains a foundation of the Italian artistic and cultural experience.[2] Even a director such as Federico Fellini, who would gain renown for his ability to create the sort of fantastic dream world of special effects expected of the cinema, was trained during the heyday of Italian neorealism with roots in a basic realist style of filmmaking.

I

Italy from Unification to World War I

1860   Giuseppe Garibaldi leads the *Spedizione dei Mille* (expedition of the thousand) Sicily. Much of southern Italy is annexed by the Kingdom of Piedmont

1866   Annexation of Venice and its territory to the Kingdom of Piedmont after war with Austro-Hungary and Prussia

1870   Rome falls to Piedmontese troops—unification of Italy complete

1874   Pope Pius IX issues *non expedit* decree, forbidding Catholics to participate in elections

1876–96 *Trasformismo* Center left-wing governments

1882   Triple Alliance—Italy merges foreign policy interests with Germany and the Austro-Hungarian Empire after French occupation of Tunis

1896   Italian army defeated at the Battle of Adua, Ethiopia

1900   King Humbert I assassinated by anarchist

1905   Pius X letter *Il fermo proposito* allowing electoral participation of Catholics with bishop's permission

1909   F.T. Marinetti's *Futurist Manifesto*

1911–12 Libyan War with Turkey (Ottoman Empire) Conquest of Libya and Rhodes

1912   Male suffrage (above age 30 or military service)

1912   Benito Mussolini editor of socialist newspaper *Avanti*

1915   Italy enters WWI on the side of England, Russia, and France after gaining postwar territorial promises in the Pact of London

1917   Austrian breakthrough Italian front at Caporetto

1918   Victory over Austrian army at Vittorio Veneto end of World War I

1919   Italy granted former Austrian possessions at Versailles peace conference Fascist movement first organized

Gabriele D'Annunzio decries the *pace mutilata* (mutilated peace) over the lack of territorial concessions in Dalmatia and Istria, occupies Fiume (contemporary Rjecka)

Italy as a nation is relatively young, only achieving total unification in 1870. In fact, the country has been more often described as a geographical rather than cultural entity.[1] Politically, Italy consisted of a collection of small feudal hereditary principalities whose history dates back to the early Middle Ages. These city states remained independent until the decline of the Renaissance with tragic events including the 1527 Sack of Rome by Spanish Imperial troops of Charles V, after which most of the peninsula's city state larger principalities and republics except the Duchy of Piedmont and the Republic of Venice fell to foreign domination. Italian political life was under the influence of one indigenous and three external governmental and societal models. The south struggled under the legacies of Hispanic feudalism from Naples to Sicily. Rome and the surrounding Papal States were ruled by the pope as a Catholic theocracy as depicted in films such as *Il marchese del Grillo/The Marquis of Grillo* (1982) or *Nel nome del Papa Re/In the Name of the Pope King* (1977). The multinational Austro-Hungarian Empire ruled northeastern Italy including the cities of Milan and Trieste. The highly centralized French model influenced the development of the Kingdom of Piedmont in the northwest. French general Napoleon Bonaparte's attempt at world conquest failed in the early 1800s, bringing influences including nationalistic impulses and a challenge to the aristocratic bases of feudal society. After the defeat of Napoleon much of Italy remained under foreign control with the exception of the Kingdom of Piedmont, which retained a larger scope of political and military autonomy.

The main ideologue of the *Risorgimento* (resurgence) or unification period was the republican revolutionary Giuseppe Mazzini (1805–72), the founder of *La Giovane Italia* (Young Italy), an organization that sought to steer Italian youth to the cause of a republican and unified Italy. Mazzini attempted to return Italy to the tradition of republican government that had served the peninsula well during the Roman republic and the Renaissance with the republican governments in vibrant city states such as Venice and Florence. The present system for electing a pope is, in fact, a vestige of Italy's republican traditions.

Despite Mazzini's republican zeal, the most successful efforts to unify Italy were from the Kingdom of Piedmont under Victor Emmanuel II of Savoy (1820–78) and Camillo Cavour (1810–61), the prime minister of the Kingdom of Piedmont from 1852 until his death in 1861. Cavour was a brilliant tactician, able to play the larger continental powers in Europe (Austia, France, Prussia) against one another for the benefit of Piedmont. By 1855–56, Cavour had contracted a shaky alliance with Napoleon III of France, and had secured English acquiescence in case Piedmont was attacked by the Austro-Hungarian Empire, which controlled much of north central and northeastern Italy including the cities of Venice, Milan, and Trieste. War with Austro-Hungary broke out in April 1859. By January 1860, a unified kingdom of northern and central Italy was formed under the Piedmontese house of Savoy.

In May 1860, Giuseppe Garibaldi (1807–82) led the *Spedizione dei Mille* (The One-Thousand Expedition) to Sicily in the hope of adding southern Italy to the Piedmontese monarchy. Garibaldi was a charismatic revolutionary leader who had fought in anticolonial causes in South America and was even reportedly offered a command in the Union Army by Abraham Lincoln.[2] In May 1860 Garibaldi sailed for Sicily with assurances of nonintervention from the British fleet with 1,000 volunteers, the *mille*, wearing their famous red shirts. By June of the same year he had conquered Sicily enjoying the tacit support of segments of the population. By September the regions surrounding Naples were annexed to the Kingdom of Italy by a plebiscite vote. In October 1860 the regions of Umbria and the Marches in south central Italy also voted in favor of annexation to the Kingdom of Italy.

In March 1861, a national parliament assembled in Turin, the capital of Piedmont and of the Kingdom of Italy, proclaimed Victor Emanuel II King of Italy with a constitution based upon the Albertine Statutes with rights such as freedom of assembly and the press but in which Catholicism was established as the official state religion and government ministers served at the discretion of the monarch rather than under parliamentary control.[3] The main regions outside the jurisdiction of the new Kingdom of Italy were the Papal States surrounding Rome, and the Veneto provinces around Venice and cities such as Trieste and Fiume along the Adriatic coast still under Austro-Hungary following Napoleon's destruction of the Venetian Republic, the *Serenissima*, in 1797. Venice was annexed by Piedmont in 1866, followed by Rome only in 1870, after Garibaldi's attempts to expel the French troops protecting the pope. Films depicting the heroic aspects of the Italian unification struggle have included the first Italian film, Filoteo Alberini's *La presa di Roma 20 settembre 1870/The Taking of Rome 1870* (1905), Alessandro Blasetti's *1860* (1933), and Roberto Rossellini's *Viva l'Italia/Garibaldi* (1961).

Italian patriot Massimo D'Azeglio reportedly remarked that after having made Italy, the *Risorgimento* now had to somehow make the Italians.[4] The comment indicates the strength of regional and linguistic differences in the peninsula. The *Risorgimento* movement leading to Italian unification had actually been led by an idealistic elite and was never a true popular mass movement.[5] Films depicting resistance to unification include Florestano Vancini's *Bronte: cronaca di un massacro che i libri di storia non hanno raccontato/Liberty* (1973), which featured Leonardo Sciascia as screenwriter. Despite the romantic nationalist zeal that had swept across Europe during the nineteenth century, first in Napoleonic France and then in other countries, Italy's regional identities of dialects and cultural and artistic heritage were simply too strong to be swept away quickly. Before unification only an estimated 2.5 percent of the population was literate.[6] The linguistic differences between the numerous Italian dialects made the establishment of national culture difficult. After unification, educational reformers such as Francesco De Sanctis (1817–83) faced the monumental task of developing a national language and culture. The process would not be complete until a standardized national Italian language adapted from the works of Tuscan literary figures of the thirteenth and fouteenth centuries such as Dante and Petrarch definitively became a daily presence in Italian homes first through radio and especially through television.

Among the most vexing issues facing the newly unified nation was the status of the Vatican and the Southern Question. Despite the armed conquest of Rome and its territory in 1870, the Vatican remained under the influence of the pope, a situation exacerbated by Pope Pius IX's *non expedit* decree forbidding Catholics from participating in national politics. Fearful of possible southern separatism, the

Piedmontese government attempted to impose a centralized administration on the southern provinces that faced the difficult task of incorporating local customs and interests reinforcing suspicions that the new Italian national state was more interested in maintaining advantages for the more industrialized north than in developing the mainly agrarian south. Agrarian reforms, promised by the new national government, never materialized as economic efforts concentrated on furthering the country's progress toward industrialization. Eventually, Italy's northern rulers left the south under the control of the *latifondisti* landowners, often the descendents of Hispanic aristocrats, who maintained a feudal system.[7] The south, or *Mezzogiorno* (midday) remained economically underdeveloped and vulnerable to the social plague of organized crime. A term for the fatalistic political attitude regarding the difficulty to change Italy, *trasformismo* (transformism) was coined during the tenure of Prime Minister Agostino Depretis (1812–87), whose liberal coalition displaced the *destra storica*, right-wing coalition, which had led the country to unification. The term *trasformismo* initially used to describe the continuation by DePretis of the policies of the previous administrations has also come to describe how Italians were so used to external, foreign control that the essence of Italian political and social life was rarely altered despite outward appearances. The provinces of southern Italy in particular had been ruled from a series of distant capitals for centuries. Thus despite the fact that the new power center in Turin was in Italy, the national government led by a monarchy in Piedmont had difficulty breaking into local political reality. Many of these themes are presented in Luchino Visconti's adaptation of Tomasi di Lampedusa's novel *Il gattopardo/The Leopard* (1958).

Italian society of the late nineteenth and early twentieth centuries presented an uneasy mixture of a feudal, rural society and a rapidly expanding urban, industrial network. Other countries, such as Great Britain, had faced similar problems and avoided major political upheaval because of a tradition of parliamentary government, a large middle class that supported parliamentary democracy, and the outlet of colonies for its more adventurous or needy citizens. Italy's parliamentary tradition was not well established and its middle class relatively small, so the division between urban and rural societies was more pronounced. The cultural and political tradition of the republican governments from ancient Rome and the Renaissance city states such as Venice and Florence had been largely erased over the centuries.

As in most of Europe in the late nineteenth and early twentieth centuries, nationalism was a dominant political force in Italy and an integral part of the *Risorgimento* ideology that had unified Italy under the Piedmontese monarchy. After centuries of foreign domination and a late unification, the Italian ruling class spent the last decades of the nineteenth century yearning for international respect and prestige. Emigration was a further problem with the departure of thousands of Italians yearly, mainly to destinations in the Americas and northern Europe. The Italian government in the late nineteenth century, like its counterparts in Europe, also faced increasing demands for social justice from workers. One solution was to copy the British model of exporting potential participants in social upheaval to colonies. The desire to become a member of the colonial club became a key goal of

Italian foreign policy. After tensions following the French colonization of Tunis, Italy joined Germany and Austria in a Triple Alliance in 1882, in the hope of gaining colonial outlets. However, the results of Italy's foreign ambitions were largely unprofitable with the embarrassing defeat of an Italian army in the Horn of Africa at Adua in 1896 and other difficulties in adventures from Albania to the Greek islands. These colonial ambitions were part of a worldwide political current that had long-lasting cultural ramifications in the development of attitudes of superiority and insufferance toward colonized peoples. In Italy such attitudes were given spurious scientific legitimacy through the work of the sociologist Cesare Lombroso (1835–1909), the inventor of the concept of anthropological criminology.[8]

The political climate from unification to the turn of the century continued to be characterized by *trasformismo* or the idea that government coalitions, no matter their political persuasion, would eventually support the status quo in order to perpetuate political patronage systems. At the turn of the century, the reformist Prime Minister Giovanni Giolitti (1842–1928) attempted to increase democratization through expansion of voting rights and social legislation such as shortening work days and child labor laws. As long as the economy performed well, the reforms proposed by Giolitti were accepted, particularly among some of the entrepreneurial class of family corporations such as the Agnelli and Pirelli who made fortunes in the new automobile industry and emulated the capitalist models in northern Europe and the United States. Between 1897 and 1907, wages increased as did productivity, although the economic progress was largely limited to the north. Once the boom slowed after 1907, and particularly after 1912, so did support for reforms. Because of Giolitti's political dependence on southern landowners and northern industrialists, his government was reluctant to stop the suppression of strikes, which would also lead to one of the first splits in the Italian Socialist Party.[9]

Until the question of intervention in WWI, the future Fascist dictator Benito Mussolini (1883–1945) had been active in the revolutionary faction of the Socialist party and the editor of the Socialist Party newspaper *Avanti*. By 1914 Mussolini joined writer Gabriele D'Annunzio (1863–1938) in nationalist politics. The nationalists, led by intellectuals such as Enrico Corradini (1865–1931), appealed to the revolutionary aspirations of disillusioned socialists and the status quo of industrial and landed interests who sought to restore public order and limit concessions to the working class. This political climate had already led Giolitti to declare war on the Ottoman Turkish Empire in 1911 and invade Libya, a decision that enjoyed large public support including Ernesto Teodoro, the 1907 recipient of the Nobel Peace Prize. However, the war's success further polarized the Italian political situation. Giolitti became isolated from the nationalists who were emboldened by the Italian campaign in Libya and consequently favored entrance into WWI. On the other end, due to a deteriorating economic situation revolutionary socialist factions led strikes and protests in the summer of 1914. This destabilizing political climate was decisive in the public relations campaign led by D'Annunzio and Mussolini for Italy to enter into WWI.

Initially a coalition of liberals, reformist socialists, and Catholics successfully opposed intervention in WWI. Together D'Annunzio and Mussolini orchestrated large public demonstrations that brought together a wide coalition in support of intervention. In 1914–15, D'Annunzio gave a series of public speeches, which were glowingly reported by Mussolini. The nationalists, freemasons, and futurists supported calls for immediate intervention in order to save national honor. F.T. Marinetti's (1876–1944) Futurists saw the war as a Darwinistic "hygiene of the world" in which they were eager to participate. The Futurists were enamored with technology and mechanized dynamism. In his speeches, D'Annunzio succeeded in communicating the Futurists' enthusiasm for modernity into neoclassical language about honor, duty, and virtue. A few liberal politicians favored intervention in the hopes that a national effort would aid the process of nation building for an Italy that had never fully accepted what they considered the "Piedmontese" unification of 1870. Some anarchists and communists sympathizers saw a cynical advantage to intervention in the hopes that protests against the war would make conditions ripe for a left-wing revolution, as was eventually the case in 1917 Czarist Russia. Together D'Annunzio and Mussolini's diverse coalition overcame the Catholics and reformist-liberals who favored neutrality. In May of 1915, Italy finally entered the war after negotiations leading to the Treaty of London. In exchange for entering the war on the British side, Italy could hope to gain the Adriatic port city of Trieste, Austrian possessions in the South Tyrol, German colonies in Africa, and former Venetian possessions on the Dalmatian coast.

After the Italian army attacked Austrian lines in the Dolomite mountain range in places such as Cima Vezzena in 1915, the war drew to a stalemate. The pivotal event of the conflict was the collapse of the Italian front in 1917 at Caporetto when men and material resupplied the Austrian lines from the Russian front after the 1916 Brest-Litovsk peace treaty between Russia and Germany/Austro-Hungary. There was a huge divide between the reality of war and pro-interventionist ideology and the enormous suffering by Italian soldiers including summary executions and decimations in order to force the Italian army to reform its lines. By the time of the armistice in 1917 Italy had suffered nearly 700,000 casualties with a mobilization of nearly 5 million men. Italian films depicting WWI include Luigi Romano Borgnetto's wartime hero fantasy *Maciste alpino/The Warrior* (1916), Giovacchino Forzano's fascist era military drama *Tredici uomini contro un canone/Thirteen Men against a Canon* (1936), Mario Monicelli's brilliantly ironic portrayal of the contradictions of the Italian military character in *La grande Guerra/The Great War* (1960), and Francesco Rosi's *Uomini contro/Many Years Ago* (1970), a wrenching adaptation of Emilio Lussu's novel *Un anno sull'altipiano* depicting the decimations and mutinies following the army's collapse at Caporetto.

When the tide of the war finally turned against Austria/Germany after the influx of troops and materiel from the United States, the following peace conference and Treaty of Versailles did concede Italy territory in the southern Alps around the city of Trento but not on the Istrian coast of the Adriatic sea (currently in Slovenia and Croatia). The protocols that the Italian government had signed with Great Britain before entry into the war were not recognized by American president Woodrow Wilson who brought ideas about national self-determination to the treaty negotiations. D'Annunzio and other nationalists, including

Mussolini, interpreted this as an affront to national dignity and an inadequate recognition of the sacrifices of an Italian army that had held the Austrian advance after Caporetto. During the war D'Annunzio had enhanced his celebrity status by dropping patriotic tricolor leaflets on Vienna from his biplane and participating in well-publicized air raids against the Austrians.

D'Annunzio described the postwar agreements that allotted few territorial concessions to Italy as a *pace multilata* (a mutilated peace). D'Annunzio reacted in 1919 by occupying the port city of Fiume, the present Rjeka on the Istrian coast with a force of former shock troops (the *arditi*), nationalists, and revolutionaries in a move unauthorized by the Italian government. He ruled Fiume for nearly a year before escaping due to mandates from the League of Nations backed by the real threat of Italian gunships. D'Annunzio's Fiume adventure would become important for development of Italian fascism. Mussolini and the Fascist Party later parroted the style of D'Annunzio's rule at Fiume with its mixture of public theater and politics. In terms of style and rhetoric, the influence that D'Annunzio had over Fascism and later over Nazism should not be underestimated. The raised right-hand Roman salute, the skull and crossbones emblem, and black uniforms of the *arditi* shock troops at Fiume were later copied by Mussolini's Fascist black shirt squads and Hitler's Nazi SS.

The Cultural Scene

In the period prior to unification in 1870 to the end of the nineteenth century, Italian life underwent a process of political and economic transformation that also influenced its cultural make-up. A main literary figure was novelist Alessandro Manzoni (1785–1873), whose Catholic novel *I promessi sposi/The Betrothed* (1840) chronicled the struggles of a young couple to wed against the wishes of their Hispanic overlords in seventeenth-century Lombardy. The novel attracted film-makers very early as demonstrated by three silent era adaptations (1909, 1913, 1923) and an adaptation by Mario Camerini in 1941. Patriotic poet Giosué Carducci (1835–1907) expressed many of the idealistic and nationalist impulses in the classical themes and romantic tinges of his poetry. Carlo Collodi's *Le avventure di Pinocchio/The Adventues of Pinocchio* (1883) was first published as a serial in a children's journal. The underlying theme of the work is to instill a sense of moral consciousness in Italian youth in the spirit of the Italian Risorgimento movement. Collodi (Carlo Lorenzini 1826–92) had been a dedicated follower of Italian republican revolutionary Giuseppe Mazzini and a veteran of the Italian wars of unification. Edmondo De Amicis's (1846–1908) novel about school boy morale *Cuore/Heart* (1886) was also reflective of the ideological current of the *Risorgimento* and sought to instill a sense of moral and national identity in Italians. De Amicis's novel *Cuore/Heart* introduced readers to the figure of the goodhearted teacher Perboni, whose lessons in Turin sought to give students from different regions of Italy an idealistic sense of national belonging and duty.

The postunification period was also marked by the worldwide interest and excitement about the possibilities of scientific discoveries and their application to cultural and political life. Many of the scientific discoveries that characterize the modern era: the telephone, cinema, radio, electricity, automobile, airplane were actually invented well before WWI including Italian contributions Antonio Meucci's invention of the telephone and Guglielmo Marconi's subsequent invention of the radio. French philosopher August Comte coined the term "positivism" to describe the enthusiasm over discoveries of figures such the English naturalist Charles Darwin and his *Origin of the Species* (1859) and *The Origin of Man* (1871). Discoveries in physics and the physical sciences brought further challenges to religious teachings of cosmology. These new theories were appreciated in Italy by the burgeoning middle class, which sought to flourish in an economic system based on consumption and development of technological capability.

The influence of the new interest in science extended to the arts and literature. The *verismo* literary movement in Italy of authors such as Sicilian Giovanni Verga (1840–1922) concentrated on replicating the scientific approach to social problems in literature through a portrayal of social ills with objective distance. *Vero* in Italian means "true." *Verismo* was the Italian corollary of the Naturalist movement of French authors such as Emile Zola (1840–1902). *Verismo* and Naturalism championed artistic styles that tried to observe reality accurately, and encourage scientific objectivity to stress the causal relation between the environment and characters' actions. Another artistic current in Italy was the *Scapigliatura*, an Italian translation for the French word *bohème*, which took its name from a novel by Cletti Arrighi (1830–1906) *La scapigliatura e il 6 febbraio* (1862). The *scapigliati* often rejected the patriotic and religious assumptions of the *Risorgimento*, seeking to emphasize the essence below the rhetoric of the newly unified Italy, a theme not often depicted in the Italian cinema with the exception of Ettore Scola's *Passione d'amore/Passion of Love* (1981). The most iconoclastic application of the new scientific influences in Italy was by F.T. Marinetti whose Futurist movement arose before WWI. Marinetti's Futurists adapted scientific terminology to the arts by idealizing mechanized forms and questioning the relevance of Italy's centuries' old artistic traditions in a rapidly changing world. In his hyperbolic enthusiasm for everything modern Marinetti rejected the past in his manifestos and free verse sound poems such as *Zang Tumb Tub* (1914). He called for the destruction of museums and the glorification of war as the "hygiene of the world"; in fact many of his Futurist followers would expire in WWI.

A most important and influential cultural figure remained Gabriele D'Annunzio (1863–1938) whose reach extended from politics to literature, the theater, and even the cinema. D'Annunzio's charismatic political influence was fundamental in the campaign for Italy to enter WWI and later in his adventure at Fiume and influence over Mussolini and Italian fascism. D'Annunzio was also an exponent of Decadentism, a post-Romantic artistic movement, which exalted an individual artist's sense of refinement and, self-importance with an interest in exotic sensuality and mystery at times bordering on self-destruction. D'Annunzio's flamboyant personality and his ability to adapt artistic currents like Decandentism into an Italian cultural context and beyond made him a pivotal Italian cultural figure in the first half of the twentieth century.[10]

Origins of Italian Cinema

The new interest for a scientific approach in social and literary matters, together with the great demand for technological advances, created an ideal setting for the birth of cinema. As early as the 1870s, the topic of animation had interested scientists and photographers. British photographer Eadweard Muybridge's *zoopraxiscope* showed the sequential movements of a galloping horse. Ohio born inventor Thomas Edison developed his *kinetoscope* and made a sequential film of a sneeze in 1893. The Lumière brothers in France invented their *cinematographe* and made short films that projected aspects of real life, linking film with reality. In 1895, the Edison Kinetoscope made a presentation in Turin. A cinematographic machine had also been developed in Italy. Also in 1895, a license for a cinematographic instrument for shooting, projection, and developing film was issued for Filoteo Alberini's *kinetografo*. Alberini, however, did not have sufficient capital to develop his project, and the arrival of the Lumières *cinematographe* in Italy halted his efforts. The *cinematographe* Lumière made its first appearance in Italy in 1896, when Lumière's Italian representative, Vittorio Calcina, promoted an enthusiastically received show in Milan.[11] Projections followed thereafter throughout Italy as the medium gained interest as a traveling attraction. By 1898, permanent cinema halls opened in Rome and in Naples. In 1899, Calcina opened the first successful public cinema hall in Turin. Because of the brevity of the cinematographic shows—maximum 20–30 minutes—the halls used for such shows integrated films with other performances. Thus, from its origins the Italian cinema shared space with vaudeville music-hall performances and comic sketches, a theatrical practice that would continue into the 1940s.

In the early 1900s, Alberini opened more cinema halls in several Italian cities. In 1905–06 Alberini and Dante Santoni founded Cines, an early Italian production film company. Alberini also became one of the first Italian filmmakers. In 1905, he directed *The Taking of Rome 1870* (1905), the first Italian feature film based on a final episode of Italian unification. Italian cinematographers and projectionists also worked to perfect the documentary format that became a genre favored as a political tool by the Fascist regime and later during the post-WWII neorealist period. In 1896, Calcina made the first Italian documentary on King Humbert and Queen Margherita at the Royal Villa in Monza. Between 1909 and 1916, Italian films entered the world market with a variety of genres including slapstick starring Frenchman Andre Deed, known as Cretinetti in Italy, who appeared in over a hundred films produced at the Itala studios in Turin. The comedy genre also featured performers such as Ferdinand Guillaume known as Polidor, perhaps best known for his cameos in Federico Fellini's *La dolce vita* (1960) and *Le notti di Cabiria/The Nights of Cabiria* (1957), or Marcel Perez known as Robinet.[12] Other figures who contributed to the Italian silent period included Emilio Ghione's role as Za-la-Mort in the eight episodes of *Topi grigi/Grey Mice* (1918) and in the *Yellow Triangle/Triangolo giallo* (1917–18). Gione's incredible facial mimicry, later used to effect by Italian comedian Totò (1898–1967), was dramatized by a special use of light techniques that favored violent contrasts of black and white in order to accentuate the sharpness of his facial features. These performers and others appeared in shorts that were produced on an industrial scale until the outbreak of WWI. Other production centered on costume dramas such as Giulio Antamoro's *Pinocchio* (1911) and *Cristo* (1916) or Mario Caserini's films such as the adaptation *Romeo e Giulietta/Romeo and Juliet* (1908) and the disaster movie, *Gli ultimi giorni di Pompeii/The Last Days of Pompeii* (1913). There were also melodramas and comedies and even films about everyday life inspired by Italian *verismo*. By 1912 and 1913, the cinema had become an accepted facet of the Italian entertainment industry. In 1913, the government instituted censorship standards and taxes on both films and tickets.[13]

In the first two decades of the 1900s, important studios were built in Naples, Turin, Venice, and Rome. In this period, filmmaking was conducted primarily inside studios with artificial lighting. Naples became particularly important because of the efforts of Gustavo Lombardo, later of the Titanus production company, who began as a foreign film distributor who founded the magazine *Lux* in 1908 with the intention of increasing the cultural status of the cinema. Lombardo produced films that had popular appeal but which were also culturally important such as *Inferno/Hell* (1912), an adaptation of Dante's *Divine Comedy* produced by Milano Film. There were also futurist films such as A.G. Bragaglia's *Thais* (1916) in accordance with the publication of the *Futurist Manifesto on Cinema* of the same year, a declaration about experimental cinema in accordance with the futurists, desire to find forms of expression that reflected the mechanized and industrial changes in Italy and the world.

The founding of the Cines studios in 1906 made Rome one of the centers of the Italian cinema industry. Cines aimed to conquer international film markets with large investments producing about 50 titles per year beginning in 1907. One of the most important filmmakers working for Cines was Enrico Guazzoni whose adaptation of the Henryk Sienkiewicz novel with strong Christian themes *Quo Vadis?* (1913) became one of the most often repeated subjects of the peplum historical genre set in ancient Rome.

Despite activity in Rome and even in Venice, Turin was the first capital of the Italian film industry during the silent period. Turin was the country's industrial center, home of the Italian automobile industry. A Turin-based production company, Pasquali and Tempo, was run by Ernesto Maria Pasquali, a journalist and playwright who created the *Polidor* comic films. He also produced costume dramas such as *Spartacus* (1913) by Enrico Vidali and *Salambò* (1914) by Luigi Maggi. Other production companies in Turin included Ambrosio and Itala Film. Ambrosio succeeded in attracting important directors such as Luigi Maggi, who made the first version of *The Last Days of Pompeii* (1908), a 400-meter-long film, which became one of the first Italian films to break into the American market. The Itala studios featured Giovanni Pastrone (1883–1959) a director who started his career with comic films and then moved into the historical genre. Following *La Caduta di Troia /The Fall of Troy* (1911) and *Agnese Visconti* (1914), he directed and produced *Cabiria* (1914), a film about the battle between ancient Rome and Carthage during the Punic War.

Giovanni Pastrone's *Cabiria* and Gabriele D'Annunzio

Cabiria was filmed in 1913 and released on April 18, 1914, in Turin, directed by Giovanni Pastrone and scripted by Gabriele D'Annunzio (see figure 1.1). An

Figure 1.1   Advertisement for *Cabiria* featuring name of Gabriele D'Annunzio.

enormous budget went to location shooting in Tunisia and in the Alps. *Cabiria* opened with a full orchestra led by respected conductor Manilo Mazza performing the *Symphony of Fire* theme composed by renowned composer Ildebrando Pizzetti.[14] The film enjoyed international box office success with reviews impressed by the producers' attempt to legitimize the cinema, to give film the same trappings and social prestige standard in operatic productions.

Cabiria links Italian nationalism to a period of the expanding Roman Republic of the second Punic War (218–202 BC) rather than a Roman Empire persecuting Christians during the reign of Nero (AD 15–68) as is the case in other early popular films such as *Quo Vadis?* Instead *Cabiria* has a hero, Fulvio Axilla, and his shaved-headed, barrel-chested Mussolini-like African servant, Maciste, in a story of a republican-era Rome fighting a rival Mediterranean empire (Carthage) and a foreign religion (Baal or Moloch). Producers correctly expected Italian audiences in 1914 to read the similarities between the Roman victory in the second Punic War over the Baalite Carthaginians and the Italian defeat of an Islamic Turkish empire during the 1911 invasion of Libya. Thus besides being a technical and artistic achievement, *Cabiria* anticipates the political and ideological currents that culminated in the efforts of pro-WWI interventionists such as D'Annunzio and Mussolini, who were instrumental in the decision of the Italian government to enter the War in 1915.

An most important ploy by *Cabiria*'s producers to attract interest to the film was to costly decision enlist the services of Gabriele D'Annunzio as screenwriter in a period when D'Annunzio's role as cultural icon had brought other producers to his door. Casa Ambrosio, a main competitor of Pastrone's Itala studios in Turin, bought the rights to many of D'Annunzio's novels and plays. Between 1911 and 1920 at least 21 films of D'Annunzian derivation were produced in Italy.[15] In his brief treatise on the cinema *Del cinematografo considerato come strumento di liberazione e come arte di trasfigurazione/Cinematography a tool of liberation and transfigurative art* (1914), D'Annunzio describes the cinema as a medium that had the capacity to replace the dramatic theater.

With *Cabiria*, D'Annunzio had no compunctions about putting his name to Pastrone's adaptation of an Emilio Salgari (1862–1977) novel *Cartagine in fiamme/Carthage in Flames*. Indeed Pastrone's name does not appear in the opening title sequences, giving the impression that the film is entirely D'Annunzio's work. Due to D'Annunzio's influence everything in the film became more florid and bombastic. Pastrone's character names—Plinio and Hercules—became D'Annunzio's Fulvio Axilla and Maciste. D'Annunzio derived the name Maciste from the Greek superlative for "Large." These changes were enough to transform the film from a standard peplum epic into a D'Annunzian artistic experience.[16]

D'Annunzio's private life and the exotic themes he treated in his work contained titillating suggestions of the forbidden or scandalous, a key to D'Annunzio's artistic career and his success as a media personality.[17] In *Cabiria* these themes and the excitement and interest they produced in the target audience manifest in the character of Sophonisba, the suicidal Carthaginian princess, whose tale was often the subject of neoclassical tragedy. The sequences involving Sophonisba are made more exotic by the fact that her death symbolizes the disappearance of an entire civilization. Carthage is destroyed because Cabiria was not sacrificed to the fire god Moloch. This plot fit into a decadentist discourse where self-annihilation is a culminating erotic experience. Sophonisba's exotic drawing room, smoking incense pots, and statuettes seem like the decorating catalogue for D'Annunzio's home on Lake Garda, the Vittoriale, with an *art nouveau* or *liberty* emphasis on rarity, extravagance, luxury, and oriental motifs. It is an atmosphere that has often been equated with illicit sex, decadence, drugs, and illness, especially in authors such as Andre Huysmans, a source for D'Annunzio. The film's decor and plot exploited the transgressive elements implicit in such a setting and behavior, which was part of D'Annunzio's appeal and mirrored his lifestyle and reputation.[18]

Despite the technical achievements of its production and special effects, *Cabiria* is not often thought of as a technological or science fiction film because of the classical historical setting. But technology and the marvel of machines and inventions, the flash of Futurist propaganda, make an entrance in *Cabiria*. D'Annunzian culture was fascinated with light, explosions, and the machine aesthetics likely borrowed from F.T. Marinetti's futurist excitement about mechanized glory. As a pilot during WWI, D'Annunzio had dropped heroic poems over Vienna, a feat that became well documented for it was one of the few examples of individual heroism that could be celebrated in that war. One scene in *Cabiria* that appealed to the turn-of-the century romantic fascination with technology is the burning of the Roman fleet at Syracuse by Archimedes's sun-reflecting mirrors. Archimedes's ecstatic joy at his technological genius recalls the later commonplace of the mad scientist who pushes the limits of nature.

The other technological wonder of the film is the depiction of the fire god Moloch as a bellowing slag pot where the Carthaginian priests burn their vicitms. Besides the technical achievements in portraying Moloch with thousands of extras and the use of high wattage flood-lights to simulate the escaping heat, the Moloch flesh furnace is a voyeuristic marvel, which plays on the primal fears of the spectator. Another of D'Annunzio's screenwriting contributions, *La Crociata degli innocenti/The Children's Crusade* (1917), is a dramatization of the Children's Crusade of 1212 depicting another group of doomed children who were sold into slavery on a pilgrimage to the Holy Land. In *Metropolis* (1926), German director Fritz Lang adopted a similar theme when the workers' children are threatened by the breakdown of the giant machine (also called Moloch) that powers the futuristic city.

The true star of *Cabiria* is Maciste, the strong man slave and the brawn to Fulvio's brains. The direct source of the character is the good giant, Ursus, who protects the Christian slave girl, Licia, in the novel *Quo vadis?* by Henryk Sienkiewicz, adapted into a film by Guazzoni in 1912.[19] Maciste's physical ability to escape from Moloch is a victory for the body and the individual against the overwhelming power of the machine. Turin, the city where *Cabiria* was produced and largely filmed, was also the epicenter of the Italian automobile industry with its Fordist manufacturing methods. In the pro-machine, futurist-romanticized culture and in the industrial and technological reality of the twentieth century, the physical body had lost power, particularly in warfare. Ironically, one of the most popular films in the Maciste film series (ten such films were produced between 1914 and 1926) was *The Warrior* (1916). In the film an Itala film troupe is caught behind Austrian lines at the outbreak of the war, providing Bartolomeo Pagano, who plays Maciste, with an opportunity to manhandle extras in Austrian military uniforms. This image of Maciste defeating the enemy in physical combat is emblematic of the divide between official and popular culture and the technological reality of the war.

The Maciste figure has been one of the most enduring in film history from the Italian peplum epics of the 1960s starring Steve Reeves as Hercules to the Hollywood films with Arnold Schwarzenegger as muscular robot in the *Terminator* series. In the Maciste cycle it was common for Maciste not only to remain removed from any long-term love interest but also to work to reunite young lovers. *Cabiria* ends with Maciste playing the lute on a honeymoon yacht of Fulvio and Cabiria with angles flying around the young lovers as they kiss.

The most enduring legacy of *Cabiria* is the apparent influence that the figure of Maciste had over Benito Mussolini, who would rule Italy as Fascist dictator from 1922 to 1943. Between 1914 and 1924, Mussolini transformed his public image from an anticlerical Socialist revolutionary into the Fascist icon of a naturally powerful tyrant dedicated to the memory and traditions of Roman glory. He even personally oversaw *Scipione l'Africano/Scipio the African* (1937), a film that revisits the historical period of the Punic War setting of *Cabiria*. The physical similarities between the *Duce* and the personality cult developed in the 1930s around Mussolini and Maciste cannot be casual. As Maciste, Bartolomeo Pagano developed a signature gait, with eyes glaring with arms folded and head thrown back, later adopted by Mussolini (see figure 1.2). It is not clear who was the source of

3 Films Pittaluga, A.I, n. 3, 1 novembre 1923 (cat. 136)

Figure 1.2 Bartolomeo Pagano (Maciste) in a pose later commonly used by Benito Mussolini.

Mussolini's shaved head, whether it came from D'Annunzio or Maciste, but again the image is consistent. *Istituto LUCE* newsreels in the 1930s feature Mussolini with a bare chest and shaved head helping farmers to collect grain looking like an aged stunt double for Bartolomeo Pagano's Maciste in *Cabiria*. The public image cultivated by Mussolini during the Fascist period as the all powerful *Duce* could be read as a Maciste-like figure speaking the language of D'Annunzio.[20]

Figure 1.3   Italia Manzini (Sophonisba) from *Cabiria*.

Cabiria portrays the political and cultural ideals marshaled by D'Annunzio and Mussolini for Italy's entrance into WWI.[21] Italy's first film, Alberini's silent *The Taking of Rome 1870* (1905), was a re-creation of Garibaldi's successful conquest of Rome in 1870, a concluding episode of the *Risorgimento* and Italian unification. *Cabiria* expressed another potential foundational narrative for the newly unified Italian nation of a pre-Christian *romanità* (Romaness), particularly important for the later nationalist culture espoused by Mussolini's Fascist regime (1922–1943), which attempted to identify the newly united Italy with the past glories of ancient Rome.[22]

Divismo

Public interest in the stars of films became a common aspect of Italian silent film. Actresses such as Francesca Bertini, Lyda Borelli, Pina Menichelli, Lina Cavalieri, Hesperia, Leda Gys, and Rina De' Liguoro gained acclaim through the phenomenon of *divismo* or star-idolatry. Even Eleonora Duse, the most popular stage actress of the time, succumbed to the allure of cinema by acting and directing *Cenere/Ashes* (1916), a film produced by Ambrosio. Lyda Borelli established the standard for dramatic performance with Caserini's direction of *L'amore mio non muore/My Love Does not Die* (1913) and *Rapsodia satanica/Satanic Rhapsody* (1915). Another key film of the Italian silent period was Nino Martoglio's *Sperduti nel buio/Lost in the Dark* (1914), a film about an orphan girl in turn-of-the-century Naples, which is credited with being one of the films that began the realistic current in the Italian cinema. The film (now lost) was remade in 1947 by Camillo Mastrocinque with Vittorio De Sica in the role of a blind gentleman who helps an unfortunate girl. Another Neapolitan, Elvira Notari, made approximately 60 films between 1906 and 1930. Notari was inspired by themes of the everyday life of the common people of Naples, especially of women, dealing with their passions and unhappiness. Elvira Notari also starred in films as an actress but her greatest contribution was as a director in films such as *Bufera d'anima/Soul Storm* (1911), *Medea di Portamedina/Medea of Portamedina* (1919), *E' piccerella/The Little Girl* (1922) and *'Nfame/Infamous* (1924).

An important *diva* was Francesca Bertini, who began her career in the theater and then moved on to the cinema to work for the Film d'Arte Production Company in Naples. She made several important films, such as *King Lear* (1910), *The Merchant of Venice* (1911), and *Romeo and Giulietta* (1912). She was then engaged by Cines where she worked with Guazzoni in *Rosa di Tebe/Rose from Thebes* (1912) and eventually became affiliated with Celio Production Co. where she worked her way to stardom and appeared in an array of female roles that increased her popularity in films including *La signora delle camelie /Lady with the Camelias* (1915), *Odette* (1915), *Fedora* (1916), and *Andreina and Teresa* (1917).

Bertini's best-known work is *Assunta Spina* (1915), an adaptation of a play by Neapolitan poet and dramatist Salvatore Di Giacomo (1869–1934). The film, which Bertini codirected with Gustavo Serena, has been praised for the manner in which the details of everyday life in Naples are presented in an unadorned fashion. The film is about a young laundress, Assunta, whose dreams for love and familial stability, the standard goals in melodramatic narrative, are shattered by the unstable male characters in her life. These include her violent tempered fiancé Michele, his jealous rival the ne'er-do-well Raffaele, and the corrupt court official Federico who convinces Assunta to accept his sexual advances in exchange for the chance to see Michele in prison. The turning point of the drama occurs when Michele slashes Assunta's face and is sentenced to two years in prison despite Assunta's attempt during his trial to accept blame for his actions. When Michele is released and kills Federico, Assunta takes the blame for the murder, her tragedy complete. The character of the long-suffering female was well established in the operatic tradition in works such as *La traviata, Manon Lescalt,* or *La Bohème* to mention only a few nineteenth-century operas that feature doomed female protagonists. Films such as Bertini's *Assunta Spina* established the cinema as a venue for what would become the *strappalacrime* (weepie or tearjerker) melodrama. Pastrone's *Cabiria* had provided Maciste, a character who may be interpreted as a metaphor for Italian nationalistic impulses. The suicidal princess Sophonisba in *Cabiria* is emblematic of the influence of trends such as decadentism and European high art in Italian consciousness (see figure 1.3). In contrast, *Assunta Spina* represents a more humble sphere in everyday Italian society. Assunta is identified with the bare streets of Naples often appearing under a portrait of the Madonna with child in her room. She is deceived and brutalized by the immature males in her life and responds with self-sacrificial fatalism.

In 1914, just before Italy's entry into WWI the Italian film industry produced 90 feature-length films and penetrated world markets, including the United States, where films such as Pastrone's *Cabiria* enjoyed long runs and wide distribution.[23] Even though production in 1920 reached prewar levels with 371 feature films produced, the increased competition from Hollywood made retention of the former market share untenable. After WWI the Italian film industry lost its position in world markets, a fate shared in countries like France, which also had vibrant prewar film industries.[24]

2

The Fascist Years (1922–43)

1921   Founding of Italian Fascist Party and Italian Communist Party.

1922   Fascist March on Rome Victor Emanuel III invites Fascist leader Benito Mussolini to form a government as prime minister

1924   Giacomo Matteotti, Socialist parliamentarian, murdered by Fascists Secession of the Aventine, opposition parties abandon the parliamentary hall to protest Fascist policies.

1925   Mussolini assumes responsibility for the Matteotti murder, further steps to dictatorhip

1926   Autarkical economic system: Quota 90 assigns value of 1 British Pound Sterling equal to 90 Italian Lire

1928   The Statuto Albertino, the Kingdom of Italy Piedmontese era constitution is attenuated

1929   Lateran accords/Concordat between Fascist state and Roman Catholic Church

1935   Invasion of Abyssinia and Ethiopia prompting League of Nations economic sanctions

1936   Aid to Falangists (Francisco Franco) in Spanish Civil War Mussolini refers to an "Axis" between Fascist Italy and Hitler's Nazi Reich in Germany in November 1 speech

1937   Communist leader Antonio Gramsci dies shortly after release from prison Italy leaves the League of Nations

1938   Mussolini takes no action against German annexation of Austria. Leggi razziali (racial statutes) restrictions on the civil liberties of Italy's Jewish population

1939   Italy occupies Albania with Mussolini's son-in-law Galeazzo Ciano as regent Pact of Steel between Germany and Italy

A number of countries (13) in Europe underwent right-wing revolutions/ change between 1922 and the 1940s.[1] In this period, politics and economics were conditioned by the social and psychological repercussions of WWI and controversy regarding subsequent peace treaties. In Italy, the standing down of the wartime economy brought about structural displacements as well as demands from workers for a reduced work week, salary increases, and land redistribution.[2] Strikes and protests, especially in the north, added to a precarious situation accentuated by the large number of veterans returning from the front to find themselves without work. The political and economic situation was extremely tense with strikes, demonstrations, and the reduction of the value of middle-class savings between 1918 and 1920.[3] The gap between the industrialized north and the more rural south became even more pronounced.

When universal male suffrage was granted in Italy in 1918 and competition began for the new voters. Despite the tremendous costs and limited gains from the war, Italian participation in the war had actually legitimized the anti-republican politics of the Decandentist writer D'Annunzio, the Nationalist/Socialist Mussolini, and the Futurist F.T. Marinetti. Catholic forces entered into politics with Don Sturzo's (1871–1959) *Partito Popolare* after the lifting of the *rerum novarum*, the papal encyclical prohibiting Catholic participation in politics. However the events that would bring Italy under Fascist totalitarian rule were already in motion.

Before WWI, Benito Mussolini had been an anarchist and socialist agitator. He resigned as editor of the chief Socialist newspaper *Avanti* out of frustration at the Socialist Party's refusal to support Italian intervention in WWI. In the political uncertainty and civil unrest following WWI, Mussolini formed his own organization, the Fascist Party, which eventually aligned with the nationalists.[4] The term Fascism comes from the Latin *fasces* (bundles) a symbol of authority in ancient Rome. The 1919 election saw gains for the Socialists and the Catholic *Popolari*. Yet the two parties were unable to form a coalition. For the next election, Mussolini moved further to the political Right so that his platform had more in common with the policies of a conservative, moderate government—fiscal restraint, law and order and a nationalist foreign policy. Mussolini also made concessions to the Socialists by promising to form Fascist worker and farmer unions in order to position his Fascist Party for a dominant role in Italian politics.

In 1919 and 1920 the economic crisis that had followed the end of the war worsened and the continuing strikes and political unrest were not suppressed by the last moderate government. The Socialists feared Allied military intervention in the event of a Marxist revolution as had occurred in Russia in 1917. In late 1920, Mussolini's Fascists began a campaign of political violence, at times with the apparent consent of public safety officials. According to Fascist propaganda between 1918 and 1922, Mussolini prevented a Bolshevik-style totalitarian revolution from taking place in Italy. In reality, Fascism brought the end of representative parliamentary government and the institution of Fascist totalitarian dictatorship. The ruling elite allowed and even encouraged Mussolini to enter into the government who was viewed as a milder, more controllable alternative to D'Annunzio, fresh from his Fiume adventure. Italian films depicting rise of Fascism include films made under the regime such as Giovacchino Forzano's *Camicia nera* (1933), Alessandro Blasetti's *Vecchia guardia/Old Guard* (1934), or postwar studies such as Dino Risi's *Marcia su Roma/March on Rome* (1962) and Bernardo Bertolucci's *1900* (1976).

The idea of violence for political ends sprang directly from the audacity of D'Annunzio's volunteers at Fiume and former *arditi*, shock troop veterans, as did the Fascist wearing of black shirts, brandishing of clubs, and forced public feeding of cod liver oil as means of political intimidation. But D'Annunzio's political methodology did not evolve in a vacuum. Trends in philosophy and sociology that influenced D'Annunzio and Mussolini included thinkers such as Gustav Le Bon (1842–1931) and his theories on the effectiveness of political violence and demagoguery to mold public opinion. Marinetti's iconoclastic call for spontaneity, impulse, and violence fostered a sense of bravado amorality as did Freidrich Nietzsche (1844–1900), with his reading of the Judeo-Christian tradition as slave morality. But Fascism also had anti-bourgeois elements, holdovers from Mussolini's days as a Socialist revolutionary. The diffidence toward the upper middle class may be interpreted in the light of Oswald Spengler's (1880–1936) reading of Western decadence, which in turn owed much to Darwinian theories on natural competition. The Fascists, as D'Annunzio's Fiume volunteers before them, saw themselves as Darwinian agents whose violence could be rationalized as a consequence of their strength and audacity. Of course it is easy to dress up in philosophical and cultural terms what may have actually been a generational conflict between Fascist black shirt squads whose fight song *Giovinezza* (Youth) was directed against their aging liberal, Catholic, monarchist or Socialist fathers.[5]

The Socialist Party did increase membership, and support strikes in Turin and Milan, Italy's two industrial centers. But a series of rifts in the Socialist leadership led to the formation of the Italian Communist Party in 1921 by Antonio Gramsci (1891–1937). The division of the Italian Left into opposing factions rendered it incapable of profiting from the political and economic situation. The government, led by the Liberal Party, failed to secure a peaceful solution and Italians responded to Mussolini's call for a return to law and order. The middle and property-owning classes were fearful that these difficult economic and political conditions could lead to a revolution patterned on the 1917 Russian Bolshevik revolution. The situation was ripe for an opportunistic and decided leader like Mussolini to impose his will and his Fascist Party on the nation.

The 1921 Italian election results saw a split between Fascists/Nationalists, Socialists/Communists, and Catholics. A pivotal event was the decision by the Fascist leadership to march from their party congress in Naples to Rome in October 1922. Once in Rome, parading Fascists occupied the post office and other government buildings. King Victor Emanuel III (1869–1947) refused to order in troops, one of the acts that sealed the fate of the monarchy after WWII. Support for the Fascists grew and in October of 1922 Mussolini was asked by the king to replace Luigi Facta as prime minister, perhaps unaware that he had just invited in a dictatorship that would last 21 years. Mussolini's appeal was based mainly on his promise of a "return to law and order," an end to strikes and the "fear of Bolshevism," a reassurance to the new middle class that they would not become "proletariarized," and finally, a promise that through dedication to military virtues Italy could become a Great Power reevoking the Roman Empire.[6]

In his first few years in power, Mussolini (often called *Il Duce*, The Leader) moved somewhat cautiously. Yet the first three years of the *ventennio*, the 20 odd years of Fascist rule, were characterized by Mussolini's consolidation of power, a transformation that took him from the figure of a suit waring premier of parliament to the uniformed *Duce* of WWII. An important first step in the Fascist promulgation of the totalitarian state was the Acerbo Bill, which guaranteed the party receiving most votes in an election two-thirds of the seats in parliament. In 1924, the Fascists attained a majority in parliament using a proportional representation law, which in various guises has continued sporadically to be a feature of the Italian parliamentary system.

Mussolini's early policies appeased politicians who had acceded to his inclusion in government. But after the murder of parliamentary opposition leader Giacomo Matteotti in 1924, an event depicted in Florestano Vancini's *Il delitto Matteotti/The Assassination of Matteotti* (1973), and the walkout of Parliament by opposition deputies, an act known as the Aventine Secession, Mussolini decided to accept responsibility for the actions of his followers. In a speech to parliament in 1925, Mussolini accepted responsibility for Fascist violence, a moment that commentators have seen as the moment of the beginning of Fascist totalitarian dictatorship. After surviving the crisis in 1924–25 involving the murder of Matteotti, Mussolini unhesitatingly asserted his power, reducing government to single-party rule and establishing the OVRA (*Opera Vigilanza e Repressione Antifascista*), a secret police service charged with repressing anti-Fascists in the country and abroad.

The Fascist movement thus led the country to dictatorship with the banning of opposition political parties after an attempt on Mussolini's life in 1926. This definitively cancelled any hopes of the two previously influential political forces, the Socialist/Communists and the Catholics. Yet Mussolini was careful not to alienate the previous governing establishment, and to this end the Fascist Party slowly purged itself of its most violent black shirt, revolutionary elements. Mussolini further secured his position, appeasing Catholic sentiment by signing the Lateran accords in 1929, creating the independent status of the Vatican under the governance of the Catholic Church, and establishing Roman Catholicism as the official state religion, quite a jump from Mussolini's early days as an anticlerical agitator. The Fascist system of Corporatism, which developed gradually and finally crystallized into the Chamber of Fasces and Corporations in 1938, professed to be a system in which political representation was based not on residence, but on occupation whether in agriculture, transport, manufacturing, or self-employed professionals. Supposedly such a system would have eliminated class conflict. But in practice Corporatism allowed the Fascist Party to maintain rigid control over the unions (eliminating Catholic and Socialist union groups), while favoring business interests.

By accepting a right-wing revolution in 1922, the governing establishment underestimated Mussolini's abilities from his past as a journalist and communicator. Other historians noted that the republican ideology of Mazzini's Risorgimento had never been a mass movement but was instead directed and controlled by an elite whose hold on popular consciousness was weak and who were overly dependent on Garibaldi's charisma, the Piedmontese monarchy, and its able prime minister Cavour.[7] Commentators have blamed the middle class for never having fully understood or practiced the ethical responsibilities necessary for the survival of republican institutions.[8] Other commentators have seen Fascism in more strictly psychological terms as a form of arrested adolescence defined by a willingness to obey the voice of authority whether that voice emanated from the *Duce* or the Church as presented in Federico Fellini's *Amarcord* (1974). The regime's policy of exiling political dissidents, among them writers such as Cesare Pavese and Carlo Levi, furthered the formation of a conformist society that perpetuated Fascist rule.

The Fascist years did bring changes for large segments of the population, particularly in demographic and economic terms. Despite the restrictions of the regime, the 1930s evidenced a movement toward urban, modern life characterized by a growth in consumer culture and sports attitudes perhaps best reflected in the romantic comedies directed by Mario Bonnard or Mario Camerini. Sociologically these trends began with the movement toward the cities, an internal migration away from the countryside caused by demographic increases. Mussolini did achieve some successes in controlling the economy during the Great Depression. The regime oversaw the draining of marshes and the propagandistic high point of improving transportation scheduling—"making the trains run on time."

Whatever the cultural or sociological interpretations, a main legacy of Fascism was an increase in the extent of state control in Italy, which fostered a sense of social, political, economic hierarchy for the creation of wealth or social status. Fascism awarded a structural bureaucratic approach to economic and social wealth. It was the culture of *clientilismo* (political patronage) rather than the entrepreneurial verve that had characterized Italian economic development in the early part of the century by bourgeois industrialist families. The totalitarian nature of Fascist government expanded with Mussolini's restrictions on freedom of the press and his autarkic policies of national self-sufficiency, which relieved the public of the responsibility of involvement in governmental or economic decisions. The world economic crisis of the 1930s brought even more state control with the formation of large state-run industrial holding companies the IMI, the IRI, (postwar ENI), and a national pension system the INPS (created in 1933) to the point that by the late 1930s Fascist Italy rivaled Soviet Russia for the level of state involvement in the economy.

In response to the Italian invasion of Ethiopia, the League of Nations instituted economic sanctions on trade with Italy. Films from the late 1930s like Mario Camerini's *Il Signor Max* (1937) have references to the consumption of embargoed foreign products as unpatriotic. Mussolini's regime reacted by turning further inward and instituted economic and cultural politics known by the catch word *autarchia* (autarky or self-sufficiency). The regime policy of national economic self-sufficiency or autarky had already been evoked in attempts to resolve a grain shortage with the Battle of Grain in 1925, even turning some city parks into grain fields. The Battle of the Lira and the freezing of exchange rates for the Italian lira with major currencies such as the British Sterling at *quota novanta* (ninety lire per British pound) and the Battle of Gold were further autarkic attempts to stop the rienforce the national currency, the lira.

After the conclusion of the war in Ethiopia (May 1936) and before the Pact of Munich (May 1938) and alliance with Hitler's Nazi Germany, Mussolini declared a period of peace, which was well received by the populace. Thus the late 1930s was somewhat ironically a period of relative popularity and have become known as *gli anni dei consenso* (years of consensus), preceding Mussolini's alliance with and subjugation to Hitler's Nazi Germany. In September of 1938, Mussolini's Fascist regime passed the *leggi razziali* (racial statutes), which prohibited Jews from intermarriage, attending public schools, holding public office. There were even limits put on the amount of real estate that an Italian Jew could possess in his own country.

The Cultural Scene

In May 1925, liberal philosopher Benedetto Croce (1866–1952), one of the leading Italian intellectuals of his generation, wrote the *Manifesto degli intellettuali antifascisti/Manifesto of the Anti-Fascist Intellectuals*. His rival, the official philosopher of the regime, Giovanni Gentile (1875–1944), wrote a corresponding *Manifesto degli intelletuali fascisti/Manifesto of Fascist Intellectuals* in the same year. When university professors were required to sign a loyalty oath and join the party, few gave up their chairs and refused. Some intellectuals who rose to prominence in the postwar period have subsequently been embarrassed by the reappearance of sycophantic letters to Mussolini or by evidence of concrete ties to the regime, although many cultural figures including Luigi Pirandello, Giuseppe Ungaretti and Carlo Emilio Gadda were at times supporters of the regime during periods of the *ventennio*.

Fascism originally had utopian and anti-bourgeois elements, held over from Mussolini's days as a Socialist revolutionary. Once in power, Mussolini was careful not to alienate the upper class and the establishment. By the 1930s, Fascist high functionaries aspired to noble titles to legitimize their position in society. The Fascist *gerarchi* leadership gained ever-closer ties to the upper echelons of Italian society best demonstrated by the showy wedding in 1930 between Mussolini's daughter Edda and Count Galeazzo Ciano, the son of an industrialist who had flown missions with D'Annunzio in WWI. Ciano later became head of Mussolini's press office in 1933, a position upgraded to the Undersecretariat for the Press and Propaganda in 1934. The position eventually came a separate ministry, the Ministry of Culture and Propaganda (Miniculpop), which oversaw an agreement reached with the United States for the limitation of Hollywood film exports to Italy to 250 films per year.[9] The Miniculpop controlled the ENIC (Ente Nazionale Industrie Cinematografiche), which distributed and produced films for the network of theaters the state had acquired after the decline of the pre-WWI Italian studio and distribution system.

Despite the desire of Fascist officials for aristocratic legitimacy, the regime did have an anti-aristocratic policy, at least linguistically. The campaign to require the second person plural *voi* as the common form of address instead of the feudal and feminine third person singular *Lei* was at its height in 1938 with complete substitution promulgated in 1939. This linguistic policy aimed to democratize Italian speech and create a Fascist culture that would not accept the feudal feminine forms of address.[10] The regime also promoted diffidence toward dialects, although the relationship between dialect and cinema was less continuous. Between 1929 and 1934 and after 1939, Italian regional dialects were featured and even encouraged in films. It was between 1934 and 1939 when Luigi Freddi was head of film directives that dialects were discouraged. The Italian practice of dubbing foreign films, rather than distributing them with subtitles began in 1932 shortly after the introduction of sound technology to film.[11]

As the regime attempted to expand its influence over popular culture during the mid-1930s, American literature, music, and style came to have a glow of the forbidden.[12] American narrative had already suggested a realist model such as that of Verga and his *verismo* style. Italian intellectuals such as Elio Vittorini and Cesare Pavese cultivated an image of America as a source of anti-Fascist culture.[13]

To counter the appeal of foreign influences, the regime encouraged a culture that sought to equate *italianità* (Italianess) with *romanità* (Romaness) and ancient Rome's aura of historical and military prestige. There was a demographic campaign of tax benefits for large families. Mussolini's *Duce* personality cult mimicked cultural commonplaces from ancient Rome. In order to instill a sense of national identity and prestige in Italian popular culture, children and teenagers were enlisted in youth groups such as the *Balilla*, the *figli e figlie della lupa* (sons and daughters of the she wolf), *Avanguardisti* (for teenage males), and *Giovani Italiane* (young Italian girls). Such groups are depicted ironically in films such as Fellini's *Amarcord* (1974). The OND (*Opera Nazionale Dopolavoro*, National After Work Group) offered working-class, adult groups with activities divided between *attività sportiva* and *culturale* (sport and cultural and activities) including theatrical groups.[14] The actor and future director Vittorio De Sica is featured singing in an OND chorus in Camerini's *Il Signor Max* (1937).

Spectator sports had been immensely important in the ideology of Mussolini's regime. With a boxing heavyweight world champion, Primo Carnera in 1933, and two World Cup soccer victories in 1934 and 1938, Mussolini trumpeted the return of the ancient virtue of the Italian people and commissioned stadiums and public sports culture. The equation of athletics with nationalism made its way to films including depictions of fascist university games in Mario Bonnard's *Io suo padre* (1938), — a film adaptation of an Alba De Cespedes novel. There was also interest in the record setting and technological culture. Minister Italo Balbo made a record setting flight by piloting a squadron to Chicago in 1933. Tazio Nuvolari (1892–1953) had a remarkable career as a race car driver in the increasingly popular formula 1 and *Mille Miglia* automobile rally races around the Italian peninsula. Bicycle racing was also immensely popular, rivaling soccer in popularity, with the exploits of champions such as Fausto Coppi and Gino Bartali firing popular imagination in races such as the *Giro d'Italia* (Tour of Italy). Sporting events were transmitted by the Italian state radio instituting a popular element in national culture.

Italy's first Nobel Prize for literature after nationalist poet Giosué Carudcci (1835–1907) was won by Sardinian novelist Grazia Deledda in 1926. Yet, a literary figure who continued to yield huge influence during the Fascist period remained Gabriele D'Annunzio (1863–1938). D'Annunzio was strongly opposed to a bourgeois state, preferring the old aristocracy of birth and means, the only class that, in his view, had any cultural validity and understood his poetic need to defend his visions of beauty and genius. D'Annunzio had also been able to identify himself with patriotism and militarism, a mantle he had appropriated after the death of poet Giosué Carducci. D'Annunzio retained an aura of personal prestige into the

1930s, living his last years in an alabaster windowed villa at Salò on Lake Garda, the Vittoriale, where the aging, photophobic poet could receive his admirers.

Equally important for his controversial views of the world and of man in this particularly critical time of Italian life is Luigi Pirandello (1867–1936), a true innovator in world theatrical history. Pirandello won the Nobel Prize for literature in 1934. His strong philosophical pessimism, by which human unhappiness is not so much a consequence of the social system, but of human nature, brought him to accept Fascism and dictatorship as the least possible evil in order to control the evil of human nature. Pirandello saw man as unable to break out of his tragic solitude or to communicate with others or even with himself. The only way of escape is either madness or a painful form of resignation. Pirandello's theatrical works like *Six Characters in Search of an Author* (1921) used traditional schemes, characters, and situations, but within such schemes, the action always transgresses and criticizes the traditional system of thought and behavior.

Another important writer was the Trieste-born author Italo Svevo (1861–1928) who dabbled in psychoanalysis and took English lessons from a young James Joyce, then living in the Adriatic port city of Trieste. Svevo's masterpiece *The Confessions of Zeno* (1923) underlines the frailty of the individual. Many important Italian poets after WWII remained active during the Fascist period, such as Giuseppe Ungaretti (1888–1970), Eugenio Montale (1896–1981), Mario Luzi (1914–2005), Sandro Penna (1906–77), Umberto Saba (1883–1957). Novelists included Alberto Moravia (1907–90), Dino Buzzati (1906–72), Sibilla Aleramo (1876–1960), Aldo Palazzeschi (1985–68). For many of these authors the Fascist period was a period of reflection and preparation for intellectual production after WWII. Other artists, like still life painter Giorgio Morandi (1890–1964), who also enjoyed increased recognition after WWII, kept to their craft choosing subject matter which could not provoke the regime. During the Fascist period, it remained possible for authors to write and publish even if they were not open supporters of the regime, as long as their works did not contain explicit political attacks. In fact censorship on literary works was not as severe as on the press, for example, for the regime actively discouraged not only publication of articles critical of the government but even crime beat reporting, which could besmirch the propaganda of the new "Fascist era." Open criticism of the regime could lead to internal exile in remote regions of southern Italy, as experienced by authors including Cesare Pavese and Carlo Levi.

Film in Fascist Italy

The years before WWI saw the expansion and consolidation of Italian cinema, not only in Italy, but also in the European and North American markets. The outbreak of WWI in 1914 interrupted this vital period of Italian filmmaking and initiated a critical period of stasis so that in the 1920s Italy lost much of its prewar international market share. Many Italian studios went bankrupt, unable to compete with Hollywood products in the Italian market after WWI. In an attempt at self-defense, Italian studios organized into the *Unione Cinematografica Italiana*, a conglomerate that subsisted until 1927.[15] In this period, Italian film producers relied on remakes of earlier successes to reduce financial risk such as Maciste muscleman peplum epics. American film studios began to arrive in Italy to make their films on location and to take advantage of Italian expertise and craftsmanship. MGM filmed the first version of *Ben Hur* (1924) in the Cines studios in Rome and other Hollywood film studios also opened production and distribution offices in Italy.[16]

Mussolini's regime initially did not demonstrate a determined control of the film industry, although this may be more a reflection of the decline of the Italian film industry after WWI than a conscious decision by the regime. Unlike Russian dictator Joseph Stalin or German dictator Adolf Hitler who had moved to support filmmaking, Mussolini was initially interested in newsreels for the propagation of his personality cult. To this end the *Istituto Nazionale LUCE*, a state-sponsored documentary consortium, was formed in 1925 and projections of LUCE newsreels became obligatory in Italian theaters in 1926.[17]

The first Italian sound film released was a musical comedy *La canzone dell'amore/Song of Love* (1930) by Mario Righetti from a treatment (*Il silenzio/Silence*) by playwright Luigi Pirandello. It was also the year of the lowest production (14 features) since the early days of the cinema.[18] Sound allowed the Italian film industry, like many industries in Europe suffering from competition with Hollywood, to offer a product in a national tongue. The themes and style of the contemporary Italian national cinema truly begin in this period and the regime's attitudes toward the cinema changed accordingly. By the mid-1930s, Mussolini was identified with a placard proclaiming that the cinema was *l'arma più forte* (the strongest weapon), although it has not been established that Mussolini ever actually made the statement. Mussolini's son Vittorio took an active interest in producing and screenwriting as well as editing the journal *Cinema*. The government founded the Venice Film Festival in conjunction with the XVIII *Biennale* (Biannual) Art exposition, with the film competition becoming an annual event in 1932. The regime also added the *Centro Sperimentale di Cinematografia* (CSC) film school in Rome in order to further develop the national film industry. The first president of CSC was the noted film theorist Luigi Chiarini, who would later direct features such as *Via delle cinque lune/Five Moons street* (1941). Joining him in lecturing were Umberto Barbaro (1902–59), Alessandro Blasetti (1900–87), and Francesco Pasinetti (1911–49). The CSC numbered future directors among its students, including Giuseppe De Santis (1917–97), Luigi Zampa (1905–91), Pietro Germi (1914–74), Roberto Rossellini (1906–77), and Michelangelo Antonioni (1912–). In 1937, the CSC began publishing a film journal *Bianco e Nero* (White and Black). In the same year, *Cinecittà* (Cinemacity), one of the world's largest film studios, was inaugurated by Mussolini in Rome for the development of a national film industry to bring the culture of Rome to the world. Several important future directors and scriptwriters worked at Cinecittà or on Vittorio Mussolini's journal *Cinema* in those years including Cesare Zavattini (1902–89), Vittorio De Sica, Alberto Lattuada (1914–), Rossellini, Antonioni, Giuseppe De Santis, and Luchino Visconti (1906–76). The Italian professional cinema of the late 1930s became a training ground for postwar Italian film directors.

After the introduction of sound, the Italian cinema enjoyed a period of innovation and high production through the efforts of producers such as Stefano Pittaluga. In 1937 only 32 films were produced in Italy and Hollywood studios enjoyed nearly three-fourths of the Italian market, compared with only 13 percent for Italian productions.[19] American films were refused distribution in 1938 when American producers rejected the Fascist government's institution of a monopoly for the distribution of foreign films. With trade barriers against Hollywood films, by 1942, the number of Italian films produced increased to 117 with Italian production accounting for over 50 percent of the domestic market.[20] One might imagine that Mussolini would have been eager to profit politically from development of the Italian film industry. This is true to a certain extent since Mussolini also fancied himself as a playwright and even took a personal interest in producing some films including *Scipione Africano/Scipio the African* (1937), directed by Carmine Gallone centering on the Roman general who defeated the Carthaginian leader Hannibal. But the regime's demands did not equal those of the Nazi government on the German film industry or Soviet demands on Russian filmmakers. On the whole, the regime encouraged Italian directors to make films that depicted Italian life in a positive light. The regime did encourage propaganda-style films with themes promoting Italian colonial exploits such as Augusto Genina's *Lo squadrone bianco/White Squadron* (1936) or Alessandrini's *Abuna Messias/Cardinal Messias* (1939). However intellectuals including Luigi Chiarini, Umberto Barbaro, and Francesco Pasinetti were able to continue their discussions of film theory in journals like *Bianco e nero*. Film directors who did not wish to blatantly praise the regime could make films that were politically "neutral" or that had elements that indirectly appealed to the regime's political agenda such as *Pietro Micca* (1938), a film directed by Aldo Vergano and written by Sergio Amidei about the Piedmontese defense against a French invasion in the early 1700s in which a humble miner blows himself up in order to deliver Turin.

Alessandro Blasetti

One avenue by which directors could avoid explicitly criticizing Fascism was the historical or pseudo-historical spectacular film, a genre with a long tradition in Italy, going back to *Cabiria* and *The Last Days of Pompeii*. Probably the best representatives of the 1930s historical dramas trumpeting the heroic and nationalistic values dear to Fascist culture ministers are the early films of Alessandro Blasetti. Like many Italian directors Blasetti started his career as a critic and journalist. Blasetti was influenced by the reaction against the Idealist philosophy of Benedetto Croce, which criticized technical elements in artistic expression.[21] In journals includings *Cinema*, Blasetti praised the style and work of Russian directors such as Sergei Eisenstein as a model to reestablish the artistic and cultural role of Italian cinema. Once Blasetti became a director, he borrowed from the formalists, particularly in terms of camera angles and shots that depicted a strong relationship between characters and their natural surroundings. Blasetti's firs effort as solo director, *Sole/Sun* (1929), now lost, portrayed the difficult life in the swamplands of the Littorio region south of Rome (later renamed Latina after WWII), drained under the Fascist land reclamation policies. *Sole* was hailed as a rebirth for Italian cinema. The film focused on seemingly nonprofessional actors and popular themes, techniques that would become trademarks of the famed neorealist period in the 1940s.

Blasetti's career during the Fascist period is remarkable for its depth and variety. After his silent debut with *Sole*, Blasetti made *Nerone* (1930) a collection of the work of comedian Ettore Petrolini (1886–1936), which included the *Bravo, grazie!* (Well done, thank you!) routine featuring Petrolini as the Roman emperor Nero, which was actually a spoof on Mussolini. Blasetti also excelled in costume dramas like the Renaissance era drama *Ettore Fieramosca* (1938) depicting the *disfida di Barletta* (the 1503 skirmish between Italian and French knights at Barletta), based on a novel by Massimo D'Azeglio. He also made the first widely distributed Italian film of the period with a female nude (actress Clara Calamai) *La cena delle beffe* (1941) as well as *Quattro passi fra le nuvole/Four Steps in the Clouds* (1942), a seemingly light comedy written with Cesare Zavattini, which challenged the regime's models of family structure.

In 1932 filmmakers were invited by the Fascist regime to commemorate the *decennale*, the tenth anniversary of Mussolini's accession to power with the 1922 March on Rome. The regime also commissioned an artistic exposition at the EUR (Roman Universal Exposition) set for 1940, which recalled the style and language of pre-WWI Futurist movement. Blasetti's contribution to the commemorative celebration of the regime *1860* (1934) is a film that offers some stylistic similarities to the neorealist films of the postwar period for the use of nonprofessional actors, on location shooting, and a focus on lower-class characters (see figure 2.1). The narrative of this film has a debt to Alessandro Manzoni's (1785–1873) *Promessi sposi/The Betrothed*, a Catholic novel about two young lovers, Renzo and Lucia, separated by foreign oppression on the eve of their wedding. In *1860* the counterparts of Manzoni's Renzo and Lucia are the Sicilian couple Carmelo and Gesuzza, who postpone their wedding when the German speaking mercenary troops of the Bourbon regime invade their Sicilian village. Padre Costanzo from *1860* plays a role similar to Manzoni's heroic priest Fra' Cristoforo by providing moral leadership and a plan for the young man to escape. In Manzoni's novel, *The Betrothed*, Renzo the inexperienced country lad enters Milan, a city where the laws and customs he is accustomed to no longer apply. In *1860* Carmelo makes a similar voyage into northern Italy, first to Civitavecchia and later to Genoa. Rather than the bread riots of Manzoni's novel, Carmelo is confused by the myriad voices of Italy's different political factions. He meets a pro-republican Mazzinan, a papist Giobertian, a Tuscan who favors regional autonomy, ecstatically singing Piedmontese troops, and republicans who argue about the primacy of Italian patriots such as Camillo Cavour or Massimo D'Azeglio. Each of these members of Garibaldi's contingent in the film represents a faction of the future Italy: Catholics, republicans, monarchists, and above all the different regions of Italy identified by accent and mannerism. In *1860* there is a strong propagandistic connection between the audacity of the Fascists and Garibaldi's volunteers, and Mussolini and

Figure 2.1   Poster from Alessandro Blasetti's *1860*.

Garibaldi as men of providence whose charisma could unify the diverse forces behind a common cause.[22]

Blasetti's next film *Vecchia guardia/Old Guard* (1935) has a more contemporary setting but retains themes openly supportive of the regime. The film focuses on a small town split between Fascist and anti-Fascist factions culminating in the death of Mario, a twelve-year-old boy at the hands of anti-Fascists, an event which Blasetti presents as a part of the build up to the Fascist March on Rome in 1922. Like *1860* the commonplace of the defense of children provides the rationale for action, although depictions of the near civil war level of violence of the period in Blasetti's film is limited to a few scenes of street fighting and forced-feeding of cod liver oil. Propaganda ministers, such as Alessandro Pavolini, did not openly object to the creation of a parallel between the Fascist March on Rome and Garibaldi's *impresa dei mille* in *1860*.[23] However *Old Guard* was initially received coolly by Fascist officials during a period as the regime was more interested in depicting Fascism's imperial aspirations than its revolutionary origins. In fact the film was released because Mussolini apparently enjoyed the film immensely.[24] The film did well in Germany where it set box office records. The fact that *Old guard* received a lukewarm government reception is indicative of some of the changes and contradictions undergone by Fascism and the party since the radical revolutionary period of 1922 portrayed in the film. By 1935, the thirteenth year of the "Fascist era," the Fascists considered themselves firmly in place as the

Figure 2.2   Poster from Blasetti's *Vecchia Guardia*.

establishment and were not eager to relive the radical origins of their accession to power.

The case of *Old Guard* gives an idea of the line to be treaded by directors during the Fascist years, even by those making pro-Fascist films such as Blasetti. Direct portrayals of Fascism were actually somewhat rare in 1930s Italian cinema.[25] In fact not that many films depicted Fascism directly during the *ventennio*, the 20-year period of Fascist rule. Besides Blasetti's *Old Guard*, there was the costly production of *Camicia nera/Black Shirt* (1933) by Giovacchino Forzano, a director who made many historical dramas. In Forzano's film an amnesiac blacksmith is brought back to his senses when reminded of catch-phrases from the 1922 March on Rome. In *Aurora sul mare/Aurora* (1935) by Giorgio Simonelli, a Fascist saves the life of the anti-Fascist man who killed his father. Another of the open portrayals of Fascism in the cinema is Marcello Albani's *Redenzione/Redemption* (1943) made under the supervision of the Fascist point man Roberto Farinacci during the last period of Fascist rule in Rome. In this film, an Italian communist deserter in WWI changes his politics and sacrifices himself for the Fascist cause just before the March on Rome. The small number of dramas directly portraying Fascism indicates that filmmakers and producers prudently preferred to dress political themes in historical garb. Indirect portrayals of the regime blurred the manner in which the Fascists attained power and helped to avoid the threat of censorship. Thus more remote historical dramas such as Blasetti's *Ettore Fieramosca* (1938), *Un avventura di Salvator Rosa/An Adventure of Salvator Rosa* (1940) and *La cena delle beffe* (1941), became one of the principal film forms of the 1930s. The ability to avoid censorship is best seen in Blasetti's *La corona di ferro/The Iron Crown* (1941), which was not restricted despite negative allusions to a historically removed tyrant facing a revolt by subjugated peoples.

Mario Camerini and White Telephone Comedies

The Italian professional cinema of the 1930s also developed the so-called *telefono bianco* (white telephone) romantic comedies[26] influenced by the light comedies of the 1930s.[27] The term *telefono bianco* derived from the tendency for these films to have a sequence where a character speaks on a white enameled telephone in a richly adorned setting. Although many directors worked in the genre, the director most identified with this type of film is Mario Camerini (1895–1981). Camerini began his career in the Italian cinema quite early, receiving credit as a screenwriter for *Le mani ignote/Unknown Hands* (1913).[28] After serving in WWI and being taken prisoner of war to Germany, he returned to Italy to work with his brother Augusto and his cousin Augusto Genina in silent films, where he gained experience in a variety of genres. Camerini directed adventure films such as *Saetta principe per un giorno/Saetta Prince for a Day* (1924), and African colonial films such as *Maciste contro lo sceicco/Maciste against the Sheik* (1924), *Kif Tebbi* (1928), and late *Il grande appello/The Great Call* (1936). However it was in the romantic and sentimental comedies that Camerini made his mark. His first films as director, *Jolly* (1923) is the tragic story of a clown's love affair with a plot much like Fellini's *La strada* (1954). *La casa dei pulcini/The Little Kids' House* (1924) is a sentimental drama set in an orphanage. *Rotaie/Rails* (1931) is the story of a struggling couple that alternates between scenes of working-class troubles and leisure-class ease, which would become a commonplace of the Camerini comedy.

In 1933 Camerini wrote a brief article that recommended using inexperienced actors because of their tendency to follow direction more closely than professional actors.[29] He emphasized the importance of improvisation in filmmaking and the necessity for the director to retain a mental montage in order to handle the mosaic of details in production. Camerini also reveals an admiration for the style of Soviet formalists specifically mentioning Vsevolod Pudovkin's *Film Technique*.[30] In later interviews Camerini would declare that one of his

DAL FILM "CINES,,

GLI UOMINI CHE MASCALZONI!

Pianoforte L. 6 --   Mandolino L. 1,50   Orchestrina L. 6 --

EDIZIONI MUSICALI SOC. AN. STEFANO PITTALUGA - TORINO

Stab. Grafico Perô - Torino, via Nizza 30 - 1932-XI

91 Copertina dello spartito della canzone Parlami d'amore Mariù di C.A. Bixio, per Gli uomini che mascalzoni (1932) di Mario Camerini (cat. 195)

Figure 2.3   Victorio De Sica (Bruno) and Lia Franca (Mariuccia) in Mario Camerini's *Gli uomini che mascalsoni.*

strengths as a director was in montage—the splicing together of different film sequences for narrative effect.[31] Fundamental for an understanding of Camerini is that he spent a period in the late 1920s working at Paramount's Joinville studios in France in the production of multiple language versions of American films for the European market. Thus Camerini had direct contact with the Hollywood style and cultural conventions centered on the sentimental treatment of a good deed rewarded with a happy ending.[32] The Hollywood–Camerini connection would continue after the wars as a number of Camerini's films were remade in the United States.[33]

Like his colleagues, Camerini could also never be sure he would not run afoul of the regime's censors. In Camerini's *Il cappello a tre punte/The Three Cornered Hat* (1935) starring Neapolitan actors and writers Eduardo and Peppino De Filippo set in the Naples of the 1600s, an arrogant governor decides to coerce favors from a peasant girl by imprisoning her husband. The husband assumes the identity of the governor and the natural imbalance caused by the governor's abuse of power is overturned for a happy ending. Camerini remade the film after WWII as *La bella mugnaia/The Miller's Beautiful Wife* (1955), a benign comedy starring Sophia Loren and Marcello Mastroianni. But in the 1930s an open depiction of the abuse of power by an absolute ruler was not welcomed by the regime. Mussolini wanted to prohibit the release of the film, but after the intervention of culture minister Alessandro Pavolini and severe cuts, the film was released in a 70-minute version.[34] After these reprimands from the Fascist authorities, Camerini was careful to cloak any criticism of the regime in his films although he ran into similar problems for his adaptation of Manzoni's novel *The Betrothed* (1941).

Perhaps Camerini's greatest legacy is for having launched the career of future director Vittorio De Sica as a leading man in romantic comedies including *Gli uomini che mascalzoni!/Men What Rascals!* (1932), *Darò un milione/I'll Give a Million* (1935), *Ma non è una cosa seria/But It's Nothing Serious* (1936), *Il Signor Max* (1937), and *I grandi magazzini/Department Store* (1939) (figure 2.3). After his success as an actor, De Sica also began to direct romantic comedies such as *Maddalena zero in condotta/Maddalena, Zero for Conduct* (1940) with Carla Del Poggio and *Teresa Venerdì/Doctor Beware* (1941) featuring the vibrant Roman actress Anna Magnani in an early film role. De Sica developed the Camerini romantic comedy model with his career-long collaborator, screenwriter Cesare Zavattini, another figure of pivotal importance in postwar Italian cinema, whose career began with Camerini.[35] The benign depictions of social tensions resolved in the Hollywood tradition of the happy ending in light comedies like *Il Signor Max* (1937) and *Doctor Beware* (1941) could be seen as indication of the *anni del consenso* period. In *Doctor Beware*, three love interests vie for the attention of an irresponsible pediatrician played by De Sica. Anna Magnani plays Loretta, a fast talking and fast living show girl. Adriana Benetti, who would also star in Blasetti's *Four Steps in the Clouds* is a poor orphan girl who eventually wins the doctor's heart and Irasem Dilian is the spoiled daughter of a rich mattress manufacturer. The film has undertones of real social commentary. There is a dire depiction of Teresa working under the lustful eye of a butcher to the vapid frivolity of the rich girl aptly named Lilli Passalacqua (Lilly PasstheWater), or the manner in which Teresa is spied upon by one of her fellow orphans, or the reliance as a universal cure all by the pediatricians at the orphanage on cod liver oil, a supplement with political overtones from its use to publicly humiliate Mussolini's opponents during Fascism's revolutionary period. Films like *Doctor Beware* were important for the later development of the *commedia all'italiana* (comedy Italian style) of the 1950s and '60s which would rekindle the technical ability shown by De Sica to provide quick and efficient characterizations that supplied often devastatingly ironic social commentary in a comic setting.

Precursors of Neorealism

Some films of the 1930s had a production style and thematic content that presaged many pre-neorealist themes of the 1940s, especially those deriving from the naturalistic or *verismo* currents in Italian literature. One of the most important innovations of the journals *Bianco e Nero* and *Cinema* was that they both called for a more realistic film style in articles theoretical enough to avoid censorship. Among the contributors to *Cinema*, the influence of Italy's realist writer Giovanni Verga was so great that they were often called "the Verga group" and praised Verga's "virgin, bare, violent language" (November 25, 1941) and another called Verga's work "revolutionary art inspired by humanity that suffers and hopes" (October 10, 1941).[36] The latter description will aptly apply as well to neorealist films of the early postwar period. In short, the *Cinema* group wanted to rejuvenate Italian cinema by modeling it after Verga's prose. In 1933, Leo Longanesi, a fervent Fascist journalist who reportedly coined the expression "Mussolini is always right," wrote about the ideal film style of taking the camera into the streets to observe reality, a statement similar to those expressed by Cesare Zavattini, the later theoretician of the neorealist style of the 1940s.[37] Many of the techniques later classified as neorealist were already firmly entrenched in the Italian professional cinema of the 1930s. By the early 1940s, the idea of neorealism as a style of cinema was gaining a strong foothold. Umberto Barbaro published an article entitled "Neorealismo" in the review *Film* in 1943.[38]

With the approach of WWII the Italian cinema also offered documentary style films such as Rossellini's depiction of a military hospital ship, *La nave bianca/The Hospital Ship* (1941), and Francesco De Robertis's *Uomini sul fondo* (1941) about a submarine crew. Such films did not accept distinctions between documentary and fictional film narratives. Pasinetti's films such as *Il canale degli angeli/The Angels' Canal* (1934) anticipate the quasi-documentary style of neorealist shorts similar to Antonioni's early ventures into the documentary genre such as *Gente del Po/People of the Po River* (1943) or his postwar *Nettezze urbane/N.U.* (1948).

Credit for the first neorealist film is often allotted to Luchino Visconti's *Ossessione/Obsession* (1943) (figure 2.4). Visconti was born into the Milanese aristocracy in 1906. The Visconti name stands alongside other great ruling families in Italian history such as Della Scala and the Medici. Luchino enthusiastically developed his cultural and artistic interest in theater and opera. Before long, Visconti was attracted to film and traveled to France to assist Jean Renoir on *Toni* (1935), a film about an Italian immigrant in France whose unhappy marriage and involvement in a violent and tragic love triangle has been seen as a precursor of the Italian neorealist style for its spare photographic imagery, multilinguistic cast, and gripping storyline about the passions of humble people.[39] Visconti eventually returned to Italy and joined the *Cinema* group led by Vittorio Mussolini. He directed several plays and then made *Obsession* (1943), an adaptation of James Cain's novel The *Postman Always Rings Twice*. *Obsession* (1943) is a stark vision of life in the Po Valley region of northern Italy with close attention to environmental details and an unflattering treatment of daily life in Italy contrary to the regime's social self-image, which removed the film from circulation. The film evidences the early contrast between melodrama and the fatalism that would become a part of the Italian art cinema decades later.[40]

A large part of the reticence that Fascist culture ministers felt for films like Visconti's *Obsession* was its frank depiction of sexual themes. In the early 1940s, themes of sexual conflict appeared in the waning years of the Fascist-era cinema with films such as Vittorio De Sica's *I bambini ci guardano/The Children Are Watching Us* (1943), a film which starts as a vacation/beach movie and progresses

Figure 2.4   Clara Calamai (Giovanna), Massimo Girotti (Gino) in Visconti's *Ossessione*.

into a devastating study on the effects on a young boy of the destruction of a middle-class family due to the mother's adultery and the father's suicide (figure 2.5). These films faced potential censorship due to plots based on themes perceived as an affront to the regime's image of the family based upon female subservience and male virility extending from the *Duce* to the masses. Yet such rebellious or antisocietal roles for females were not unusual in the Fascist-era cinema. Roberto Rossellini featured his then girlfriend Roswita Schmidt as a sexually promiscuous Red Army commissar moll in *L'Uomo dalla croce/Man of the Cross* (1943). Alessandrini had featured a similarly emancipated Alida Valli in another anti-Soviet film *Noi vivi/We the Living* (1942) and *Addio Kira* (1942) based on an Ayn Rand novel. In both these films the heroines come from a foreign national and political culture, Russian Bolshevism, and their role was to present the evils of the alternate totalitarian political system.

One of actress Clara Calamai's films before Visconti's *Obsession* was *Boccaccio* (1940) directed by Marcello Albani in which Calamai assumes male dress in order to impersonate her uncle, the fourteenth century writer Giovanni Boccaccio, because she is jealous of the female conquests of her cousin, Berto. This early reference to Boccaccio gives an indication of the continuing importance of female roles in the Italian cinema, a tradition from the days of the diva-like Francesco Bertini, which would continue after the war. By the 1920s and early 1930s the corpulence/beauty model of the silent-era divas has been overturned. In popular culture such as film there was an identification of female beauty with slenderness rather than the traditional appreciation of a wider girth as defense against disease

203 Cineromanzo *I bambini ci guardano* (cat. 336)

Figure 2.5   Poster from Vittorio De Sica's *I bambini ci guardano/The Children are Watching Us (1994)*.

and starvation. In Hollywood musicals of the 1930s, the kicking rockette choruses mimicked the lever actions of factory machine and fused female sexual energy with the machine imagery.[41] A female figure communicating industrial and technological imagery supplanted the traditional identification of female physical weight with health and procreative power. Besides chorus lines in this Fordist context, the standard for a 1930s female physical display in the cinema was Claudette Colbert's hitchhiking stocking readjustment scene in Frank Capra's *It Happened One Night* (1934), mimicked in the Italian cinema by Assia Noris in Camerini's *I'll Give a Million* (1935).

Overall the 1930s and early 1940s were an incredibly vibrant period for the Italian cinema, which like French cinema under Nazi Vichy rule, enjoyed increased production due to autarkic policies that kept Hollywood films out of theaters. This climate allowed experimentation in genres such as biopics, operatic musicals, and literary adaptations from directors including Carlo Ludovico Bragaglia, Carmine Gallone, Mario Mattoli, Amleto Palmeri, Fernando Poggioli, and Gennaro Righelli. For example, Enrico Guazzoni, noted for his work in peplums made a biopic about the Italian inventor of the telephone, Antonio Meucci, *Antonio Meucci il mago di Clifton/Meucci the Wizard of Clifton* (1940). The high level of professionalism is best demonstrated by the *calligrafismo* (refinement) style of directors who took extreme care in the details of literary adaptations in films such as Mario Soldati's adaptations of Antonio Fogazzaro's novels *Piccolo Mondo Antico/Old Fashioned World* (1941) and *Malombra* (1942). The strength of Italian production in comedies, biopics, and even historical epics evidence continuity in the Italian cinema and the development of a cadre of professionals who would take the lessons learned during the 1930s and early 1940s into the postwar period. Of course production decreased due to the interruption of the war, whose end in 1945 meant the beginning of the next step in the realist movement: neorealism itself.

3

World War II

Italy's ties to Germany strengthened in the late 1930s as both countries assisted future Spanish dictator Francisco Franco's nationalist forces in the Spanish Civil War (1936–39). Mussolini saw the Rome–Berlin Axis as a chance for Italy to achieve Great Power status, a desire only partially satisfied by Mussolini's conquest of Ethiopia in 1936 and his exuberant rhetoric claiming that the Empire had finally returned to the "seven hills of Rome" after 20 centuries of history. As WWII broke out, Mussolini initially kept Italy out of the conflict. But Hitler's early string of successes in Poland, Denmark, Norway, Belgium, and France convinced Mussolini to enter this war on what he mistakenly judged to be the winning side in part to order to avoid the limited territorial concessions of the *pace mutilata* (mutilated peace as defined by D'Annunzio) peace treaty following WWI.

The tide of the war began to turn against the Axis powers of Germany, Italy, and Japan by the fall of 1942 with Allied victories on the North African front and the Russian counteroffensive. In February 1943, the Russian Red Army retook Stalingrad sealing the fate of the thousands of troops Mussolini had sent to the Russian front. On July 10, 1943, Allied armies landed in Sicily reportedly aided by informants connected to imprisoned Sicilian mafia bosses from New York.[1]

After the Allied liberation of Sicily, Mussolini suffered a no confidence vote by the Fascist Grand Council in which Galeazzo Ciano, Mussolini's son-in-law, voted against Mussolini. Ciano was always a bit at odds with the utopian, anti-bourgeois attitudes, or memories, of his maximalist father-in-law. The tension between the aristocratic status quo and Fascist iconoclasts was never fully resolved. The anti-aristocratic attitudes resurfaced in the last days of Fascism when Ciano, who had apparently voiced criticism of the alliance with Germany, was executed for his disloyalty after his vote in the Fascist Grand Council allowing inquiry into Mussolini's actions following the Allied invasion of southern Italy in 1943. These events were fictionalized in Carlo Lizzani's *Il processo di Verona/The Verona Trial* (1963).

On the pretext of a meeting, Italian king Victor Emmanuel III reportedly had Mussolini arrested and taken to prison (reportedly in an ambulance!). Victor Emmanuel then appointed WWI hero and conqueror of Abyssinia, General Badoglio (1871–1956), as head of an interim government before fleeing to Puglia, a region in southeastern Italy not under German or Anglo-American military control. Between July 25, 1943, and September 8, 1943, the Italian peninsula reeled in political instability. General Badoglio secretly negotiated an armistice with Anglo-American forces. When news of negotiations for an armistice between the Italian monarchy and the Allies was radio broadcast by Badoglio on September 8, neither Anglo-American forces nor the Italian Army which had received ambiguous instructions from the king's generals were able to prevent German forces from gaining military control over much of the peninsula. These events were dramatized in films including Luigi Comencini's *Tutti a casa/Everybody Go Home* (1960) and Francesco Rosi's *Le Quattro giornate di Napoli/The Four Days of Naples* (1962).

On September 12, Mussolini was rescued by German paratroopers from the prison-fortress at Gran Sasso in the Abruzzi region. He was installed as the leader at the Republic of Salò, a Nazi/Fascist German vassal state based at Lake Garda in northern Italy. Thus from 1943 until 1945, Italy was effectively divided in half. The Anglo-Americans controlled much of the south. Northern Italy remained under Nazi Germans and Italians loyal to Fascism under the Republic of Salò. The Allied invasion of southern Italy, the king's appointment of Badoglio, Mussolini's flight, and the return of Italian Communist Party chief Palmiro Togliatti (1893–1964) from exile in Russia set the stage for the loose confederation of anti-Nazi/Fascist forces between Catholics, Communists, and liberals known as the Resistance. Following instructions from Moscow, Togliatti had announced the *svolta di Salerno* (the Salerno about face), which instructed Communist Party members and sympathizers to cooperate with monarchists and other anti-Fascist forces. Partisan resistance groups under the general heading of the Committee of National Liberation (CLN) enlisted the participation of former Italian soldiers, interested in avoiding the Republic of Salò draft. These groups undertook a resistance campaign of anti-Nazi/Fascist sabotage. These events were depicted in numerous films of the neorealist period such as Roberto Rossellini's *Roma città aperta/Open City* (1945) and *Paisa'/Paisan* (1946) and more recently in films including Guido Chiesa's *Il partigiano Johnny/Johnny the Partisan* (2000). The end result was that the operations of the CLN weakened Nazi/Fascist control in the north and helped prepare the way for an Allied push northward since the Allied advance had stalled in the mountainous Italian peninsula with troops diverted for the main thrust into Germany with the Normandy D-Day landing in June 1944.

The success of the underground Resistance added significantly to the prestige of the Italian Communist Party, which had provided important members of the Resistance leadership. In March of 1944, the CLN mobilized general strikes in the north calling for an end to the war. Catholic forces joined in the Resistance as the Vatican began to position itself for a postwar world to defer embarrassment regarding the perceived inaction of Pope Pius XII (1876–1958) against Nazi–Fascist policies. By the end of the war there were popular uprisings in Milan, Domodossola, Turin, and Genoa. Allied liberators not only had to expel the Nazi German troops, but also disarm the victorious Resistance fighters and control their own often undisciplined multinational forces. Many of the Allied troops in Italy had been culled from around the world, and included brigades which committed atrocities against the Italian populace as depicted in Vittorio De Sica's film *La ciociara/Two women* (1960). By April 1945, the war entered its final stages in Europe. Mussolini tried to escape incognito into Switzerland but was captured, killed near Dongo, and brought back to Milan and hung by his feet with his faithful mistress Clara Petacci and others at Piazzale Loreto, the site of an earlier Fascist atrocity. Mussolini's attempt to flee is dramatized in Lizzani's *Mussolini ultimo atto/The Last Days of Mussolini* (1974).

The existence of a near state of civil war during 1943–45 between monarchists in southeastern Italy, partisan groups fighting Fascist sympathizer draftees of the Republic of Salò (which included important postwar figures such as dramatist Dario Fo) and German regular troops proved that there had been an indigenous reaction against Fascism. The fact that some Italians had acted against Nazi/Fascism independently helped to create a political mythology that somewhat assuaged the feeling of collective responsibility after the war. The myth of the Resistance allowed Italians to attenuate the level of war guilt felt in Germany, for example, for the industrial scale of the atrocities committed against Jews and other ethnic groups in the Holocaust. It is estimated that through the complicity of the Italian Fascist forces in northern Italy after September 8, 1943, approximately 8,500 Italian Jews were deported primarily to the Nazi death camp at Auschwitz; as dramatized by the Italian cinema in films including Carlo Lizzani's *L'oro di Roma/Gold of Rome* (1961) and vividly recounted in Ruggero Gabbai's documentary of survivor testimonials, *Memoria/Memory* (1997).[2]

Some events in Italy during this period have been overshadowed by the historical attention to Nazi atrocities and the heroic reputation of the Resistance. These include infighting between Red (Communist) and White (Catholic) factions in the Resistance itself, which resulted in atrocities including the incidents depicted in Renzo Martinelli's film *Porzus* (1997). There was also the resistance of Italian regular army units against the Nazis following September 8, 1943, which led to reprisals including the mass execution in Cefalonia of approximately 5,000 Italian soldiers unwilling to enlist in the Salò army or accept deportation to work camps in Germany,[3] an event not fully examined by the Italian entertainment industry until the television miniseries *Cefalonia* (2005). Another often overlooked aspect of the period was the ethnic cleansing of hundreds of thousand of Italians from the coast of Istria in contemporary Slovenia and Croatia. Yugoslavian Partisans troops loyal to Communist leader Josip Broz Tito reportedly murdered between 5,000 and 15,000 Italian civilians, dumping their bodies in the *foibe* (caves), which characterize the terrain of the region,[4] an event alluded to in Luigi Zampa's postwar demarcation drama *Cuori senza frontiera/The White Line* (1949) and dramatized more completely in the television miniseries *Il cuore nel pozzo/Heart in a Well* (2005).

After the fall of Mussolini's Fascist regime and its shortlived heir the Republic of Salò, there followed a period of civil strife, political reprisals and summary executions with numbers of victims approaching the controversial figure of 20,000.[5] Palmiro Togliatti, leader of the Italian Communist Party, called for a general amnesty in June 1946, helping to end reprisals. In May of 1946, King Victor Emmanuel III abdicated in favor of his son Humbert, a move insufficient to quell the memory of the Savoy monarchy's policies during Fascist accession and rule. The process of establishing a post-Fascist order was not entirely smooth and gave rise to the term *camaleontismo* (turncoatism) to describe the opportunism of ex-Fascists to identify with the new political order. There was also a certain cynicism in the electorate exemplified by the short-term rise of the *Fronte del Uomo Qualunque* (The Whatever Man Front) led by writer Guglielmo Giannini (1881–1960). Despite the fall of the Fascist regime, many prewar laws have remained on the books for decades as many Italians with close ties to the regime adapted to the new political reality, themes depicted in Luigi Zampa's adaptation of a Brancati novel *Anni difficili/Difficult Years* (1948).

The Cultural and Literary Roots of Neorealism

Although the term neorealism was coined in the early 1940s, the postwar moment of neorealism has deep roots in Italian culture. Alessandro Manzoni's (1785–1873) novel *I promessi sposi/The Betrothed* contains characters from all classes in a plot with a Catholic undercurrent that has influenced the narrative structure of many Italian films. Manzoni was in turn influenced by eighteenth and nineteenth-century currents in realism such as the work of the English novelists Daniel Defoe (1660–1731) or Henry Fielding (1707–54), who like later French authors, such as Stendhal (1783–1842), portrayed middle, and lower-class characters in stories that reflected the social and economic conditions of their time. Sicilian author Giovanni Verga (1840–1922) developed *verismo*, from *vero* (true), similar to naturalism but without naturalism's scientific language. Verga emphasized the strong primitive impulses and passions of Sicilian peasants in their natural environment in a linguistic style that pretends that the author is absent and reality is portrayed objectively. Instead of describing the inner feelings and thoughts of the characters—as any omnipresent and omniscient author usually does—Verga presents only what can be seen or experienced from the point of view of an objective observer, a style that had great influence on the Italian cinematic style of neorealism.

The Italian neorealist period was also influenced by American writers such as Sherwood Anderson, John Dos Passos, William Faulkner, Ernest Hemingway, and John Steinbeck, who were translated into Italian by two of Italy's most important writers, Cesare Pavese (1908–50), and Elio Vittorini (1908–66). Many Italian authors in the 1930s read American literature as a form of protest against the Fascist dictatorship. The Italians admired the spare, nonrhetorical style of the American authors and their frank treatment of all subject matter, regardless of how common, grim, or violent. Partly influenced by these American writers, Italian writers such as Pavese and Vittorini refused to follow government directives asking for propaganda writings that would convey a rosy or exalted view of life under Fascism. The neorealist school of literature is not as well defined as its counterpart in film but among its writers figure the abovementioned Cesare Pavese and Elio Vittorini, Alessandro Varaldo (author of one of the first Italian detective novels *Il settebello* (1931)), Vasco Pratolini, Renata Viganò, Ignazio Silone, Italo Calvino, and Carlo Levi. Neorealist prose developed as the successor of *verismo* and was characterized by a low-key opposition to Fascism, a concern for the problems of industrial workers and peasants and lower class as opposed to aristocratic heroes. Neorealism rejected the rhetorical flourished of authors such as D'Annunzio and described the settings and events of day-to-day life in frank terms, often reproducing the popular speech of the protagonists. Several of the neorealist literary works achieved international fame. Vittorini's *Conversazione in Sicilia/In Sicily* (1941) and Pratolini's *Cronache di poveri amanti/A Tale of Poor Lovers* (1946) were widely translated. Silone wrote two anti-Fascist novels that enjoyed great success also in the United States: *Fontamara* (1933) and *Pane e vino/Bread and Wine* (1937). Other writers include Vitalino Brancati with his novel about the Fascist era *Bell'Antonio* adapted to film starring Marcello Mastroianni by Mauro Bolognini in 1960. Carlo Levi, a Jewish doctor and painter from Turin, sent by the regime into internal exile in the tiny village of Aliano in southern Italy, wrote about his experiences in *Cristo si è fermato a Eboli/Christ Stopped at Eboli* (1946) adapted to film by Francesco Rosi in 1979. These novels described the poverty and ignorance that afflicted southern Italy in an objective manner that contrasted with the style of overt anti-Fascist propaganda or self-indulging moralistic rhetoric. These novels succeed in "letting the facts speak for themselves" in the tradition of *verismo*. Italo Calvino's novel *Il sentiero dei nidi di ragno* (1947) from the point of view of a young boy and Renata Viganò's *L'Agnese va a morire/Agnese will die* tale centered on a woman partisan were both written in simple, unaffected prose. Primo Levi's (1919–87) accounts of his deportation to a Nazi death camp in *Survival in Auschwitz/Se questo è un uomo* (1947) brought the objective style of neorealist writing to its starkest expression in which Levi, a chemist by training, described the horrors of the Nazi death camp with spare but powerful prose. Levi's account of his long journey back to Italy at the end of the war *La tregua/The Truce* was adapted to film by Rosi in 1997.

Neorealism in Film

More than any one stylistic element, there is a certain attitude that best describes neorealism, especially in film. That attitude includes a strong desire to uncover the truth about the widespread suffering in Italy, and to identify with the plight of the victims. Neorealism also criticizes the view of society as a mere collection of individuals who condone indifference to others' suffering. According to Cesare Zavattini, the screenwriter for Vittorio De Sica and a chief theoretician of neorealism, many social problems persist because of a lack of awareness of the plight of others. Neorealism wants to help overcome this barrier by showing how others live, suffer, and hope.[6]

Naturally, any neorealist project would have to involve filming situations that were not always visually pleasing. The journal *Cinema*, in October 1943, carried this statement by Italy's nineteenth-century literary scholar Francesco De Sanctis, "It is said that the ugly is not material for art and that art represents the beautiful. But [. . .] there is nothing that is in nature that cannot be in art."[7] De Sanctis (not to be confused with the director Giuseppe De Santis) was influential among the *Cinema* group and his above-quoted statement helped provide aesthetic justification for neorealism's desire to portray poverty. De Sanctis's words were echoed later on by the director Alberto Lattuada in what may be called the neorealist manifesto: "So we're in rags? Then let us show our rags to the world. So we're defeated? Then let us contemplate our disasters. So we owe them to the Mafia? To hypocrisy? To conformism? To irresponsibility? To faulty education? Then let us pay all our debts with a fierce love of honesty, and the world will be moved to participate in this great combat with truth."[8] When Cesare Zavattini was accused of being exclusively concerned with portraying a poverty and misery-stricken Italy, he replied, "We have started with misery simply because it is one of the most dominant aspects of our present society." Rossellini, when asked to define neorealism, called it "an interior state, a way of feeling, a humble representation of the world, an act of courage that aspires to accept man as he is."[9]

What is common about all of the above descriptions of neorealism is the clear sense of a mission to enact a social as well as aesthetic renewal in Italian culture. Another statement by Zavattini is revealing: "To describe poverty is to protest against it."[10] In fact neorealism was a cinema of protest, of liberation not only from Fascism but from injustice in general. Neorealist directors hoped that, by identifying with victims of suffering and injustice, they could instill in their viewers a positive response, a movement toward reform. That they were able to seek such a response without turning their films into propagandistic documentaries is to the credit of neorealism.

A major element of the "newness" of the new "realism", was the reaction to the wartime political situation. Never before had a realist movement in film or literature been so attached to the contemporary political situation as to actually encourage reform. The greatness of neorealism lies in the fact that it managed a detailed portrayal of the contemporary Italian sociopolitical situation. In this spirit of renewal and experimentation, the practical reality of the Italian cinema in the immediate postwar period was that many stylistic similarities among the neorealist films were determined by the lack of funds. Part of the vibrancy of the neorealist films may be explained by the fact that often the directors produced their own films on very limited budgets. Directors used cost saving measures that actually have been recognized as a style of filmmaking with the use of on-location shooting in authentic settings, nonprofessional actors, an emphasis on popular speech, a rejection of elaborate or contrived plots, frequent employment of improvisation, and a reliance on post-synchronous sound, a technique that would actually characterize much of postwar Italian production. Some of the neorealistic techniques were developed out of necessity due to a lack of resources like functioning studios or even a steady supply of electricity. For example, Rossellini had to use on-location shooting for *Open City* (1945) because the Cinecittà Studios in Rome were unusable. The making of these films has become a subject in recent Italian cinema such as Carlo Lizzani's *Celluloide* (1996) a dramatization of the making of *Open City* or Maurizio Ponzi's dramatization of the wartime Italian film industry, *A luci spente* (2004). By and large the "rough" neorealist style was a well-planned reflection of both a serious social consciousness that wanted to tell the truth about an "Italy in rags", an aesthetic ideal that turned "ugliness" into art. This combination produced films of great power and beauty. The neorealist film movement rushed into Italy on the heels of the departing Nazi troops. The sense of relief coming from the realization that Mussolini, the Fascists, and the Nazis had been defeated was matched only by a conviction that the story of widespread suffering needed to be filmed immediately.

Roberto Rossellini and *Open City* (1945)

War films from the Fascist period may be divided into several categories. There were costume dramas with thinly veiled pro-regime themes such as the Mussolini-influenced *Scipione l'Africano/The Defeat of Hannibal* (1936) by Carmine Gallone, one of the most costly films of the Fascist period, as well as films like *L'Assedio dell 'Alacazar/Alcazar* (1940) directed by Augusto Genina. The third current was the documentary drama featuring the Italian armed forces such as *Uomini sul fondo* (1941) and *Alfa Trau* (1942) directed by Francesco De Robertis, who also released a war dramas started during the war, *Uomini e cieli* (1947) after 1945.

Roberto Rossellini has been called the "father of neorealism".[11] His first directing experience was in short documentaries for the *LUCE* newsreel institute. Rossellini co-wrote Goffredo Alessandrini's *Luciano Serra pilota/Luciano Serra Pilot* (1938), a vehicle for the swashbuckling actor Amadeo Nazzari, which won the Mussolini Cup at the Venice Film Festival. In fact Rossellini's first features were all Fascist-era war films: *La nave bianca/The White Ship* (1941), *Un pilota ritorna/A Pilot Returns* (1942) co-scripted by Michelangelo Antonioni and Tito Silvio Mursino, a pseudonym for Vittorio Mussolini, son of the *Duce* and editor of the influential journal *Cinema*.[12] Rossellini's *Uomo dalla croce/Man of the Cross* (1943) is a film about a heroic priest accompanying Italian troops in the invasion of Russia. *Open City* (1945) has enough thematic and stylistic elements in common with *Man of the Cross* for *Open City* to be considered its remake.[13] Thus by the time Rossellini made *Open City* in 1945, he was at least on his fifth war film.

Many films presented valid aspects of the Resistance such as the multi-director documentary and recreation film *Giorni di gloria/Days of Glory* (1945), Camerini's *Due lettere anonime/Two Anonymous Letters* (1945), Giacomo Gentilomo's *O sole mio* (1945), Blasetti's *Un giorno nella vita/A Day in the Life* (1946), Max Neufeld's *Un uomo ritorna/Revenge* (1946), Enrico Cerlesi's *Uno tra la folla/One among the Crowd* (1945), Giorgio Ferroni's *Pian delle stelle* (1946), Carmine Gallone's *Avanti a lui tremava tutta Roma/Before Him all Rome Trembled* (1946). Alberto Lattuada would mix themes of neorealism and the Resistance in *noir*-tinged plots, later known as *neorealismo nero* (black neorealism) with films such as *Il bandito/The Bandit* and *Senza pietà/Without Pity* (1948).[14] Luigi Zampa's added *Un Americano in vacanza* (1945) and *Vivere in pace/To Live in Peace* (1947). Aldo Vergano's *Il sole sorge ancora/Outcry* (1946) in particular has a storyline with many elements that encapsulate the experience of the Resistance during WWII with the direct participation of partisan veterans including Gillo Pontecorvo as well as other future directors: Carlo Lizzani, Giuseppe De Santis, and future film critic Guido Aristarco. However Rossellini's *Open City* has been singled out as the film that best portrays the short-lived alliance between Catholics and Communists against the Nazi/Fascists. Like Vergano's *Outcry*, Rossellini's *Open City* portrays a Catholic priest and a communist dying for the same cause. Rossellini's film rises above political infighting with a theme of universal brotherhood in a film that effectively depicts all views of the wartime struggle.

Figure 3.1   Anna Magnani (Pina) in Roberto Rossellini's *Open City*.

Part of the legend of *Open City* derives from the difficulties making a feature film in the immediate aftermath of the war. In 1943 after hearing that Mussolini had been arrested and deposed by King Victor Emmanuel III, Rossellini stopped production on his next planned project, *Desiderio/Woman* (1946), a melodrama about the daughter of a stationmaster eventually completed by Marcello Pagliero, the actor who plays the partisan Manfredi in *Open City* and the future director of *Roma città libera* (1946). Rossellini left Rome for the Abruzzian countryside and Tagliacozzo, to prepare for this film and be closer to the Allies and perhaps to sort out his personal situation given his track record making Fascist-era war films. In September 1943, German troops occupied Rome and would remain until Anglo-American troops liberated the city in June 1944. Following the September 8 radio announcements by General Badoglio of the fall of the Mussolini government in Rome, German troops requisitioned material from Roman film studios and invited directors to move north to Venice, where the Republic of Salò would attempt to create film studios. Many figures in the Italian film industry went into hiding or like Vittorio De Sica took refuge with the Vatican's film production company Orbis making *La porta del cielo/The Gate of Heavan* (1945), a film about a trainload of pilgrims to the shrine of Loreto, partly in order to avoid being sent north to work in the Salò Republic film industry.[15]

Open City depicts the interim period between German occupation and Allied liberation. "Open City" is a diplomatic term that refers to a city that in time of war has been declared by both sides to be free from all acts of military aggression. The title is an ironic testimony to the violence that marked the occupation period with a story of attempts of the Nazi occupation forces to capture CLN members carrying out guerrilla warfare. Nazi troops occupied Rome, and the Gestapo Headquarters in Via Tasso was full of prisoners being interrogated, tortured, and killed. A climax was reached in March 1944 with the *fosse ardeatine* massacres, when Nazis executed 335 Italians, including women and children, in retaliation for a bombing in Via Rasella, which claimed the lives of 33 Nazi soldiers. Events like the *fosse ardeatine* massacres or the round up of Jews from the Roman Ghetto for deportation to Auschwitz gave neorealist directors a sense of mission about the sort of films they should make after the war.

Rossellini's initial idea was to make a short film, a documentary, celebrating the Italian Resistance fighters, the college-age youths of the GAP (*Gruppo Azione Partigiana*) responsible for the Via Rasella bombing. However, Rossellini had Catholic backers who were interested in making a film about the life of Don Morosini (1913–44), a priest among the executed during the Ardeatine caves massacres. Rossellini's left-leaning screenwriter Sergio Amidei was also interested in the story of CLN hero, Celeste Negarville, who later became mayor of Turin. The character Pina, played by Anna Magnani, was based upon the story of Teresa Gullace (1907–44), a pregnant mother of five reportedly shot by Nazi guards as she attempted to throw food to her detained husband. The final script combines these influences with a nod to the themes of a standard *telefono bianco* story of the showgirl Marina, played by Amidei's girlfriend Marina Michi. Marina's betrayal of the resistance leader Manfredi fits into the plot lines of 1930s dramas in which a foreign-influenced *femme fatale* or *fatalona* tempts a valiant protagonist. This narrative had been a feature of Fascist era war dramas like Alessandrini's Rossellini scripted *Luciano Serra pilota/Luciano Serra Pilot* (1938) or Genina's *Lo squadrone bianco/White Squadron* (1936), two films with settings in Italian colonies in Africa. The final version of the script of *Open City* actually also has a great deal in common with the plot of Manzoni's Catholic novel *The Betrothed*. The plot revolves around a couple prevented from marriage by a foreign occupier. As in Manzoni's novel there is a bread riot and a heroic priest who stands up against the selfish ideology of the occupiers (in this case the Nazi's Social Darwinism instead of the feudal arrogance of the Hispanic noblemen in Manzoni's novel) with a final threat of divine retribution from a heroic priest.

Rossellini did rely on the so-called methodological signatures of neorealism such as popular dialects, on-location shooting, non professional actors, and post-synchronous sound. Many of the "neorealist" elements in the film were actually a result of logistical necessity. Rossellini reportedly acquired film stock on the black market with bits spliced together giving the film a documentary, newsreel feeling. Ambient sound and actors' voices were dubbed in later, after the film was edited, a technique common in the Italian film industry. The natural lighting acclaimed in *Open City* is a result of the lack of studios and a shortage of electricity, which the troupe allegedly pilfered from an American army club where they met an officer in the U.S. army, who reportedly later oversaw the successful distribution of the film in the United States where it won the equivalent of an Academy Award for best foreign film. Actually the lack of conventional resources may have been a blessing in disguise, for without them Rossellini was better able to recreate reality in the bare terms idealized by the *Cinema* group.

The neorealist casting of non professional actors was actually a practice followed more rigorously by Vittorio De Sica and screenwriter Cesare Zavattini than by Rossellini in *Open City*. Rossellini cast Roman showgirl Anna Magnani and Roman comedian Aldo Fabrizi, both established box office draws in the Italian cinema before the decline in production due to the war (figures 3.1 and 3.2). Fabrizi and Magnani had already appeared together in Mario Bonnard's film *Campo de'fiori/The Peddler and the Lady* (1943), a comedy in which Aldo Fabrizi's virtuous fishmonger is tempted to reject the *popolana* played by Magnani. Aldo Fabrizi's comedic talents are evident in the slapstick sequences in *Open City*, when Fabrizi as Don Pietro strikes a bed-ridden invalid with a frying pan or when he moves a religious statue away from another statue of a female nude, a sight gag lifted from Chaplin's *City Lights* (1931). Fabrizi also brought his gagman, the future director Federico Fellini, to the production as screenwriter. The genius of *Open City* is the manner in which Rossellini and Amidei were able to combine such stories under extremely difficult conditions into a coherent film that has come to exemplify the near mythology created around the Resistance period.

In *Open City* the Italians are involved in two struggles; one against the Nazis and the Italian Fascists; the other against a severe shortage of food and essentials. The film opens with documentary-style footage showing Nazi troops searching for Giorgio Manfredi, a Communist member of the CLN forced to remain in hiding near the Spanish steps, a landmark that evokes memories of the German and Italian intervention in the Spanish Civil War, where Manfredi had fought on the republican side. Manfredi continues his Resistance activity with

Figure 3.2   Aldo Fabrizi (Don Pietro) in Roberto Rossellini's *Open City*.

the help of the priest, Don Pietro. Manfredi's safety is threatened after he quarrels with his lover, the showgirl Marina, whose drug addiction is supported by Ingrid, a Gestapo agent. Meanwhile, the children of the neighborhood where Manfredi is hiding gamely form their own Resistance troop and stage bomb attacks against German positions. The adults of the historical GAP resistance group of the Via Rasella bombing are transformed into children in Rossellini's film. When German forces get wind of Manfredi's whereabouts they conduct a dragnet of the neighborhood. Eventually both Manfredi and Don Pietro are apprehended and put to death by the Nazi forces, Manfredi after grisly torture and Don Pietro at the hands of the hungover German officer Hartmann commanding a reticent Italian firing squad.

Open City is by and large a story of defeat. Rossellini boldly embraced a realist style, taking the cameras into the misery-stricken streets and homes of the capital with wartime life in all its grimness, tragedy, and humor. Rossellini recreated the wartime suffering and tension so accurately that many viewers thought that they were actually seeing documentary footage. Yet *Open City* allows a measure of optimism by stressing the cooperation between seemingly unlikely allies such as the Communist Manfredi and the Catholic priest Don Pietro. The theme of choral solidarity and cooperation is carried over from Rossellini's Fascist-era films and would become a continuing characteristic of his later work.

Rossellini's portrayal of the Resistance to the Nazi occupation of Rome is not limited to the views of his heroic characters, for he also ably presents the viewpoints of defeated figures, like the Nazi officer Bergman who gives an explanation of his racist ideology and the torture of Manfredi as a test case for the differences between "slave" and "master" races. Bergman also provides a prediction of eventual conflict between the Catholics and Communists temporarily united by the Resistance. The film effectively deals with issues of German war guilt in the drunken tirade of the German officer Hartmann, who eventually kills Don Pietro. Hartmann decries the results of the violence of two world wars that produced a harvest of hatred. Italian war guilt is depicted in the character of the Italian policeman who does not stop the bread riot or the Italian soldiers on the firing squad who shoot at the ground instead of at Don Pietro's back. With his able characterizations of both sides, Rossellini reveals an ability to use a few short sequences to convey entire historical issues from the Resistance period.

The film ends with a message of Catholic consistency. In fact, Rossellini's entire war trilogy—*Open City, Paisa'/Paisan, Germania anno zero/Germany Year Zero*— has themes of Catholic ideological restoration. Alberto Tavazzi, the actor who played the chaplain from *Man of the Cross*, Rossellini's 1943 film about an Italian army unit on the Russian front, appears briefly in *Open City* as the priest who gives Don Pietro the last rites. The last characters seen in the film are the children as they march toward a panorama of Rome dominated by the dome of St. Peter's Basilica. Out of the current defeat comes the hope that the children's cooperative struggle against injustice and oppression will have prepared them to carry their mentors' efforts to a positive conclusion in the rebuilding of an Italy dominated by Catholic values. In fact, postwar Italy would be dominated by the Christian Democrat Party.

The Vatican, with its Orbis production company, was quite active in film production in the war years, producing films such as *The Gate of Heaven* (1945) by De Sica, Blasetti's *A Day in the Life* (1946) about a convent of nuns who hide resistance fighters, and the documentary *Pastor Angelicus* (1943). These films, which have an undercurrent of independence from the Fascist regime, could be read as an attempt to reposition the Church for a post-Fascist Italy. These films were coscripted by Diego Fabbri, an author with close ties to the Vatican, who also worked on Giorgio W. Chili's episodic film *I dieci comandamenti/The Ten Commandments* (1945), an episodic film featuring leading actors from the prewar Italian cinema including Amadeo Nazzari and Massimo Girotti appear in episodes illustrating the moral lessons of each commandment. Fabbri would also later collaborate on *Fabiola* (1949), a Catholic peplum directed by Blasetti with a story set during the Roman empire's persecution of Christians with a plot recalling *Quo Vadis?*

Open City was highly acclaimed in Europe and the United States winning the Grand Prize at the Cannes Film Festival and the equivalent of the Academy Award for best foreign film. The film has a reputation for not receiving much attention on the Italian market, a comparison that holds only if the film's box office receipts are compared to the Hollywood films that flooded the country after the war as the latter had been denied distribution in Italy since 1938. However if *Open City* is compared to other Italian films, it did well, although the box office data for 1945 is a matter of some controversy. Some sources have *Open City* finishing first among Italian domestic films of 1945.[16] As mentioned above other sources have it finishing second to *The Ten Commandments* and ahead of Gennaro Righelli's *Abbasso la miseria/Down with Misery* (1945) a *telefono bianco* style comedy starring Vittorio

De Sica and Anna Magnani, and another De Sica comedy with Clara Calamai *Lo sbaglio di essere vivo/My Widow and I* (1945) directed by Carlo Ludovico Bragaglia. This undervalued comedy in the tradition of *Teresa Venerdì/Doctor Beware* is based on an Aldo De Benedetti play and features Vittorio De Sica in the role of an honest man who is treated with disrespect by his friends and family until he is falsely jailed for embelzzelment, after which he is celebrated as a man of the world. The film is a brilliant satire of social snobbery and moral hypocrisy in anticipation of the *commedia all'italiana* (Italian style comedy) of the 1950s and 1960s.[17]

Rossellini's second film in his war trilogy, *Paisan* (1946), has a title that derives from the term *paesano* used by American GIs, which in Italian means, among other things, "comrade, friend", particularly in southern Italy. *Paisan* is a collection of six episodes that trace the northward movement of the Allied forces in Italy from 1943 to 1945 in Sicily, Naples, Rome, Florence, the Apennine Mountains, and the Po River Delta. The Sicilian episode depicts the battle for Sicily between Nazi and Allied forces, and the reaction of the native Sicilians to the American troops. The Naples episode is about destitute Neapolitan children trying to steal from unwary American GIs. The final sequence in Naples offers a haunting view of the cave dwellings of those left homeless by the war. In the Rome episode Rossellini tells the story of an American soldier's bitter sweet romance with an Italian girl who has fallen into prostitution, played by Marina Michi, the same actress who appeared as the Nazi collaborating showgirl in *Open City*. The Florence episode finds the Allied advance stalled by Florence's Arno River. The plot revolves around the attempt of an American nurse to get news about an Italian partisan leading CLN attacks behind enemy lines. The fifth episode written by Federico Fellini allows a respite from the war. Three American Army clergymen—a Jew, a Catholic, and a Protestant—visit an isolated monastery in the Apennines and are surprised by the otherworldly outlook of the monks in the midst of the war. The sixth and final episode returns to warfare with a depiction of the efforts of American OSS (the precursor of the CIA) commandos and partisan forces facing defeat from a better-equipped and better-organized German army in the Po river valley of northern Italy.

Paisan is somewhat less optimistic than *Open City*. Most of the episodes end in defeat with less emphasis on hope for the future. This is particularly evident in the roles of children who, rather than being symbols of hope as in *Open City*, are tragic victims of the military and economic consequences of warfare. Nevertheless, the love stories in several episodes remind that even in the midst of war, hope survives in the strength of human emotions. Furthermore, *Paisan*'s collection of separate episodes allows a greater complexity of characterization and point of view. For instance, rather than the single opposition of good and evil (Partisans versus Nazis) in *Open City*, in *Paisan* a new force, the American army, is introduced and portrayed in ambiguous terms. The Americans are usually generous and good-willed, but because of their lack of exposure to foreign cultures they can also be insensitive to the fears and anxieties of the war-weary Italian population. Finally, in focusing on the war and foreign occupation in different regions of Italy (rather than just one city as in *Open City*), *Paisan* introduces a historical dimension by recalling Italy's long foreign domination prior to the unification of 1870. *Paisan* expands the documentary tendency of realist film by including a larger historical dimension and introducing ambiguity and complexity of characterization and point of view. The film had a huge influence on filmmakers such as Gillo Pontecorvo, a prime exponent of postwar Italian political filmmaking as well as André Bazin the theorist of the French New Wave school of the late 1950s because of the spare nature of the film's style and story lines.[18] The third film of Rossellini's war trilogy *Germany Year zero* (1947) was filmed in postwar Berlin and centers on a thirteen-year-old child, Edmund, who undergoes a series of symbolic and frightening encounters with family members and acquaintances, which culminate in the boy's suicide when he cannot reconcile the Social Darwinist education he had received from the Nazis with the defeat of his father and nation.

4

Reconstruction and the Late '40s

1946   National Referendum selects republic over monarchy
       Umberto II leaves Italy
1947   De Gasperi visits the United States to accept the Marshall Plan of economic
       aid
1948   Political elections, the Christian Democrats defeat a coalition of the PCI
       and the PSI
       Unsuccessful assassination attempt against Communist Party leader Palmiro
       Togliatti
1949   Italy joins NATO (North Atlantic Treaty Organization)
1950   CD-led government institutes the *Cassa del Mezzogiorno* public works pro-
       gram to promote southern Italian economic development

In 1946 a referendum was held with universal suffrage to decide whether the
future Italian constitution would be monarchical or republican. The voters'
choice of a republic paved the way for a republican constitution with a weak exec-
utive branch and a parliament divided into two bodies with a large number of
deputies. The victory for a republic demonstrated not only a desire for a break
with the past but also some of the divergences between the north, which favored
the republic, and Rome and the south, which favored a monarchy.[1] The
Resistance had been more of a northern than southern phenomenon. Liberation
began in July of 1943 with the Anglo-American invasion of Sicily, with northern
Italy remaining under Nazi occupation longer than the south. In Southern Italy
the monarchy was identified with political stability and a continuation of the
political patronage system, a traditional source of employment. There was even a
short lived movement to have Sicily join the United States after the war.

By May 1947, Prime Minister Alcide De Gasperi established a government
comprising Christian Democrats and their political allies.[2] When the first parliamentary elections were held on April 18, 1948, the DC won 48.5 percent of the
vote and the coalition of the PCI and the PSI received approximately 30 percent.
Italy became politically divided between the PCI and the DC. An important factor
for the DC victory was the split of the Socialist Party in January 1947 into pro-Soviet

and pro-Western factions. The Christian Democrats presented the elections as a choice between Western-style capitalism and Communism in anticipation of the coming Cold War between the Soviet block of Iron Curtain nations under Russian occupation in Eastern Europe and the countries in Western Europe liberated from the Nazis by Anglo-American forces. The Christian Democrats relied heavily on their identification with the anti-Communist policy of the United States. The Russian engineered Communist coup in Prague in 1947 confirmed suspicions about the Communists' intention to foment a worldwide communist revolution. With the Marshal Plan, the United States provided billions of dollars for Italian reconstruction. Over the reconstruction period the Italian government followed policies based on classical liberal economic theory with an emphasis on free trade, attenuation of state participation, and mobility of labor. Postwar unemployment remained high through 1948 until the postwar boom. But there were also concessions to the Left such as legislation regarding minimum wage, holidays, and cost-of-living adjustments. Despite the changes the new Italian republic remained under a system of legal statutes made by the Fascist regime.

In an attempt to bridge the gap between northern and southern Italy, in 1950 the government instituted the *Cassa del Mezzogiorno* public works project. But the funds of the *Cassa* were tied to the political patronage system. These practices were a continuation of the *clientellismo* (political patronage) culture, which had perpetuated under Fascism but whose roots were actually centuries old. *Lottizzazione* (division of government contracts by party loyalty) and *clientelilismo* characterized the Italian political talent for *trasformismo* (status quo politics). However there were also protests in southern Italy when sharecropping or dispossessed peasants occupied arable lands during 1944–46. A crowd of May Day celebrants were massacred at Portella delle ginestre in Sicily on May 1, 1947, allegedly by a guerilla group tied to the bandit Salvatore Giuliano, an event depicted in Francesco Rosi's film *Salvatore Giuliano* (1962) and a situation alluded to in films such as Giuseppe De Santis's *Non c'è pace tra gli ulivi/No Peace under the Olive Tree* (1950).

The DC reacted to the increase in civil strife with marginally successful land reforms, causing a backlash from their own supporters. The DC's delay of reform measures broadened their electoral hold on the conservative elements and effectively halted the rise of the monarchists and separatists in Sicily. Alcide De Gasperi, the Christian Democrat leader, hoped to avoid future DC losses by an attempt to reintroduce proportional representation with what has come to be known as the *legge truffa* (swindle law), echoing the Acerbo proportional representation law of 1923 passed under Mussolini. However after the proportional representation law was passed in 1953, the DC coalition with the monarchists and the neo-fascist MSI narrowly missed the required 50 percent needed to attain seats through the proportional representation law. These political battles demonstrate how the wartime coalition of the Resistance came to mirror the Cold War bipolarism that dominated international politics after WWII.

The success of the wartime CLN Resistance coalition had created a national desire for moral, political, and economic renewal. The prestige of the Resistance served as a basis for a culture of collective understanding and reaction against the rhetoric of Fascism. In the postwar period, Italian culture came under the influence of the dictates of the Soviet Union, the Vatican, and the United States in popular and economic culture. The Communists clung to the image of the Soviet Union as a societal model. In an effort not to repeat the mistake of 1921 when Communist maximalists split with the Socialists, which helped the Fascists attain power, Communist leader Togliatti opted to tone down revolutionary rhetoric. The Catholic Church valued the status it had gained under the 1929 Lateran accords/Concordat and had to counter the impression of Pius XII's seeming inaction against Nazi–Fascism. The Church reacted to the political success of atheistic socialism by excommunicating all PCI and PSI voters in 1949. Catholic elements supported the Christian Democrats who were willing to incorporate the main points of the 1929 *Concordat* into the post war constitution. The third influence economically and culturally came from the United States, which in the postwar period exercised varying degrees of cultural and political hegemony over Italy and Western Europe. America provided a powerful model for the development of an international consumer culture driven by a mass media. These three cultural and ideological forces (Church, Soviet Union, United States) were also well represented in the cinema and popular culture. The Vatican sponsored parish/oratorio screenings. The Italian Communist Party did the same at their network of *Casa del popolo* (house of the people) recreation centers. The ideological undertone of Hollywood's optimistic cinema dominated commercial theaters, television, and the advertising industry.

In Italy, many authors who contributed to postwar culture had been active during the Fascist era, such as Ignazio Silone (1900–78), Carlo Levi (1902–75), Elio Vittorini (1908–66), Cesare Pavese (1908–50), Carlo Cassola (1917–87), Curzio Malaparte (1989–57), Alberto Moravia (1907–90) Vasco Pratolini (1913–91), Corrado Alvaro (1895–56), and Sibilla Aleramo (1876–60). After WWII these authors offered a new tone to Italian culture that sought to break with the rhetoric of the past. All of these novelists shared a commitment to the portrayal of grim, exploitative situations from which rebellious protagonists gain a renewed sense of humanism and meaningful action. Similar themes are evident in Primo Levi's (1919–87) Holocaust account *Survival at Auschwitz* (1947). Giovanni Guareschi (1908–68) with his *Don Camillo* (1948) series wrote comic tales, adapted with great box office success for the Italian cinema, that depicted the geopolitical cultural split between Catholics and Communists in the Cold War in the microcosm of a small town in the Po valley. Italo Calvino wrote a foundational novel depicting the Resistance period, *Il sentiero dei nidi di ragno* (1947). Carlo Emilio Gadda's (1893–1973) detective novel *Quer pasticciaccio brutto di Via Merulana/That Awful Mess on Via Merulana* (1957) depicted the often contradictory and messy reality of the Fascist period and was later adapted for the screen as an Italian *noir, Un maledetto imbroglio/ The Facts of the Murder* (1959) by Pietro Germi. There was also international recognition for the vibrancy of Italian postwar literature as poet Salvatore Quasimodo (1901–86) won the 1959 Nobel Prize for literature. The Italian theater featured the work of Neapolitan author Eduardo De Filippo (1900–84), brother of the actor Peppino De Filippo, who often played straight man to Totò, and author of plays such as *Napoli milionaria/Side Street Story* (1950) adapted as a musical in 1950 and *Filumena Martiruana* (1945) adapted by De Sica as *Matrimonio all'Italiana/Marriage Italian Style* (1964).

Film: The Late 1940s

Luchino Visconti

With his film *Ossessione/Obsession* (1943), Luchino Visconti put into practice the realist theories of the *Cinema* group trained in the Italian professional cinema of the late 1930s and early 1940s. During the war Visconti was an active participant in the Resistance and was eventually captured and imprisoned in Rome by the Nazis, who planned to execute him. He managed to escape from prison just before the American Fifth Army entered Rome in 1944. In 1946, Visconti contributed to the multi-director documentary recreation film about the Resistance, *Giorni di Gloria/Days of Glory* (1945). After the war, Visconti returned to theater productions in Rome. At the same time, Visconti's interests continued to focus on two key figures who were to influence his next film, *La terra trema/The Earth Trembles*; novelist Giovanni Verga and the Communist theorist Antonio Gramsci. In 1948, Visconti turned his attention to the problems of Italy's rural poor with *The Earth Trembles* (1948), an adaptation of Verga's novel in the *verismo* style, *I Malavoglia/The House by the Meddlar Tree*. Visconti originally intended to make a film trilogy about Sicily based on Verga's novels but only completed *The Earth Trembles* (1948), an epic-length film set in the Sicilian coastal village of Aci Trezza about a young fisherman Antonio Malavoglia who tries to raise his family out of poverty by fighting the exploitative owners of the village fishing boats. Antonio decides to take out a loan with the family house as collateral in order to buy his own boat. But the project ends in failure because Antonio is unable to enlist the support of the other fishermen in Aci Trezza.

Visconti's film is a faithful adaptation of Verga's novel and is close to Verga's realistic portrayal of the Sicilian poor, showing their passions, superstitions, and stoic nobility, which often involves a passive acceptance of fate. Visconti, influenced by Verga's attempt to accurately reproduce the speech of the Sicilian peasants, employed an entirely nonprofessional cast speaking their own Sicilian dialect. Incidentally the language used by actors is different enough from standard Italian that when the film was released in Italy, occasional voice-over commentary by Visconti was added to help non-Sicilians follow the story.

Visconti's film makes extensive use of close-ups with depictions of the day-to-day life of its characters. Visconti's pacing in the film anticipated the art cinema style with less emphasis on action and more emphasis on character development. The film has many long sequences that may at first viewing seem "unnecessary" for the development of the plot, but that are actually crucial to Visconti's study of the daily life in Aci Trezza. The film's patient depictions of the daily habits of the fishermen and their families recall the detached scientific tone of anthropological or wildlife documentaries. Following the ideas of Communist theorist Antonio Gramsci, Visconti's film concentrates on a rural rather than an industrial situation, and pays close attention to the regional question by emphasizing Sicilian mannerisms and speech. *The Earth Trembles* is a convincing portrayal of a social struggle that fails to produce significant change. Nevertheless, at the end of the film it is evident that despite his defeat, the main character, Antonio, is still determined to overcome the exploitation in his village. In practical terms, the film was one of the first box office disappointments of the neorealist period.[3]

Giuseppe De Santis

Giuseppe De Santis, like De Sica, Visconti, Rossellini, Vergano, and Antonioni, gained valuable experience in the Italian professional cinema of the 1930s. Like Visconti he began his directing career in the multi-director Resistance film *Days of Glory* (1945) before making his first feature *Caccia Tragica/Bitter Hunt* (1946). The film starring Massimo Girotti, is in the *neorealismo nero* vein similar to the gangster film genre and reveals the the struggles between friendship, collaboration, and political duty during the Resistance. De Santis's later film *Riso amaro/Bitter Rice* (1949) also mixes elements of neorealism with the gangster or *noir* crime film genres depicting the seasonal harvest of the *mondine*, female rice pickers, who worked in the Po Valley in northern Italy. De Santis depicts sequences of the indigenous culture, such as the call and response songs of the *mondine* rice pickers while also displaying an understanding of pop culture in the early postwar years. He recognizes the attraction of American popular boogie woogie culture with the sexually charged performance of actress Silvana Mangano emblematic of the the natural background of the rice fields within a community of hard-working and sexually vibrant women rice pickers. Silvana also represents the desires of the Italian working classes for a life removed from hard work and the threat of poverty. She yearns for the materialism of consumer culture and admires *foto-romanzi* (pulp magazines) like *Grand Hotel*. Silvana is attracted by the ne'er-do-well thief and womanizer Walter played by Vittorio Gassman whose cynical attitude toward crime and mannerisms recall standard characterizations in Hollywood *noir* gangster films. In *Bitter Rice*, Walter is a contrast to the model of solidarity and hard work from the suitor Silvana rejects, the goodhearted soldier Marco, played by Raf Vallone.[4] The trio (Mangano, Gassman, Vallone) would appear later in similar roles the melodrama, *Anna* (1952).

De Santis's social message in *Bitter Rice* is that the individual can be saved through collective action. De Santis remained a committed leftist even after the Soviet suppressions of popular revolts in Hungary (1956) and Czechoslovakia (1968). *Bitter Rice* shares a common theme with other neorealist-era films such as Pietro Germi's *Gioventù perduta/Lost Youth* (1947) with Carla Del Poggio and the Antonioni's episodic docu-drama about the nihilistic youth of postwar Europe *I vinti/The Vanquished* (1951), which deals with individual alienation in post war popular culture. *Bitter Rice* was also influential for the manner in which it conveyed an ideal of female physicality, which incidentally provoked threats of censorship in the United States.[5] De Santis also developed innovative camera techniques such as his extended crane shot that moves from a close-up of a single character (full or medium figure) without any specific spatial or temporal localization, to the discovery of a space, often unlimited, natural landscape, and of a group or "chorus" to a close-up of another or the same character. The purpose of each shot was to underline De Santis's belief in the essential need for an individual to be closely connected to a community. A similar crane shot was later made famous in the opening long-shot sequence of Orson Welles's *A Touch of Evil* (1958).

Vittorio De Sica and Cesare Zavattini[6]

Vittorio De Sica (1901–74) appeared as the male lead in comedies of the 1930s including the so-called *telefono bianco* (white telephone) comedies directed by Mario Camerini such as *Men What Rascals!* (1932), *I'll Give a Million*, and *Il Signor Max* (1937). De Sica's directing career in collaboration with screenwriter Cesare Zavattini (1902–89), began with Camerini-style romantic comedies including *Teresa Venerdì/Doctor Beware* (1941).[7] De Sica seemed to break with the Camerini romantic comedy model when he and Zavattini turned to melodrama with *I bambini ci guardano/The Children Are Watching Us* (1943) and *La porta del cielo/The Gate of Heaven* (1945). De Sica and Zavattini's early postwar films *Sciuscià/Shoeshine* (1946), *Ladri di biciclette/The Bicycle Thief* (1948), and *Umberto D.* (1951) continued in the melodramatic vein and would become seminal films of Italian neorealism.[8]

The assumption that prewar and postwar Italian films are essentially different is central to discussions of Italian neorealism. Rather than representing a break with the past, the films De Sica and Zavattini made during their neorealist period develop themes that were staples of their earlier collaborations with Camerini, in which De Sica starred as leading man and Zavattini was the scriptwriter. But the trajectory from from Camerini to De Sica and Zavattini is most clearly evident in their use of plot elements. In Camerini's films of the 1930s, comedic elements derive from a Boccaccian exchange of roles between people of different economic classes. In *Men What Rascals!* for instance, Bruno pretends to own a luxury car in order to impress Mariuccia. In *I'll Give a Million*, the millionaire Gold assumes the identity of a pauper in order to find true love. In *Il Signor Max*, Gianni impersonates an upper-class boat passenger in order to impress lady Paola. In *The Big Stores*, Lauretta steals an outfit in order to impress Bruno. In each film the theft of a class-related object (car, outfit, camera), makes the masquerade credible.

De Sica continued this theme/motif in his own films *Maddalena, Zero for Conduct* (1941) with the theft of a letter, *Doctor Beware* (1941) in which the title character impersonates the sister of a doctor. In *The Children Are Watching Us* (1943), *Sciuscià/Shoeshine*, and *The Bicycle Thief*, an adaptation of a Luigi Barolini novel, the theft is finally presented from the perspective of the owner. By the time that De Sica directed *The Bicycle Thief*, a film in which an unemployed Roman searches for his stolen bicycle, he had been involved in at least eight films that centered on a class-identifying object.

In the bicycle theft scenes in *The Bicycle Thief*, De Sica relied on montage in the Russian formalist sense more than his other neorealist colleagues.[9] This could be expected recalling that Camerini considered his strength as a director to be in montage. The roots of this stylistic method are in the shot–countershot exchange that establishes the protagonist's desire for the object in question. In Camerini's montage of *Men What Rascals!* Bruno admires his boss's automobile, in *Il Signor Max* Gianni gazes longingly at flowers, suits, cigarette cases, or the mannerisms of bourgeois society. In *The Bicycle Thief*, De Sica follows Camerini's style by emphasizing bicycle imagery at the pawnbroker, on city streets, at the marketplace, and at the stadium. As in Camerini's cinema, the function of bicycle imagery in *The Bicycle Thief* is to reify the economic and social ramifications of the class-identifying object.

In all these films, the hero's ability to acquire the object in question in all of these films elevates his sexual status. Mariuccia accepts a ride from Bruno in *Men What Rascals!* once he replaces his bicycle with his boss's car, and Gianni is successful with Donna Paola in *Il Signor Max* after he adopts the dress of the leisure class. These sexual motifs are repeated in *The Bicycle Thief* when Maria sacrifices the family's bed sheets for the bicycle or rides on the handlebars of Antonio's bicycle after he accepts the job and reaffirms his dominance as head of the household.

Despite sexual elements that are central to the plots of their films, both Camerini and De Sica limit female displays. True, in *I'll Give a Million* Anna (Assia Noris) raises her stockings as Claudette Colbert does in Frank Capra's *It Happened*

Figure 4.1   Lamberto Maggiorani (Antonio) and Enzo Staiola (Bruno) in Vittorio De Sica's *The Bicycle Thief.*

One Night (1934) and the bikini-clad Anna is brought out before a crowd on a float. However, each display scene is presented as if Anna were being violated. Also, Anna, displays her legs involuntary, because she is caught in a thorn bush, and she is forced to parade in a swimsuit because of pressure from her boss at the circus.

Like Camerini, De Sica's early films consciously limit female displays. This ran contrary to the current in neorealist films that featured Marina Michi as a show-girl in *Roma città aperta/Open City* (1945), Silvana Mangano in *Bitter Rice* (1949), and even Ingrid Bergman in *Stromboli—Terra di Dio/Stromboli* (1949). In De Sica's neorealist films, the reduction of sexuality arguably begins with *The Children Are Watching Us*, in which sex has a negative connotation. Prico's mother's display on the beach draws the attention of affected bourgeois admirers and foreshadows the abandonment of her son. In *The Bicycle Thief*, such de-emphasis on female imagery begins as Antonio accepts his work assignment under a poster of Gale Storm in an evening gown advertising the American film, *Forever Yours/Gioia di vivere* (1945). Such female imagery continues during the scenes when Antonio works pasting posters of Rita Hayworth around Rome. The act of pasting reduces the sexual provocation of the image as the *femme fatale* from King Vidor's Hollywood film about a promiscuous wife, *Gilda* (1946), is reduced to a wet and floppy poster. In the basement vaudeville sequence, the rehearsing dance girls are dressed in everyday attire rather than in titillating costumes. The female imagery is similarly unprovocative in the *casa chiusa* bordello, where the thief seeks refuge. Although the wallpaper is of female nudes, the images are barely distinguishable and without great voyeuristic appeal in a full shot of a dining room.[10] In Camerini and in De Sica, the female body exists as an object whose value is determined by male viewing.[11] However both directors significantly reduce the emphasis on female bodily displays and focusinstead on the class-identifying object, the bicycle.

In general, the plots of Camerini's films question the prewar status quo of the property-conscious bourgeoisie. In the political climate of 1930s Italy, this criticism was well received in part because it was tied to the regime's autarkic policies under League of Nations economic sanctions after Mussolini's invasion of Ethiopia. By the late 1930s, there were restrictions on foreign goods in Italy, including the luxury items favored by the leisure classes. Such goods had a negative political connotation in Camerini's films such as *Il Signor Max*, in which the affectations of the aristocracy are critiqued through the use of foreign words, products, and mannerisms. These class status objects and behavior are juxtaposed with what the patterns and what the working-class newspaper vendor protagonist of *Im Signor Max* is supposed to desire.

In *The Bicycle Thief*, there is a shortage not only of luxury goods but also of basic necessities. In Reconstruction Italy, the *borsa nera* (black market) was an important source of all goods, including basics. The black market became a running motif in Italian films of the early postwar period in films such as Lattuada's *Il bandito/The Bandit* (1946), Righelli's *Abbasso la richezza/Peddlin' in Society* (1946), and Camerini's drama *Molti sogni per le strade/Woman Trouble* (1948). There is even a postwar black market drama *L'angelo e il diavolo/The Angel and the Devil* (1946)directed by Camerini based on a story by Zavattini.

In De Sica's *Shoeshine* and particularly in *The Bicycle Thief*, organized crime and the black market replace the class-conscious and propertyowning bourgeoisie seen in Camerini's comedies. In *The Bicycle Thief*, the black market's new role as status quo is revealed by its to the police. In Camerini's comedies, by contrast, the police reestablish property and class-relationships disrupted by the theft of the class-identifying object, as in *Men What Rascals!* in which Bruno is arrested after crashing his boss's car. The police are also societal guarantors in De Sica's *The Children Are Watching Us* where they reestablish family order by rescuing Prico after his mother abandons him.

In *The Bicycle Thief* the black market's position as the protected status quo can be inferred from the police commissioner's indifference to Antonio's report and during the scene at the Piazza Vittorio market, where Antonio and friends search for the bicycle amid aisles of spare parts of dubious origin. When Antonio finally finds the thief in the Via Panico neighborhood, a mob forms, led by a figure wearing classic mafia style dark glasses and talking in a southern accent. Antonio's son, Bruno, locates a policeman, but he only seconds the neighborhood threats rather than arresting the thief. This encounter destroys Antonio's moral compass.[12] In desperation he decides to copy the black market model and fails because he lacks their organization and community protection.

Another example of Camerini's influence is the portrayal of proletarian political organizations in De Sica's film. Camerini's *Il Signor Max* (1937) features De Sica as Gianni, a newspaper vendor who impersonates a rich playboy to attract a leisure-class love interest, Lady Paola. The film depicts the fascist *OND* (*Opera Nazionale Dopolavoro*)—working-class, adult versions of youth groups such as the *balilla* and *giovani italiane*, which promoted the autarkic program of the regime. In *Il Signor Max* an *OND* chorus of fresh faced, uniformed bus drivers sing Giuseppe Verdi's fatalistic slavery lament *Va' pensiero*, thereby underscoring an acceptance of class division. Lady Paola's servant Lauretta is attracted to Gianni's *OND* community and quits her job, rejecting the model of female emancipation through work outside the family. However rather than promoting traditional family values, a mendacious *OND*, corporate model replaces the façade of the leisure-class model. The root of the mendacity is that Gianni is not even an official member of the *OND* chorus, limited to public transportation workers like his uncle. Gianni's coworkers lie and break the rules for him at the newspaper stand and train station. Gianni's uncle lies about the stability of Gianni's character to Lauretta.

The Bicycle Thief continues the depiction of proletarian unions or political institutions along lines established in *Il Signor Max*. Antonio searches for his friend Baiocco in a *casa del popolo* basement meeting hall, where the local cell of the Communist Party holds a meeting. A bespectacled, Antonio Gramsci-like figure explains the communist interpretation of the unemployment situation in terms of the necessity for public work projects with the Ministry of Labor. His audience is the same intent, male, working-age group that had stormed the job placement office and perhaps attended the Party rally. Antonio interrupts the meeting, but the communists, like the police, tell him to be quiet and leave. Antonio's friend is on the other side of the hall preparing a vaudeville stage show with the popular song, *Se mi volessi bene veramente (If you really loved me)*. The earnest *OND* chorus from *Il Signor Max* is replaced by a mistimed vaudeville whose female dancers are twirled like puppets by an incompetent singer. If the Party really loved Antonio they would offer him more help. Instead, the communists and the vaudeville troupe argue about who has the right to use the stage, leaving the impression that like the vaudeville troupe, the communist cell is only interested in putting on a show.[13] Antonio's garbage men friends help him to search for his bicycle. However, their honest approach to report the serial number to the police is naive.[14] The successful worker organization in *The Bicycle Thief* is the black market neighborhood, which, like the *OND* in *Il Signor Max*, is willing to lie for its comrade and to collude with the police to intimidate Antonio. As in *Il Signor Max* the strength of proletarian unions and political groups is not found in values of collective justice and worker solidarity but in their favor-mongering willingness to evade or subvert the enforcement of legality.

In Camerini's films that star De Sica, the Roman Catholic Church as an institution is largely absent.[15] There is a Catholic subtext in *I'll Give a Million*, whereby poverty is presented as a virtue that contrasts sharply with the affectations of the bourgeoisie. In Camerini's films, De Sica's dashing hero usually lives on the fringes of respectable society, eager for sexual adventure, his parents absent or avoided. The redemption and forgiveness that resolve the misunderstandings separating the young lovers reiterate regime- and Church-ordained dogma on family stability. The resolution of every Camerini comedy is the creation of a stable pair bond.

Similarly, De Sica's early efforts as director, such as *The Children Are Watching Us* and *Doctor Beware*, also champion the goal of a solid family unit. In *The Bicycle Thief*, Antonio Ricci's role as breadwinner echoes the identification of the nuclear family unit and its patriarchal structure as a microcosm of the super-structure of Fascist society.[16] However the black market scenes in *The Bicycle Thief* are based on an amoral familial model. However, this is not a holdover from the Fascist regime's family-centered social legislation. After the suffering of the war the family was simply one of the few universally accepted and viable institutions in Italian life.[17]

In contrast to Camerini, in his early films De Sica's continued to portray the Church as an institutional guarantor of familial stability. In *The Children Are Watching Us*, the priests who run the orphanage for the abandoned boy, Prico, are rare, stable characters in the film. And in De Sica's *The Gate of Heaven* (1945), a train of sick and penitent pilgrims travel to the shrine of Loreto to implore the Virgin for forgiveness and healing.

The recursion to Catholicism in the neorealist period is a reaction to the failure of the D'Annunzian and Fascist culture to ingrain nationalist myths into the Italian psyche. There is also an *Azione Cattolica* undertone concurrent with the Vatican shift from Concordat politics to a tepid anti-Fascism after the Allied invasion in 1943. However, in contrast to *The Children Are Watching Us* or *The Gate of Heaven*, in *The Bicycle Thief* Catholic prestige is not institutional. De Sica's themes of Catholic solidarity and brotherhood in poverty return to the interpersonal settings of Camerini as demonstrated in the bourgeois charity sequence in *The Bicycle Thief*. After unsuccessfully pursuing the thief for a second time, Antonio accosts, attempts to bribe, and finally threatens the beggar at a church where the needy attend a service before receiving a ration of pasta and potatoes. Despite the church setting, this charity operation is run by a lay order, an indirect reference to the DC victory in Italy's first postwar election in 1948.[18] A lawyer shaves the beggar as an act of penance. A man in bourgeois coat and tie, not a priest, reads a liturgy on spiritual serenity. When the film was released, the Catholic press objected to the cynical repetition of Don Luigi Moresco's "Mass of the poor," by a congregation hungry for material rather than spiritual reassurance.[19]

The film has anticlerical elements in the urination scene and the manner in which the crowd/congregation are locked inside the church.[20] Nonetheless there is a Catholic undertone in *The Bicycle Thief*.[21] For instance, the policeman's search of the thief's room reveals a miserable existence, and an embarrassed Antonio discovers that the man who had stolen his bicycle appears to be an epileptic struggling to earn a living. Whether motivated by fear or grace, Antonio heeds the policeman's warning about the penalty for calumny and decides not to press charges. Antonio is repaid when he steals a bicycle and is caught and beaten by an angry crowd. The bicycle's owner compassionately looks at Antonio's son, Bruno, and decides not to press charges. One of Antonio's captors admonishes him in the last line of the film "Può ringraziare Dio (You can thank God)." Antonio's receipt of mercy may be interpreted as a demonstration of worker solidarity that once given was justly returned. However, the brand name of the bicycle, *fides*, faith or trust, points to a Catholic reading.[22] Antonio, the common man, survivor of the trials and shortages of the war, searches for faith in Reconstruction Rome. After finally finding work after a two-year wait, Antonio dreamed of prosperity. In the restaurant he drunkenly calculates the economics of happiness in terms of wages, overtime, and a family allowance. However, one day on the job and a weekend in Rome teach the supremacy of the black market model. Divine Providence imparts a further lesson in humility, redemption, shame, and forgiveness.

Italian films before the war relied on the popular tradition of the hero as defender of the weak. The muscleman Maciste rescues Cabiria in Giovanni Pastrone's *Cabiria* (1914, rereleased in 1931). There were Italian army war heroes or historically removed costume drama heroes in Goffredo Alessandrini's *Scipione l'Africano*/Scipio the African (1937) or Roberto Rossellini's *Un pilota ritorna*/ *A Pilot Returns* (1942). In Rossellini's *L'uomo dalla croce*/Man of the Cross (1943) and *Open City*, the role of hero is transplanted to goodhearted priests and commoners, a model already developed in Alessandro Blasetti's *1860* (1933) with a debt to the self-sacrificing character of Fra' Cristoforo from Alessandro Manzoni's Catholic novel *The Betrothed* (1827).

De Sica had acted in some 28 feature films between 1932 and 1939, and stated that he had been typecast in the prewar romantic comedies as a caricature of the debonair *bello dannunziano*, the D'Annunzian handsome man.[23] This hero rescues loveinterests or orphaned girls in the Camerinian comedies and comes from the tradition of the strong man, who defends the weak and poor. In *Doctor Beware* the De Sica character surprises Teresa as she plays a scene from *Romeo and Juliet*. Instead of Romeo to Teresa's Juliet, the doctor claims he once played Ursus, the good giant from *Quo Vadis?* who is the source for the strongman character Maciste in Pastrone's *Cabiria* (1914). Therefore the Camerini hero traded Maciste's muscles for a bourgeois pedigree in the professional class. However De Sica's subsequent directorial efforts steadily turned away from the Maciste *bello dannunziano* heroic model. His early films feature nuns in *Un Garbaldino in convento/A Garibaldian in the Convent* (1942), schoolgirls in *Maddalena zero in conduct*, a female orphanage in *Doctor Beware*. These films were part of the schoolgirl comedy genre, in which a gender shift occurs as heroes become heroines and hegemonic positioning is challenged.[24] In De Sica's neorealist period, the Maciste *bello dannunziano* hero is completely absent. The protagonists are boys such as the defenseless Prico in *The Children Are Watching Us*. This thread continues in the postwar *Shoeshine* and especially *The Bicycle Thief* where Bruno, the only employed member of his family, assumes the heroic role by rescuing his father at the last minute from the black market and vigilante mobs (see figure 4.1).[25] Such dependence on innocent characters and children in particular seem to be a universal trend in Italian film that persists to this day. *Cabiria* (1914) centered on the rescue of a lost girl. Blasetti's *1860* (1934) and *Vecchia guardia/Old Guard* (1935) both center on the tragic death of young boys. Even Visconti's *Ossessione/ Obsession* (1942) has shots that evoke sympathy for the damned lovers with references to children.

There is a melodramatic undercurrent in *The Bicycle Thief* whereby the Ricci family struggles against a hostile world to achieve economic security.[26] If *The Bicycle Thief* is a melodrama this raises the question of who is the villain? All factions of Italian society treat Antonio disrespectfully: the party, Church, police, mafia. Yet the chief candidate for villain in the film is the Italian state as the collective expression of society. There is also an antistatist current in Camerini's comedies. In fact, as mentioned above his *Il cappello a tre punte/The Three Cornered Hat* (1935) incurred the wrath of Fascist censors.[27] De Sica continued Camerini's criticism of extra-governmental functionaries such as the Giovanni Gentile-like high school teacher in *Maddalena zero in condotta* or the bankers in *Doctor Beware* and *The Children Are Watching Us*. Also like Camerini, by targeting extra-governmental officials, De Sica revealed the abuses of a bureaucratic mentality without risking state censorship.

The Bicycle Thief continues this negative portrayal of functionaries. Antonio struggles with the inefficiency of the state employment office in order to find work. When the bicycle is stolen, Antonio confronts the state's inability to control crime. As he exits the police station, he sees stacks of unread reports gathering dust on the shelves, repeating the images of stacks of bed linen and rows of bicycles at the pawnshop.[28] There are also depictions of inefficient public infrastructure: long bus lines, lack of running water, myopic functionaries crouching over their casebooks at the pawnbroker, the job center. Leftists could see the protagonist's struggle to claim his right to work in *The Bicycle Thief* as a criticism of the inefficiency and waste of the capitalist market system which rewards the hoarding of goods and denies necessities to the lower classes. The images of shortages are an indictment of the Italian state's reluctantance to allocate Marshall Fund resources for public infrastructure after the war in favor of anti-inflationary monetary policy. However, because of Mussolini's autarkic economic policies, the Fascist regime was also identified with state intervention. The tight monetary policy of postwar Christian Democrat governments was, in part, a break with the past.[29] Thus, De

Sica condemns both the Italian state's autarkic past and the liberal policies of the present government, a political stance that Tomasulo identifies as fitting the "social democratic modification of high capitalism."[30]

Given the Fascist regime's ideology, one would expect to find references to sports in the De Sica/Camerini comedies of the 1930s and 1940s. Camerini's films include representation of sports. There is a parade of bicycle racers at the opening of *I'll Give a Million*, the aristocratic fascination with bridge or horseback riding in *Il Signor Max*, and a spoof of the sickly physical education instructor in De Sica's *Maddalena zero in conduct*. The Bicycle Thief also portrays sports as a vital cultural phenomenon.[31] When the drunken Antonio visits the Santona fortuneteller, the soundtrack breaks into the chirping bird network signature of the RAI radio broadcast of Sunday's football game between the teams of Modena and Roma. Sunday is set aside for the stadium as well as for church. While wandering the streets, Antonio and Bruno see a truckload of exhuberant Modena supporters anticipating the match of the day. In the immediate postwar period, bicycle racing, with football, was among the most popular spectator sports in Italy. *The Bicycle Thief* has a brief shot of a group of bicycle racers during the final theft sequence. Desperate for a bicycle, Antonio endures the sight of bicycles being used for leisure as a final blow to his conscience. The image of the bicycle and the rivalry between racers Gibo Bartali and Fausto Coppi became linked to Italian national pride in a period of general depression and misery. Because of his background and personality Gino Bartali was often identified with the DC, and Fausto Coppi was often identified with the PCI. Bicycle racing gained political significance after the 1948 assassination attempt on Italian Communist Party leader Palmiro Togliatti. On the same weekend, Bartali won the Tour de France and reduced tensions by dedicating his victory to a recovering Togliatti.

De Sica's films were part of a current of realism or *verismo* that appeared as a reaction to the D'Annunzian rhetoric that dominated Italian culture early in the century and in the centuries-old mimetic traditions in Italian artistic expression. The plots of Camerini's comedies featuring the problems of humble protagonists provided a preparatory platform for De Sica's work in the neorealist style which would develop with more tragic plot elements and ambiguous endings that would become a trademark of the Italian art film.

As with the backdrop surrounding the wartime production of *Open City*, De Sica's ability to make *The Bicycle Thief* was an achievement in itself. He had to partially produce the film himself after it was rejected by Italian producers and Hollywood producers who suggested casting leading man Cary Grant as the protagonist. De Sica's faith in the project and his development of a neorealist style with Zavattini was eventually rewarded with critical awards including the equivalent of the Oscar for Best Foreign Film. *The Bicycle Thief* has a reputation for not being appreciated by the Italian public, and although it placed fifth in the Italian domestic box office of 1948 the film created some controversy among ministers of the Christian Democrat government who sought to deprive De Sica of government subsidies for this film and his later neorealist efforts for their stark portrayal of the social ills of Italy.

5

The 1950s

1954 Trieste returned to Italy
1955 Italy joins the United Nations
1957 Treaty of Rome creates European Union with Italy as founding member nation
1958 Rapid development of Italian economy
John XXIII succeeds Pope Pius XII Merlin Law passed closing the state-run *Casa chiuse* brothel network

In the early postwar period the Christian Democrats constructed centrist coalitions under the leadership of Alcide De Gasperi, Mario Scelba, and Antonio Segni. The first DC premier, De Gasperi, had somewhat neglected the grass roots organization of his party, depending on Catholic Church parishes to mobilize support for Christian Democratic candidates. As the DC stagnated, the Communist Party worked to construct an efficient party machine as a part of the worldwide communist revolutionary movement. Recognizing this weakness, Amintore Fanfani broadened the DC constituency by increasing its popular base. Fanfani, an economics professor, felt that the DC could prevent a leftist takeover in Italy only by supporting moderate social reform and controls on major industries.

The conservative atmosphere of the 1950s had been welcomed by the Vatican. The Church had retained privileges in the 1929 Concordat/Lateran Accords and many prelates were determined that the Church should continue to influence temporal affairs in postwar Italy. The DC assignment of a semi-political role for the Church was dependent on Vatican policies and the personality of the pope. Nevertheless an alliance with the Vatican turned out to be less problematic for the DC than the alliance with the interests and policies of the Soviet Union for the PCI. The Italian Left underwent a crisis after Soviet premier Nikita Krushchev's secret speech to the Soviet Communist Party Congress in 1956. When Khrushchev revealed Stalin's purges, the monolithic leftist ideological front in Italy had to react to the news that the WWII hero "Baffone" (Uncle Joe) had been a paranoid tyrant who had ordered not only the purges of the Party in Russia but also forced starvation in Ukraine and russification policies throughout the Soviet Union. Adding to the public relations woes of the PCI was the Soviet invasion of Hungary in 1956 and suppression of riots in Poland, which brought further political repercussions for the Italian Left. For example, Italian director Gillo Pontecorvo had been a leader in the Resistance with impeccable leftist credentials, yet he left the PCI following the Hungary invasion. The rigidity of the Communist Party and its insistence on the paradoxical idea of democratic centralism did not sit well with Pontecorvo or with the Socialist Party, which since the days of Mussolini had at times been a swing constituency in Italian politics.[1] When Pietro Nenni, the Socialist leader, condemned Soviet oppression in Eastern Europe, he distanced the PSI from the PCI. The Christian Democrats did not miss this opportunity to isolate the Communists by courting Nenni's Socialists, who began to look favorably upon Italy's ties within Western Europe and with the United States in the NATO military alliance. Italian Communist leader Togliatti held to the Soviet line until 1964 when he issued his *Memoriale di Yalta*, which called for autonomy of national Communist parties.

The Development of Neorealism

Neorealism was a cultural development that expressed an Italian reaction against the legacy of the Fascist period and the defeat of the war. However, there were also other attempts to revive Italian cinema. As early as 1945 the Italian film industry started making films that sought to reclaim at least part of its prewar market position, a difficult task given the influx of Hollywood films that had not been widely distributed in Italy since 1938. Mario Mattoli made a popular musical *Partenza ore 7/ Departure Seven O'Clock* (1946) and anticipated the populist melodrama of the 1950s with *La vita ricomincia/Life Begins Anew* (1945), a film distributed in the United States, which brought its star, Alida Valli, to the attention of Hollywood producers. Mattoli saw his films as a counterpart to the political valence of neorealism and as evidence that the Italian film industry was quickly recovering from the interruption of the war and eager to continue where it had left off.[2] In fact even in the year in which the war officially ended there were a number of Italian films produced that aimed at maintaining the prewar position of Italian cinema in the domestic market including musicals such as C.L. Bragalia's *Torna a Sorrento/Return to Sorrento* (1945), M. Costa's *Il barbiere di Siviglia/The Barber of Seville* (1945), and Giacomo Gentilomo's *O sole mio* (1945). This current would continue throughout the early postwar period with operatic films such as Carmine Gallone's *Rigoletto* (1946), the Dionisetti biopic *Il cavaliere del sogno/Life of Donizetti* (1946), and M. Costa's *Follie per l'opera/Mad About Opera* (1948).

Neorealist films have a somewhat undeserved reputation for being box office disappointments in Italy. In the Italian 1946, for example,—*Il bandito/The Bandit* (1946), *Paisà'/Paisan* (1946), and *Il sole sorge ancora/Outcry* (1946)—have identifiably neorealistic characteristicsas do other important films of the neorealist period including *Roma città aperta/Open City* and *Ladri di biciclette/The Bicycle Thief*, which were among the top Italian domestic films in the year of their release. The reputation of neorealist films and their directors was heightened in Italy due to their success abroad De Sica's *Sciuscià'/Shoeshine* (1946) and *The Bicycle Thief* and Rossellini's *Open City* all won prestigious foreign film awards in the United States and in France.

Despite the critical triumph of neorealism, particularly abroad, the actual content of the Italian film industry did not change significantly from the 1930s to the 1950s but rather remained a flow of peplum epics, melodramas, historical dramas, and comedies.[3] There were box office successes such as *Aquila nera/Return of the Black eagle* (1946), a swashbuckling adaptation of a Pushkin adventure story directed by Riccardo Freda, who would continue to work in genre productions such as the peplum and horror into the 1990s. Adaptations of Russian historical novels would be among the most popular Italian films of the early postwar period including the Italian produced *War and Peace* (1955) directed by King Vidor. Eventually much of Italian production returned to the type of film popular before the conflict including the comedies starring Neapolitan comedian Totò (Antonio de Curtis) (1898–1967), who continued the popularity of his prewar films *San Giovanni decollato/St. John the Baptist Beheaded* (1940) with *Totò le Moko* (1949), a spoof of the French crime thriller *Pepé le Moko* (1936), or *Fifa e arena* (1948) a spoof of a bullfighter film *Blood and Sand* (1941), and *Totò terz'uomo* (1951) a parody of Carol Reed's *The Third Man* (1949), or in the vacation/beach movie *L'imperatore di Capri/The Emperor of Capri* (1949). The lighter subject matter of one of the first Italian color films starring *Totò a colori/Totò in Color* (1952) by Steno indicates the mood of the Italian film going public. Toto's adaptation of the cadences of the Neapolitan dialect to the Italian language delighted audiences with his ability to bring a marvelous nonsense to any situation. He would remain a fixture of the Italian cinema until his death in 1967, even appearing in Pier Paolo Pasolini's satire of postwar ideological disputes *Uccellaci e uccellini/Hawks and Sparrows* (1966). Even at the turn of the millennium, Totò's films are among the most frequently broadcast on Italian television.

There was also a continuation of the historic and operatic and biopic genres. Luciano Emmer made films such as *Leonardo da Vinci* (1952) and *Giotto* (1969). Directors such as Carmine Gallone had made prewar biopics—*Christopher Columbus* (1937) and *Giuseppe Verdi* (1938)—and continued in the operatic musical genre after the war with *Rigoletto* (1946), *La forza del destino/The Force of Destiny* (1949), *Enrico Caruso leggenda di una voce/The Young Caruso* (1951), *Canzoni di mezzo secolo/Half a Century of Song* (1952). Musicals in particular would become a mainstay of Italian production. Three of the top films of 1953 were operatic musicals: *Giuseppe Verdi* (1953), *Puccini* (1953), and *Aida* (1953). A notable Italian musical production was *Carosello napoletano/Neapolitan Carousel* (1954) starring Sophia Loren in an episodic film that depicts the history of Naples from the 1300s to modern times through song in the Neapolitan tradition. Italian singing stars were able to make the jump to cinema. Operatic performer Mario Lanza and singer/composer Domenico Modugno starred in the musical *Arrivederci Roma/Seven Hills of Rome* (1957). Modugno starred in Piero Tellini's undervalued musical *Nel blu dipinto di blu* (1958), a film that mixes elements of *neorealismo nero* with the mastery of Modugno's singing and songwriting.

There were also films that had an ideological basis in Catholic restoration. Besides Rossellini's *Open City* and De Sica's *La porta del cielo/The Gate of Heaven* (1945), many films combined Catholic themes with a neorealist style. These include Augusto Genina's *Il cielo sulla palude/Heaven over the Marshes* (1949) about the young saint Maria Goretti, Blasetti's *Un giorno nella vita/A Day in the Life* (1946), in which a convent of nuns are massacred after hiding Resistance fighters, and Blasetti's *Fabiola* (1949), one of the first postwar European colossal coproductions, an adaptation of a Catholic novel in the tradition of the silent sand and sword, peplum epics .

The grim postwar reality of neorealist films—such as De Sica's *Shoeshine* (1946) about a pair of struggling Neapolitan shoeshine boys who try to buy a horse or *Umberto D.* (1952) about a retiree whose pension was so meager he could not afford room and board for himself and his dog—was so close at hand that Italians were not always interested in reliving it as entertainment. The result was that neorealism gained a reputation as unpopular cinema, when its motivating impulse had been to depict the conditions of those often ignored. As economic conditions improved, writers and directors who had contributed to the postwar moment of Italian neorealism began to adapt the style of neorealism to a more personal sphere in the development of what would become art cinema. Films such as Rossellini's *Viaggio in Italia/Voyage to Italy* (1953), Visconti's *Bellissima* (1951), and *Senso/Livia* (1954), Antonioni's *Cronaca di un amore/Story of a Love Affair* (1950), *La signora denza camelie/The Lady without Camelias* (1953), *Le amiche/The Girl-Friends* (1955), and *Il grido/The Shout* (1957) display an interest in the psychological or spiritual dimension of characters often featuring long-shot camera sequences. This preference for the personal, the private, the psychological, or the spiritual over the social and the public was viewed as a betrayal of neorealist ideals by several leftist critics, particularly the *Cinema Nuovo* group directed by critic Guido Aristarco in discussions of Fellini's film *La Strada* (1954). Yet this interest in psychological introspection adopted the neorealist style of long takes for the examination of everyday reality, which would become an important stylistic imprint of Italian art cinema.

The lesson of neorealism, however, did not die in Italian cinema. The profound value of Visconti's "moral attitude" toward reality or of Rossellini's "documentary observation and analysis" influenced filmmakers of the time. Even a film such as Camillo Mastrocinque's Totò vehicle *Siamo uomini o caporali/Are We Men or Corporals* (1955) contains stark references to wartime suffering and postwar poverty, which are shot in a simple style. Many Italian directors, influenced by the neorealist style, adapted neorealist characteristics to their films. The storyline of Carmine Gallone's *Avanti a lui tremava tutta Roma/Before Him all Rome Trembled* (1946) features Anna Magnani in a film about an English soldier in wartime Rome among an opera troupe performing Giacomo Puccini's opera *Tosca* thus offering an opportunity to mix the operatic musical and the wartime neorealist drama. Macario, a vaudeville comedian, appeared in *Eroe della strada* (1946), a film that adapted Macario's talents to the themes of the neorealist style. De Sica and Aldo Fabrizi appeared in a choral comedy about Italian prisoners of war in California *Natale al campo 119/Christmas at Camp 119* (1946).

Neorealism's impact and style lived in the work of the directors who had been active members of the original neorealist group: Antonioni, De Sica, Rossellini, Visconti, and Zavattini. Other Italian directors who worked under neorealist directors were profoundly influenced by the experience or legacy of neorealism, as is the case of Federico Fellini, Pier Paolo Pasolini, Ettore Scola, Sergio Leone, Francesco Rosi, and Gillo Pontecorvo and his writing partner Franco Solinas.

Italian neorealism also had a worldwide impact as a model for an oppositional cinema against the Hollywood commercial cinema. The working methods of neorealism offered a way to produce films without large financial resources. The stories of common men, often played by nonprofessional actors, inspired filmmakers in Europe such as the directors of the French New Wave school of the late 1950s and early 1960s championed by critic Andre Bazin, who were heavily influenced by Rossellini's *Paisan*. Neorealism's influence can also be seen in the *Cinema Novo* of Brazil, the Free Cinema of Britain, the *Nova Vlna* of Czechoslovakia, the Third Cinema of Argentina, in Egyptian neorealism, the Mexican films of Buñuel such as *Los Olvidados/The Young and the Damned* (1950), and even to the present day in the films from the emerging cinemas in countries with extremely strict censorship codes, for example, turn of the millennium Iran, or whenever a film/television serial is made based upon simple production values that attempt an objective depiction of everyday existence.

With the box office disappointment of De Sica's *Umberto D.* (1952), the fortunes of neorealism declined and there was a dearth of funds for new productions in the neorealist film style. In 1948, only 54 films were made in Italy whereas 874 films were imported (668 from the United States) and only 13 percent of box office receipts went to Italian filmmakers. The Italian film industry was faced with the prospect of low production yielding few profits compromising future production.[4] In 1949, the Italian government took steps to protect a previously vibrant national industry by passing legislation that granted tax reductions for films of Italian origin. This law took effect in 1950 and remained until 1955 when it was replaced by the 1956 law that raised the number of days per year when Italian theaters were required to book Italian films.[5] However government patronage came with strings attached in the form of the reticence of ruling DC coalition governments to support films depicting social problems. Subsidies for Italian film production were dependent on "artistic and technical merits" to be determined by government officials. In 1949, the arrangement became known as the "Andreotti law" (named after long-serving cabinet minister and later premier, Giulio Andreotti) and his reaction to the films of Vittorio De Sica—*The Bicycle Thief* and *Umberto D.* (1952). In Andreotti's words in a letter to De Sica, "If it is true that evil can be fought by harshly spotlighting its most miserable aspects, it is also true that De Sica has rendered a poor service to his country if people throughout the world start thinking that Italy in the 20th century is the same as *Umberto D.*"[6] Controversy over tax breaks and subsidies also clouded Pietro Germi's semi film noir about a troubled youth, *Gioventù perduta/Lost Youth* (1947), a situation that would repeat for Germi's emigration drama *Il cammino della speranza/The Road of Hope* (1950).[7]

After *Umberto D.* (1952), critics lamented that De Sica's postwar films, *Miracolo a Milano/Miracle in Milan* (1951) and *L'oro di Napoli/The Gold of Naples* (1954), did not continue the socially progressive tone of early neorealist films such as *The Bicycle Thief*. De Sica and Zavattini made arguably the last neorealist film *Il tetto/The Roof* (1956) about the struggles of a young family to find housing, although there would be later attempts at neorealist revival with films such as Lizzani's *Il gobo/The Hunchback of Rome* (1960) or the Pasolini-Bolognini collaboration *Notte brava/Bad Girls Don't Cry* (1959). Critics questioned the political implications of De Sica's transition from 1930s matinee idol to postwar neorealist legend, accusing him of being a technician of Fascist-era cinema whose neorealist films were an exceptional moment in his output. Actually De Sica and Zavattini would continue to examine themes of social criticism in their comedies: *Miracle in Milan* (1951), *Gold of Naples* (1954), *Il giudizio/The Last Judgement* (1961), *Il boom* (1963), or even *Caccia alla volpe/After the Fox* (1966).

The decline of neorealism had a corollary in Italian politics. The postwar harmony between Left and Right had devolved into the rivalry of the elections of 1948 and the repercussions after the attempt on Communist leader Palmiro Togliatti's life the same year. Cold War ideology even seeped into film theory and criticism. It is true that the films of De Santis and perhaps early Visconti had an overtly Marxist tone. However, with Rossellini and the later Visconti, the Marxist influence decreased. Rossellini's films starring Ingrid Bergman—*Stromboli* (1950), *Europa 51* (1952), and *Voyage to Italy* (1953)—are perhaps the more typical Rossellini, the work of a mature artist with an ability to concentrate on personal and spiritual issues, in contrast to Rossellini's Fascist-era war films or his early heroic, socially committed neorealist films—*Open City* and *Paisan*. Many films from 1950 to 1951 (Rossellini's *Francesco Giullare di Dio/The Flowers of St. Francis*, Visconti's *Bellissima*, Fellini's *Luci del varietà/Variety Lights*, De Sica's *Miracle in Milan*) were less manifestly left-wing than earlier neorealist films. Marxist critics such as Guido Aristarco sought to counter what they perceived as a reactionary development in popular culture. Neorealist film had much in common with the developments in Italian narrative during the Fascist and postwar periods, which came out of the *verismo*/Naturalist style. Writers projected autobiographical memory onto historical memory with works such as Levi's *Christ Stopped at Eboli*, Vittorini's *Conversazioni in Sicilia/Conversations in Sicily*, Ignazio Silone's *Fontamara*, or Primo Levi's *Survival in Auschwitz*.[8] Yet Marxist film critics insisted upon an ideological interpretation of the importance of neorealist films that sought to bring to film theory the independence that had already occurred in politics, since the political coalition between Catholics and Communists forged out of the Resistance had disintegrated. The result was that by the early 1950s Italian film critics were making arguments about artistic merit that seemed to parrot the ideological divisions of the Cold War.[9]

The impetus of left-wing critics was driven by the legacy of the founder of the Italian Communist Party, Antonio Gramsci, who was born in Sardinia in 1891 and studied in Turin where he became a journalist. He was imprisoned by the Fascist regime for ten years and died shortly after his release in 1937, thus becoming a Communist martyr and an inspiration to the Resistance and postwar Communist ideologues. Gramsci sought to develop an Italian Marxism applicable to Italy's social and economic situation, which at the time was more rural than urban. Gramsci favored a revolutionary strategy that would involve not only the industrial proletariat (the vanguard of Marx's vision of a communist revolution) but the rural peasantry as well, as would eventually be the case of underdeveloped countries that experienced Marxist takeovers as in—mid-twentieth-century China or Cuba.

Gramsci wrote extensively on a myriad of subjects, particularly Italian cultural and intellectual history. These writings have been collected in his *Quaderni del carcere/Prison Notebooks.* Gramsci understood that Italy presented another unique phenomenon: regionalism. Before its political unification in 1870, Italy was a conglomeration of different regions, many of which had long been subject to foreign domination. This division could not simply be swept away by a military and political act (the unification of 1870). Gramsci also theorized that political culture was dominated by the concept of *hegemony*, which indicates the power of a dominant class over subordinates that is not limited to economic power but extends to the tendency of subordinates to interpret reality and act in accordance with the dominant mindset.[10] Gramsci envisioned his revolution in Italy not as an explosive coup d'état but as a very gradual acquisition of cultural hegemony. Gramsci's long-term strategy became the official stance of the Italian Communist Party so that, under Gramsci's successor Palmiro Togliatti, the Party began a process of opening up to democratic compromises with other Italian political parties such as the Christian Democrats, the Socialists, the Republicans, and the Liberals.

The attempt by Italian Marxist critics to claim the legacy of neorealism is evidence of a larger power struggle in Italian culture. The role of the intellectual in Italian society has been active ever since figures such as Dante (1265–1321) initiated the dialogue on Italian national language or Machiavelli wrote to influence Italian politics. Gramsci exhorted the Marxist intellectuals to bring ideas and art to the masses and to achieve political power through a subtle but determined opposition to the cultural and economic demands of the dominant hegemony, which until the 1960s had been the more conservative politics of the DC party. With the diffusion of Gramsci's ideas and his heirs such as Galvano Della Volpe (1895–1968), there was a moment of transition to Marxism in the evolution of historical thought in literary criticism and aesthetics. The line that led from nationalist, romantic, idealist Francesco De Sanctis to the liberal Benedetto Croce took a potential turn to the Marxist Gramsci. As a critic of the *Risorgimento* and of the bourgeoisie of the time, De Sanctis had judged works of Italian literature by their value to and influence on the ideas regarding Italian unity. After the war, the domination of the literary hearts and minds of the Italian intellectual and academic community came increasingly under the hegemony of Gramsci's theories.[11] Italian neorealist film, like its counterparts in Resistance literature, insisted that works of art be politically committed or "engaged" according to Gramsci's cultural theories. This was the strength of Resistance culture but it was also its undoing, for when Europe returned to peacetime political and social patterns, the legend of the Resistance engagement lost its dramatic appeal.

Ultimately the period of Italian neorealism was not without flaws. The treatment of the topic of the Holocaust, for example, was not fully examined by Italian neorealists. The first Italian film on the Holocaust *L'ebreo errante/The Wandering Jew* (1947) was made by Goffredo Alessandrini, who like Rossellini had been active making war films during the Fascist era. Alessandrini's film is a portrayal of the myth of the wandering Jew who expiates his sins in the Nazi camps, and despite its intentions has anti-Semitic overtones. Italy was almost without films on the Holocaust until Pontecorvo's *Kapò* (1959), and a sequence of Jews praying before deportation in Roberto Rossellini's *Il Generale della Rovere/General Della Rovere*

(1959) based on an Indro Montanelli story, and Carlo Lizzani's film about the deportation of Roman Jewry, *L'oro di Roma/The Gold of Rome* (1961).

The Visconti–Fellini Debate

In 1951, Visconti made *Bellissima* from a script by Cesare Zavattini. This film signaled a transition from the political themes of neorealism to the more psychological themes of the 1950s.[12] *Bellissima* is about a Roman stage mother's unsuccessful attempts to turn her little girl into a movie star, with brilliant performances by Anna Magnani and Walter Chiari and a cameo of Alessandro Blasetti as a film director. The film demonstrates Visconti's commitment to neorealism but also his inclination to produce the sort of psychological study that would become a sign of art cinema in the 1960s. Zavattini's script of *Bellissima* provided a simple plot that recalls elements from *The Bicycle Thief* with a focus on a dramatic pair, mother–daughter, instead of father–son, who are victims of social circumstances. Visconti's film focuses on the mother's marital crisis and the potential exploitation of her child so that *Bellissima* becomes a story of a stage mother's inner anguish. The mother, Maddalena, is obsessed by the magic power of the cinema to offer riches, happiness, and fame. Her failure to turn her child into a star is contrasted with the powerful parental figure offered by John Wayne to Montgomery Cliff in John Ford's seminal western *Red River* (1948), which receives an extended cameo in Visconti's film.

A rivalry developed at the 1954 Venice Film Festival between supporters of Fellini's *La Strada* and Visconti's *Livia*, an adaptation of a Camillo Boito story about an unhappy affair between a Venetian countess and an Austrian officer who deserted from the Austro-Hungarian army during the battle for Italian unification in the 1860s. Visconti took his abilities from directing opera to film in a manner that set the standard for future art cinema. His attention to detail and ability to connect the character of the confused countess played by Alida Valli with the settings of Venice and his attentions to the minute details of nineteenth-century life make the film a visual feast.

Visconti was known to have Marxist leanings due to his portrayal of Sicilian fishermen in *La terra trema/The Earth Trembles*, a Gramsci-inspired adaptation of Verga's novel *I Malavoglia/The House by the Meddlar Tree*. Federico Fellini on the other hand, had started his show business career as a caricature artist and gag man in prewar Rome.[13] His early screenwriting collaboration with Rossellini from *Open City* (1945) *The Flowers of St. Francis* (1950) has clear Catholic overtones, where themes of social status and economic justice are secondary to spiritual and moral consistency.

Arguments over *La Strada* or *Livia* at the Venice Film Festival exemplified the ideological split between Catholics and Marxists in the early postwar period. Fellini's *La Strada* (1954) has elements of a subtle political fable that anticipates and reports the ideological contradictions on both wings of the political spectrum. The film was criticized because it had no visible social agenda and instead focused on spiritual matters.[14] The social urgency of neorealism was absent from the film and the characters, two circus performers, were lumpenproletarians, unconnected with the working class, which had been the focus of the heroic period of neorealism in films such as De Sica's *The Bicycle Thief* and Visconti's *The Earth Trembles*. Critics complained that despite the ability of the cast and director the only function of films like *La Strada* was to produce an emotional reaction, as in De Sica's playful magical adaptation of neorealist themes in *Miracle in Milan* (1951) and Rossellini's devil fable *La macchina ammazzacattivi/The Machine that Kills Bad People* (1952). Soon thereafter critics began to write about *pink neorealism* as directors began to incorporate more audience pleasing elements in their films.[15]

There is irony in the fact that leftist critics preferred Visconti's *Livia* to Fellini's *La Strada*. Both films treated themes of spiritual realization and *Livia's* portrayal of a historically removed ruling class was far from the stark style and economically depressed setting of Visconti's earlier neorealist film *The Earth Trembles* (1948). Fellini's film presents a separation of physical and spiritual values, which hints at the two factions that dominated postwar politics: the Communists and the Catholics. In Fellini's *La Strada*, Zampanò is completely physical, concerned only with the basic economic rudiments of existence. On the other hand, Gelsomina, played by Fellini's wife Giulietta Masina, is a character with spiritual aspirations. Her moral sense is reinforced by an encounter with the Fool who dressed as an angel descends from his tightrope to encourage her talents (see figure 5.1).

Figure 5.1   Giuletta Masina (Gelosomina) and Anthony Quinn (Zampanò) in Federico Fellini's *La Strada*.

Fellini would be criticized for his lack of progressive politics throughout his career. His films were a combination of the writing influences of the moralistic themes from Ennio Flaiano and more fantastic elements from the writer Tulio Pinelli. Guido Aristarco commented that Fellini's work had a tone of decadentism that recalled the poetry of Giovanni Pascoli (1855–1912) with themes of mystery and sentimentality making Fellini a Catholic irrationalist in the tradition of the spiritual wing of Idealism deriving from Kierkegaard, the philosophical forefather of existentialism. Aristarco and Kracauer saw an existentialist quality in the endings of Fellini's early films—*La Strada* (1954), *Il bidone/The Swindle* (1955), *Luci del varietà/Variety Lights* (1950), *Lo Sceicco bianco/The White Sheik* (1952), *Le notti di Cabiria/The Nights of Cabiria* (1957), and *8½* (1963)—which have an itinerant circular nature in which the main character eventually returns to the initial situation. Fellini's reduction of plot and character development implies a deterministic, fatalistic, unchangeable human condition.[16] In Fellini's films, a character may search for grace and achieve a realization but never successfully acquire either transformation or growth, although this narrative pattern is actually a larger characteristic of narrative in Italian cinema.[17]

The source of Fellini's lack of ideological rigidity must be examined in the context of the world that shaped his personality. In Fellini's early films whenever a protagonist has a moment of self-realization, an intellectual or spiritual breakthrough, it often leads to death, suffering, or at best emargination. For example, Leopoldo from *I Vitelloni/The Young and the Passionate* (1953) is a provincial intellectual and aspiring author. His dreams of literary fame end after the traveling impresario who promises to produce his plays turns out to be interested only in a homosexual encounter. After this disappointment, Leopoldo returns to the safety of his family and neighborhood, where he still retains a reputation as an artist. In *La Strada* (1954), the Fool offers Gelsomina the parable of the little stone, meant to aid her spiritually and intellectually. However, the Fool's idea that even a stone has a role in the universe does not enable Gelsomina to free herself from Zampanò, who eventually murders the Fool, leading to the madness of Gelsomina. Augusto, in *The Swindle* (1955), is a successful conman as long as he does not ponder the moral implications of his actions. Once he does, he is also abandoned and killed. In *The Nights of Cabiria* (1957), the prostitute Cabiria first dreams of saving enough money to leave her profession, and then she is swindled out of her house and money, and nearly murdered, before eventually returning to the economic condition in which she began the film.

Fellini's later films such as *La dolce vita* (1960) and *8½* (1963) have characters whose economic resources allow them the luxury to be more conventionally intellectual (figure 5.2). The protagonist of *La dolce vita*, Marcello, cannot resist the epicurean lifestyle and easy money from his job as a Roman tabloid journalist. His initial pretense of becoming a novelist, a serious artist, is obliterated in his vapid existence during the last episodes of the film. Marcello is asked how much he would charge to write flattering reviews for an actor and he responds without hesitation, selling his pen and hence any claim to intellectual purity. Steiner, the other intellectual figure from *La dolce vita*, had encouraged Marcello's literary ambitions and invited him to an elitist cocktail party in the hope that Marcello would be inspired to abandon his unprestigious profession. Yet, at a party, Steiner

Figure 5.2   Marcello Mastroianni (Marcello) and Anita Ekberg (Silvia) with Walter Santesso (Paparazzo) far right in Federico Fellini's *La dolce vita*.

plays ominous tape recordings with tones of the savagery that lurks beneath the façade of civilization. Steiner is overcome by the artistic intuition of his two young children who are awakened by the noises of a storm, foreshadowing the irrational impulses that lead him to murder them and commit suicide. If Marcello represents the inability of aspiring intellectuals to resist the temptation of the world, Steiner symbolizes an intellectual intransigence to deal with instincts and emotions. It seems that Fellini's aim was not to emphasize his characters' success in societal or economic terms. Instead he demonstrates an interest in the spiritual rather than the material, which may be a reflection of Catholic tenets in Fellini's worldview. As a reaction to his upbringing during the *ventennio* (the near 20-year Fascist regime period 1922–43), Fellini was hesitant to accept anything that tries to define itself with too much authority.[18] A reticence to accept any official discourse whether it derives from the political Left or Right does not imply a lack of intellectual vigor, only a skepticism of all forms of official discourse and a greater emphasis on the mysteries of his own personality and memory.[19]

De Sica, Television, and Popular Film in the 1950s

After the war, along with his interest in directing neorealist films, Vittorio De Sica repeated the distinguished but useless gentleman roles that had given him a start in the 1930s in *Abbasso la ricchezza/Down with Riches!* (1946), and *Roma città libera* (1946), *Sperduti nel buio/Lost in Darkness* (1947). He also assisted in the direction of Dulio Coletti's adaptation of De Amicis's *Cuore/Heart* (1948) as the good hearted Professor Perboni, and appeared in *Lo sconosciuto di San Marino* (1948), *Domani e' troppo tardi/Tomorrow Is too Late* (1950), and the undervalued *Buongiorno elefante!/Hello Elephant!* (1952). In 1951, De Sica directed *Miracle in Milan* from a Zavattini script. The film attempted to combine the stylistic imprint of neorealism and a stark story about squatters on the edge of Milan with fantastic narrative turns like a magic goose that grants the wishes of the hero Totò. The film is a masterpiece of irony, humor, and cinematic experimentation and an attempt by a master of neorealism to adapt their style to the changes demanded by audiences in postwar Italy in a manner that would influence the genre later known as the *commedia all'italiana* and the comedy serials starring comedians such as Totò, Aldo Fabrizi, and Peppino De Filippo. But like Rossellini's attempt to marry neorealism with the humor of a devil tale in *The Machine that Kills Bad People* (1952), *Miracle in Milan* was not a box office success.

In 1952, De Sica declined an offer to direct an adaptation of the Giovanni Guareschi novel *Il piccolo mondo di Don Camillo/The Little World of Don Camillo*, eventually made into the box office hit *Le petit monde de Don Camillo/Don Camillo* (1952) by Julien Duvivier with French comedian Fernandel and veteran Italian actor Gino Cervi in the title roles of the mischievous priest Don Camillo and his rival the communist mayor Peppone. Instead of directing what would be the first of a series of Don Camillo films, De Sica chose to return to a pure neorealist style with *Umberto D.* (1952), a film that put into practice Zavattini's theories about simple narratives in unadorned settings. *Umberto D.* features nonprofessional actors in the story of a retiree whose meager pension does not allow him to keep even his dog. As with *The Bicycle Thief*, the simplicity of the narrative reveals deep human dramas and social conflict. After *Umberto D.* performed poorly at the box office barely finishing in the top one hundred grossing domestic films of 1952, De Sica attempted to recoup his losses by accepting an American production *Indiscretion of an American Wife/Stazione Termini* (1953) scripted by Luigi Chiarini and Cesare Zavattini and starring Montgomery Cliff and Jennifer Jones with dialogue by Truman Capote. The film was hampered by the cuts made in the films by American producers, and became another box office setback for De Sica.

De Sica starred as a Carabiniere officer in Luigi Comencini's *Pane, amore e fantasia/Bread Love and Dreams* series as well as in numerous other films, becoming an almost ubiquitous presence in the Italian cinema. De Sica's next directorial effort *The Gold of Naples* (1954) marks a tuning point in Italian film history for De Sica's concessions to popular taste with popular actors such as Totò and Sophia Loren, the latest revelation of the Miss Italy beauty pageant (figure 5.3). The episodic film *The Gold of Naples* (1954) examines imbalances in social and economic power relationships that are redressed through the power of nature, themes with a long history in Italian culture most notably in the writings of Boccaccio. In the first episode, a bully dominates the family of a humble man (Totò) until he shows signs of physical weakness and is expelled. The second episode is the story of a husband who attempts to compensate for his lack of physical appeal to his attractive

Figure 5.3 Publicity still of Sophia Loren.

wife (Sophia Loren) by buying her a ring, which she leaves at the bedside of her lover. In the third episode, De Sica plays the role of an aristocratic failed gambler reduced to playing cards with the doorman's son, who beats him mercilessly. In the fourth episode, a prostitute, played by Silvana Mangano, marries a man who feels guilt because a girl he jilted committed suicide. Arguably the last neorealist film, De Sica's *The Roof* (1956), about a young family's attempt to build a house on public land, came years after public and box office results had pointed to a more commercial entertainment best evidenced by the changes in De Sica's choice of projects.

Critics have often equated the end of neorealism with a decline in the quality of Italian commercial film in the mid-1950s. By decline one usually means increased imitation, commercialism, cheap melodramas, and an avoidance of serious themes. However, the 1950s was actually a period of great opportunity and vitality for the Italian film industry. The Hollywood studio system was facing the repercussions of the Paramount antitrust decision of 1948, which broke up the distribution networks between Hollywood studios and theater chains. The Hollywood film industry also would begin to suffer a decrease in domestic spectatorship due to competition with television.

Italian state television RAI (*Radioaudiovisione italiana*) first made limited television broadcasts in 1954. As in the United States, the Italian public immediately responded to the new medium and the quiz shows, such as *Lascia o raddoppia* (*Double or Nothing*), which copied American television. One program in which Italians expressed a higher level of indigenous culture was *Carosello/Caroussel*, a program of advertisements that ran from 1957 to 1977 featuring the leading directors and actors from the Italian entertainment industry in a format that recalled the *commedia dell'arte* and the tradition of theatrical revues. The San Remo music festival, first broadcast by radio, became a national institution when it was televised featuring singers/songwriters such as Domenico Modugno (1928–94) and his festival-winning song *Nel blu dipinto di blu* (1958), adapted into a musical by Piero Tellini the following year. Italian musicals as vehicles for popular singers would appear sporadically until the 1990s with films such as *In ginocchio da te* (1964) starring singer Gianni Morandi. Despite the popularity of quiz shows and *Carosello*, Italian television would not be a significant competitive force for the Italian film industry until enough Italian households owned a television set, an event that did not occur until the 1960s. This "television gap" accounted for some of the strength of the Italian film industry into the early 1960s. The decline of the Hollywood studio system reeling from competition with television allowed the Italian cinema industry an opportunity to break into world markets. In 1960 the Italian film industry would be second only to Hollywood in the number of films produced.

Italian directors focused on the energy of the next generation with a style of filmmaking known as *neorealismo rosa* (pink neorealism), which attempted to recast purist elements from neorealism such as stories about the common man stories in a more commercial light. Gillo Pontecorvo's (1919–2006) first feature *La grande strada azzurra/The Wide Blue Road* (1957) is a story about the struggles of a fishing cooperative in Sardinia reminiscent of Visconti's tale of Sicilian fisherman in *The Earth Trembles*. Yet unlike Visconti's neorealist classic, Pontecorvo's debut had color and featured known performers Yves Montand and Alida Valli.

The most popular of the pink neorealism films were Luigi Comencini's direction of De Sica in the *Pane, amore . . .* series (four films between 1953 and 1956) featuring former beauty pageant contestants turned actresses—Sophia Loren and Gina Lollobrigida—or the *Poveri ma belli/Poor but Beautiful* (1956) series starring Marisa Allasio. Sophia Loren, Gina Lollobrigida, and Marisa Allasio were part of a generation of Italian actresses who displayed an increased physicality in their performances. Their careers were aided by their personal relationships with important producers. Sophia Loren married producer Carlo Ponti and Silvana Mangano married De Laurentiis. These actresses became known by the term *maggiorata fisica* (buxom beauty), a term taken from the *Il processo di Frine* episode starring De Sica and Lollobrigida in Alessandro Blasetti's film *Altri tempi/In Olden Days* (1952).[20] Italian neorealist films had actually anticipated the *maggiorata fisica* current with Silvana Mangano in *Bitter Rice* (1949), where physically female protagonists communicated the attraction of cartoon pinups or fuselage bombshells as well as a neorealism message. In neorealism, female display was just one of the many aspects of the portrayal of reality. But in the 1950s and 1960s the emphasis on physically imposing actresses such as Loren or Lollobrigida was a response to the audience's interest in viewing sexuality on the screen and consequently also had a larger social and economic context. After the war the female image in Italian cinema returned to the physically larger ideal reminiscent of the buxom, operatic *dive* of the silent period, as corpulence and even muscularity were revived as standards of sexual display. Thus from the late 1940s and early 1950s a stream of physically imposing Italian beauty contest winners became successful actresses. This cinematic female ideal embodied by actresses such as Silvana Mangano, Gina Lollobrigida, Sophia Loren, Silvana Pampanini, and their rotund imagery replaced the more slender mechanized standard of female beauty of the tiller girls of the late 1920s and 1930s.[21] A large part of the appeal of neorealist films and later Italian cinema in the American market was the casting of physically imposing leading ladies whose physical characteristics mirrored their personalities.

During the postwar period, directors of Fascist-era comedies and costume dramas—Blasetti and Camerini—began directing films that focused on the youthful energy of a postwar Italy. Blasetti's *In Olden Days* (1952) also developed the genre of Italian episodic films featuring comic actors and beauty pageant winners whose format had much in common with the Italian *novellistica*, short story, tradition. The *maggiorata fisica* phenomenon even influenced the Italian *strappalacrime* or tearjerker genre. Lattuada's *Anna* (1951), the top domestic film of the year starring Silvana Mangano, mixes the sexual power of Mangano's charismatic screen presence with melodramatic elements apparent in the *strappalacrime* (weepie) genre films, for example, Raffaello Matarazzo's *Catene/Chains* (1949), *I figli di nessuno/Nobody's Children* (1951), or Renato Castellani's *Due soldi di speranza/Two Cents Worth of Hope* (1952).

There was a reaction against this *maggiorata fisica* cinema with its focus on buxom leading ladies. Fellini's early films portray anti-bombshell cinema, against the trend of female ornamentation of the *maggiorata fisica* in the 1950s, particularly in the films featuring his wife Giulietta Masina: *La Strada* (1954) and *The Nights of Cabiria* (1957). Fellini's film *La dolce vita* (1960) featuring Swedish actress Anita Ekberg offers a parody on the entire *maggiorata fisica* phenomenon and the dominance of the Italian box office by American films: low-brow melo-dramas, and the sand and sword epics such as Camerini's *Ulysses* (1954) starring Kirk Douglas and Silvana Mangano. Fellini's ironic look at the Italian film industry extended to *La tentazione del Dottor Antonio/The Temptation of Doctor Antonio*, an episode in *Boccaccio '70* (1962) in which a zealous censor played by Peppino De Filippo is reduced to madness by hallucinations of a monumental image of Swedish actress Anita Ekberg on a 30-foot billboard. Fellini lampoons the *maggiorata fisica* current with a parody of Nathan Juran's science fiction paranoia film *The Attack of the 50 Foot Woman* (1958).

A different reaction to the *maggiorata* current and an indication of the new path to be taken by the former neorealist directors came in the work of Michelangelo Antonioni. He began his directorial career with a *noir* murder tale, *Story of a Love Affair* (1950) starring Massimo Girotti and the first Miss Italy winner in 1947, Lucia Bosè. But rather than emphasize the physical beauty of his female star, Antonioni adapted the long-shot style of neorealism with sequences that encouraged the spectator to consider the psychological make up of the characters.[22] Antonioni would become one of the most renowned art film directors with films of dramatic psychological introspection such as *The Girlfriends* (1955) and *L'Avventura* (1959) with Monica Vitti, a film that turns the beach/vacation movie into a study of the alienation brought by the new wealth of Italy's postwar middle class in films under the photographic direction of Gianni Di Venzano. Antonioni's films emphasized a separation from the natural world brought by the industrial changes in films such as *Eclisse/The Eclipse* (1962) and *Deserto rosso/Red Desert* (1964). Antonioni's themes of psychological angst and spiritual yearning could be interpreted as a continuation of similar themes explored by Rossellini in the early 1950s. Monica Vitti's role in *Red Desert* is actually quite similar to Ingrid Bergman's housewife in crisis in *Europa '51*.[23]

The 1950s also saw a revival of the *peplum* genre with a remake of *Gli ultimi Giorni di Pompeii/The Last Days of Pompeii* (1950) by Paolo Moffa and a mixture of the *maggiorata film* with the peplum in films such as *Messalina* (1951) starring Mexican actress Maria Felix, *La regina di Saba/The Queen of Sheba* (1952) by P. Francisi, and *Teodora, imperatrice di Bizanzio/Theodora, Slave Empress* (1953) by Carmine Gallone. The action adventure peplum would become a steady component of Italian production, for example, *Le fatiche di Ercole/Hercules* (1958) by Pietro Francisi, *Nel segno di Roma/Sign of the Gladiator* (1959) by Riccardo Freda and G. Brignone, and *La vendetta di Ercole/The Vengeance of Hercules* (1960) by Vittorio Cottafavi.

6

The Early 1960s

Mid 1950s–early 1960s   The economic boom
1961   *Mater et magistra* issued by Pope John XXIII
       Vatican II Council
1963   John XXIII Church encyclical *Pacem in Terris* revokes excommunication of
       Communists
       Aldo Moro (DC) premier of Center Left government
1964   *Piano Solo* coup extreme Right attempt led by General De Lorenzo foiled
1966   Flooding in Florence and Venice

Italian politics in the early 1960s was characterized by reformist trends. In 1962, the Socialist Party entered into a coalition government led by the Christian Democrat Aldo Moro in 1962 after another split between pro-Soviet and pro-Western factions in the Socialist Party caused by the PSI approval of NATO, which had prevented the Soviet Union from spreading west after WWII. There were reactions to this political trend from the extreme Right, in particular, in the failed coup attempt let by General De Lorenzo in 1964, spoofed by Monicelli in his film *Vogliamo I colonelli/We Want the Colonels* (1973).

Reforms extended to religious life in the country. When Pope Pius XII died in 1958, his successor Angelo Roncalli, John XXIII (1881–1963) (*il papa buono*—the good pope), moved to liberalize the Roman Catholic Church. John XXIII's Vatican II Council of 1962 sought to establish the Church as a source of spiritual and moral guidance for all elements of society regardless of political affiliation. The previous pope, Pius XII, had favored an Italian government that was more overtly pro-Catholic, like the rightist Franco and Salazar regimes in Spain and Portugal respectively, instead of the republican secular vision of government with a plurality of participation promoted by Italy's first postwar coalition, Alcide De Gasperi's DC Party. John XXIII's papal encyclical *Mater et magister—Mother and Teacher* (1961) brought the end of the universal use of Latin to celebrate the Catholic mass and was interpreted as a papal blessing on the Center-Left governments. John XXIII also removed Luigi Gedda as president of Catholic Action, weakening the organization's conservative wing. In 1965, John XXIII even ended the publication of its *Index* of prohibited books, infamous over the centuries for having censored the works of important thinkers including Galileo. The hold over Italian culture by

Catholicism would be satirized in the films of Fellini such as *8½* (1963). Changes in Italian society in the 1960s saw a decline in applications to religious orders and in church attendance. Some of the social functions performed the Catholic Church in Italy, such as hospital or elderly care and childhood education, would increasingly be assumed by private organizations or the Italian state. A new Concordat would eventually be signed between the Vatican and Socialist premier Bettino Craxi in 1984, which ended the Roman Catholic Church's status as Italy's state religion. Despite attempts by the Church to change, its strongest elements retained traditional values as demonstrated by the influence of the charismatic Francesco Forgione (1887–1968), a Capuchin friar known as Padre Pio, canonized by John Paul II in 2002. The most influential attempt to retain the traditional role of the Church was by groups such as the *Comunione e liberazione* (communion and freedom) founded by Don Giussani (1922–2005).

For a combination of demographic and economic reasons, such as the creation of the European Common Market, by the early 1960s an Italian contemplating emigration considered Italy's industrial north or northern Europe as a destination along with the Americas or Australia. During and immediately following the periods of highest immigration to America in the early years of the century, America had been a fixture in the works of intellectuals such as Elio Vittorini, Carlo Levi, Ignazio Silone, Mario Soldati, and Cesare Pavese. In the 1930s, the Fascist autarkic boycott of American films actually increased the appeal of seemingly youthful and modern American art. After WWII, Hollywood flooded the Italian market with films unreleased during the embargo years 1938–44 to the point that some critics talked about a dominating American cultural influence over Italy.[1] However, after WWII and particularly in the 1960s there was an eroding of the myth of America among Italian intellectuals. Writers such as Emilio Cecchi had already written of *America amara* (bitter America) and the disappointment at the contradictions of American society.[2] Actually anti-American sentiment has a long history in Italy and in Europe—from the opposition to American President Woodrow Wilson's insistence on national self-determination at the post-WWI peace negotiations, which led D'Annunzio to decry a *pace mutilate* (mutilated peace), to the propaganda of Mussolini's Fascist regime, which defined countries with representative democracies as decadent pluritocracies, to the hostility of the postwar international Communist movement, which found its desire to impose Communist dictatorships blocked by the military, economic, and cultural forces of the United States. By the 1960s, Italian intellectual *esterofilia* (admiration of foreigners), in accordance with Gramsci's theories about the importance of cultural hegemony, turned increasingly to the models of totalitarian dictatorships of the Soviet Union, Castroist Cuba, or Maoist China in reaction to American cultural influence.

The Economic Boom

During the late 1950s and early 1960s, the Italian economy grew dramatically, a situation that occurred in many countries in Europe. Italian industrial production would later become the seventh largest in the world as exports increased and investments expanded. The European Common Market was established by the Treaty of Rome in 1957 as an economic zone for countries protected by the NATO alliance opposing the Cominterm economic union of the Soviet satellite states in Eastern Europe. The European Common Market stimulated economic vitality by reducing trade barriers within Europe. The Italian government also extended the *autostrada* (freeway), system which encouraged car ownership and stimulated economic activity. The energy exploration efforts of Enrico Mattei (1906–62) helped overcome the country's dearth of natural resources through the development of domestic natural gas and the stipulation of oil refining and exploration contracts with oil producing nations. Mattei died in mysterious circumstances in a plane crash, an event adapted for film by Francesco Rosi: *Il caso Mattei/The Mattei Affair* (1972).

In hindsight, the rate of economic expansion in Italy between middle and late 1950s to the early 1960s was an epochal event. Between 1900 and 1950, the national income had only grown by 62 percent. In the following ten years, between 1950 and 1960, the economy grew by 47 percent, nearly equal the increase from the previous half-century.[3] The number of unemployed decreased dramatically from 1.8 million in 1956 to 623,000 by 1962. The boom was mainly an industrial expansion. For the first time the numbers of industrial workers surpassed those of agricultural workers nationwide, challenging Gramsci's theories about rural revolution. The boom was a largely northern phenomenon centered on the industrial and transportation hubs of Genoa, Turin, and Milan—Italy's so-called industrial triangle. During the boom period in the automotive or chemical industry, Italy became a technologically advanced nation. However these advances did not extend to much of the central and southern regions excluded from the economic expansion. Economic disparities translated into comparatively lower standards of living for southern laborers who sought employment in northern Italy or abroad. These conditions were examined in immigration dramas such as Germi's *Il cammino della speranza/Path of Hope* (1950) or Visconti's *Rocco e i suoi fratelli/Rocco and his Brothers* (1960). The differential in economic development between the industrial North and the more stagnant South led nearly hundreds of thousands of able workers to leave the south for the north. Emigration abroad continued as well with nearly over one million Italians leaving mainly for destinations in the Americas, northern Europe, and Australia between 1958 and 1963. Internal emigration led to attitudes of resentment and even racism toward southern Italians by northerners. Ironically northern Italian economic expansion depended on the south depleting itself of its most energetic citizens.[4]

Italian Cinema Boom

The Italian cinema of the late 1950s and even into the 1960s was characterized by market share increase against Hollywood. By 1960, Italian films had acquired nearly 50 percent of the Italian domestic market, a position unseen since before WWI. The vitality of Italian production in the 1960s owed much to retrenchment of the American film industry after antitrust legislation dismantled the Hollywood studio system distribution network by not allowing American studios to own theater chains. Competition with television was also a key factor in Hollywood's retrenchment. State television broadcasting began in Italy in 1954. Household ownership of a television set however was still not a peninsula-wide phenomenon in the early 1960s. This delay allowed Italian producers to place products not only domestically but also to fill a void in the world market. The Italian cinema was in a position of increasing market strength aided by the continuation of laws requiring theaters to show Italian films a fixed number of days per year. Not only was Italian cinema commercially vital, but its greatest authors were able to reach a wide public. In 1960 in particular films by important directors were also box office hits with Fellini's *La dolce vita*, Visconti's *Rocco and His Brothers* and De Sica's *La Ciociara/ Two Women* finishing as the top three domestic films of 1960.

In the late 1950s and early 1960s, foreign producers also came to Italy in high numbers. The Hollywood studio MGM had already shot a remake of *Quo Vadis?* in Rome in 1949. Throughout the 1950s, Hollywood producers were attracted to Italy as a location by American tax loopholes for producing films abroad. The technical expertise of Italian set designers attracted big budget Hollywood productions to the Cinecittà studios in Rome renowned for the artistic abilities of Italian set designers and wardrobe technicians. Italian colossal productions had been a staple of the Italian cinema from its earliest days and continued after the war with films such as *Aquila Nera/Return of the Black Eagle* (1946), *Fabiola* (1949), *War and Peace* (1955), and *La tempesta/The Tempest* (1958), and Alberto Lattuada and Richard Fleischer's biblical coproduction starring Anthony Quinn, *Barabba* (1961).This influx of activity known as "Hollywood on the Tiber" allowed many Italian technicians an opportunity to gain the experience and expertise essential to the boom in Italian film production in the 1960s.[5] Big budget Hollywood studio productions—*Ben Hur* (1959) and *Cleopatra* (1963) or coproductions such as *El Cid* (1961) and *Barabba* (1961)—were filmed partly in Rome's Cinecittà studios with the active participation of Italian designers and assistant directors. For example, Sergio Leone reportedly replaced William Wyler to direct the chariot race sequence of *Ben Hur* and although uncredited, codirected the peplum disaster film and Italian box office hit *Sodom and Gomorra* (1962) with Robert Aldrich.[6] This tradition of reliance on Italian craftsmanship has continued sporadically and would reappear decades later when Australian actor/director Mel Gibson came to Rome to enrich his film *The Passion of the Christ* (2004), a film shot largely in Rome featuring Italian artistic iconography and craftsmanship.

American studios also set films in Italy initially attracted by the critical success of the films of neorealist directors such as De Sica and Rossellini or the box office success enjoyed by the racier imagery in titles from the neorealist catalogue such as De Santis's *Bitter Rice* and the popularity of Italian *maggiorata fisica* actresses such as Sophia Loren and Gina Lollobrigida. A sense of nordic romanticism pervaded a spate of American productions set in Italy such as Vittorio De Sica's direction of Montgomery Cliff in *Indiscretion of an American wife* (1953), the Gregory Peck and Audry Hepburn film *Roman Holiday* (1953), David Lean's direction of Katherine Hepburn and Rosano Brazzi in *Summertime* (1955), the Clark Gable and Sophia Loren vehicle *It Started in Naples* (1960), or the Rock Hudson and Gina Lollobrigida comedy *Come September* (1961).

The result of this increased activity was that the 1960s Italian film industry had talented and experienced professionals who would serve Italy's film industry for decades to come. Important Italian technicians honed their craft during this period including cinematographer Giuseppe Rotunno who worked with Visconti on *The Leopard*; Otello Martelli with De Santis and Fellini, Vittorio Storaro with Bernardo Bertolucci; Tonino Delli Colli and Giuseppe Rotunno with directors Pier Paolo Pasolini, Sergio Leone, Fellini, and Roberto Benigni; Gianni Di Venzano and Ugo Pirro with directors Carlo Lizzani, Mario Monicelli, Lina Wertmüller, Francesco Rosi, and Michelangelo Antonioni. There were also noted film score composers: Fiorenzo Carpi (1918–97), Nino Rota (1911–79) the author of the sound track of Fellini's films as well as Francis Ford Coppola's *Godfather* films, Ennio Morricone (1928–), best known for his sound tracks to Sergio Leone's Clint Eastwood westerns, and later Nicola Piovani (1946–) known for his work on the films of Roberto Benigni.

The Italian film industry produced comedies, dramas, and episodic films with a new generation of actors—Nino Manfredi, Ugo Tognazzi, and Marcello Mastroianni—who joined the already established actor Vittorio Gassman and the actresses of *maggiorata fisica* fame—Sophia Loren and Gina Lollobrigida—as box office draws. The Italian film industry also responded to the demand for Italian horror (spaghetti nightmare) films: Englishwoman Barbara Steele starring in Mario Bava's *La maschera del demonio/The Mask of the Devil* (1960), *peplums* starring American muscleman Steve Reeves in films such as Piero Francisi's *Ercole e la regina di Lidia/Hercules Unchained* (1958) or *Le fatiche di Ercole/Hercules* (1958), spy films, reality documentary shocker films such as Jacopetti's *Mondo cane/A Dog's Life* (1962) series, and the spaghetti westerns by Sergio Leone (1929–89) including the Clint Eastwood trilogy *Per un pugno di dollari/A Fistful of Dollars* (1964), *Per qualche dollaro in più/For a Few Dollars More* (1965), and *Il buono, il brutto e il cattivo/The Good the Bad and the Ugly* (1966).

Much of the critically acclaimed experimentation in art cinema was aided by the strength producers derived from the profits in genre production in westerns and comedies (the top five Italian films of 1965 were all spaghetti westerns). In some of these genre productions and even in art cinema, the Italian film industry relied on the technical shortcuts familiar from the neorealist period, such as using post-synchronous sound allowing producers to hire multinational casts who would have box office appeal in their country of origin. Thus, at times the casts of some Italian films did not have even a common working language since casts were chosen to appeal in different countries. The case of the interaction between Clint Eastwood, who did not speak much Italian, and Sergio Leone, who did not speak much English, is a case in point. Federico Fellini was noted for tales of having actors count from one to ten instead of saying lines since the dialogue would be added post-production. At times Italian actors even assumed anglicized stage names in the hopes that the film would pass as a Hollywood production all over the world. For example, the first prints of *A Fistful of Dollars* (1964) reportedly gave the director Sergio Leone and much of the cast anglicized names. The star and director of the *Trinity* western series, Enzo Barboni and Mario Girotti, spent their careers working under the anglicized names E.B. Clucher and Terence Hill.

Commedia all'italiana (Comedy Italian Style)

In the boom years of Italian cinema also featured the genre of the *commedia all'italiana* (comedy Italian style) with characters from different social classes whose interaction resulted in brilliant social satire. The physicality and humor in Luigi Comencini's *Pane, amore e fantasia/Bread, Love and Fantasy* (1953) series starring De Sica, Loren, and Lollobrigida had themes of natural sexual energy that recalled the Italian *commedia dell' arte* theatrical traditions and its sources in classical Roman and Greek theater. These currents had been a vital part of the Italian theatrical comic tradition from the use of Plautian imagery and themes in the Renaissance comedies of authors like Niccolò Machiavelli or in the short stories of Giovanni Boccaccio. In these stories physicality and youth and the power of nature served as a breaker of class barriers. The early films of the *commedia all'italiana* maintained the vibrant style of the neorealists but added comic and visually pleasing elements in films like Risi's continuation of Comencini's *Pane, amore, e* (1955) series or in Risi's *Poveri ma belli/Poor but Beautiful* (1957).

A foundational film of the *commedia all'italiana* style is Mario Monicelli's *I soliti ignoti/Big Deal on Madonna Street* (1958) penned by the scriptwriting team Age (Agenore Incrocchi), Cecchi D'Amico, and Furio Scarpelli (figure 6.1). The film is a parody of Jules Dassin's French thriller *Rififi* (1954), a story of a failed heist with doomed protagonists in the tradition of French *policier* crime films. In *Big Deal on Madonna Street*, Monicelli parodies the fatalism of the French crime genre with a story about a team of bumbling antiheroes who abandon the caper once they discover a freshly cooked meal of *pasta e ceci* (noodles and chick peas) in the refrigerator of the house they unsuccessfully tried to rob.

Monicelli's film adapts the ancient character types from the theatrical tradition of the *commedia dell'arte* to the cinema. Beppe, the failed boxer played by Vittorio Gassman, has much in common with the *commedia dell'arte* stock character of the Capitan, derived from the *miles gloriosus* of classical comedy. The *miles gloriosus* is a self-appointed leader who claims foreign origins so that he can assume a higher status and expert knowledge unavailable locally. The *miles gloriosus* also claims to be a great soldier but is a danger only to himself and is ready to change sides at the hint of danger. In *Big Deal on Madonna Street* Beppe pretends to be a rich, sophisticated, educated northerner. But he fails as a boxer after a show of false bravado and is demasked by Nicoletta, the Venetian maid of the house he is planning to rob. In the *commedia dell'arte*, the Captain often works in tandem with Pantaloon, an older figure. Pantaloon and the Soldier cook up schemes that inevitably fail after they betray each other for love or the promise of riches. The equivalent of Pantaloon in *Big Deal on Madonna Street* is Cosimo, physically older than the rest of the gang (except Campanelle) and the original mastermind of the heist, he is tricked and betrayed by Beppe.

Figure 6.1   Vittorio Gassman (Peppe) and Totò (Dante Cruciani) in Mario Monicelli's *I soliti ignoti.*

The rest of the cast of *Big Deal on Madonna Street* recalls the *commedia dell'arte zanni* (clowns). In the *commedia dell'arte* theatrical tradition each *zanni* clown can represent a different geographical region of Italy. The regional stereotypes in *Big Deal on Madonna Street* struck a common chord in the Italian popular imagination during the massive intra-national emigration of the postwar period. The most recognizable of these is the *Pulcinella*-like character, Dante Cruciani, the Neapolitan safe cracker played by Totò. Totò started his career impersonating *Pulcinella* and his character in *Big Deal on Madonna Street* has many of the same attributes of the Neapolitan *Pulcinella* character who often has a secret and a large family. Another *zanni* clown is Campanelle who recalls the *commedia dell'arte* clown Harlequin, the eternally dispossessed worker from Bergamo. Campanelle, like Harlequin, dresses in baggy pants; he keeps a low center of gravity and is constantly searching for food. Ferribotte, the Sicilian emigrant, seems to be a Sicilian *zanni* who always keeps the women in his family hidden under lock and key.

Usually a rare competent character in the *commedia dell'arte* is the maid Colombina. In *Big Deal on Madonna Street* the maid Nicoletta, like the *commedia dell'arte* Colombina character, is sharp-witted, quick speaking, and demasks and demotes Beppe. As the only rational and lucid character in the cast everything depends on Nicoletta/Colombina's participation. The figure of a dominant female in Italian popular cinema capable of subverting existing economic and societal power structures derives from the ancient tradition in Italian comedy from the *commedia dell'arte* and the *novellistica*; a Marxist reading of the *commedia all'ital-iana* is possible in which the hegemonic class prevents new ideas, such as women's liberation, by advocating ideas or conditions based on the previous order.

Big Deal on Madonna Street appeared at the height of the Italian economic boom of the late 1950s, when the working classes gained the chance to experience a more materialistic lifestyle. Ironically during a period of such economic change the most popular form of Italian cinema, the *commedia all'italiana* (comedy Italian style) relied heavily on the archaic roots of the Italian literary and theatri-cal tradition. The return to stock characters in the cinema was a comfort, even a reassurance of cultural identity in the impending consumerism, migration, and continuing industrialization of the Italian economy. In the last sequence of the film, Beppe hides from the police by entering a construction worker queue where he will work as a salaried laborer as did so many Italians of the period.

Many films in the early 1960s had plots that recalled the *commedia dell'arte* story lines or *novella* (short stories) tradition including Gianni Puccini's *L'attico/The Penthouse* (1962), *Una vita difficile/A Difficult Life* (1961) by Dino Risi about a giornalist who cannot maintain a family and decides to become the ser-vant of a rich man, the episodic film *I mostri/15 from Rome* (1963) by Dino Risi, *Le ore dell'amore/The Hours of Love* (1963) by Luciano Salce. Other films featured direct social commentary on the changes brought to Italy by the boom. In Carlo Lizzani's adaptation of Luciano Bianciardi's novel *La vita agra/The Bitter Life* (1964), a miner played by Ugo Tognazzi fired from his job in southern Italy comes to Milan to blow up the offices of the company that fired him. He is eventually integrated into the boom economy as an advertising man, leaves the girl he met in Milan, and brings his family north to be part of the new economy.

A key film in this period was Dino Risi's *Il sorpasso/The Easy Life* (1962) scripted with Rodolfo Sonengo (figure 6.2). The film is a mix between a road movie and a beach/vacation film that provides a snapshot of the changes in Italy in the economic boom years. Critics have commented that the true star of *The Easy Life* is the convertible sports car driven by Bruno (Vittorio Gassman) a man interested in perpetuating his youth despite a failed marriage and teenage daugh-ter. The car is a symbol for the dynamism, sexual vitality, and unpredictability of the social changes unleashed by the economic boom of the times. Bruno's values of speed and casual encounters are fatal to the naive law student Roberto (Jean-Louis Trintignant) who loses his bearings once the protective veneer of tradition is removed from his life. Roberto becomes tragically embroiled in a culture that rewards youth, consumption, and speed, themes and trends that would increas-ingly dominate Italian culture into the new millenium. *The Easy Life* also echoed intellectual concerns about consumer culture from literary figures such as Edoardo Sanguinetti and Elio Vittorini.[7]

Part of the *commedia dell'arte* and *novellistica* story line is the tendency to emphasize female physical and economic dominance with a corollary portrayal of the male as an inept fool. Such themes were brilliantly conveyed by De Sica in another episodic film *Ieri, Oggi, Domani/Yesterday, Today and Tomorrow* (1963) and in *Marriage Italian Style* (1964) based upon De Filippo's play *Filumena Marturiana* or in the multi-director effort *Boccaccio '70* (1962) by De Sica, Fellini,

Figure 6.2   Jean-Luois Tritignant (Roberto) and Vittorio Gassman (Bruno) in Dino Risi's *Il sorpasso/The Easy Life* (1962).

Monicelli, and Visconti. The film's title is an explicit reference to the debt of the *commedia all'italiana* and the earlier tradition of the Italian short comic tale, the *novella*, by authors such as Giovanni Boccaccio.

A main actor of the *commedia dell'italiana* who perfectly represented this type of comic masculinity was Alberto Sordi (1920–2003), who began as an extra on Gallone's *Scipione l'Africano* (1937) and went on to act in nearly 150 films including Fellini's *Lo sceicco bianco/The White Sheik* (1952) and *I vitelloni/The Young and the Passionate* (1953) and De Sica's *Il giudizio universale/The Last Judgement* (1961) and *Il boom* (1963). Sordi is best remembered for playing an Italian male overwhelmed by the expectations of society (figure 6.3). In Steno's *Un americano a Roma/An American in Rome* (1954), Sordi parodied American sloppy eating habits, bizarre dress, and fascination with technology and machinery in a meeting between *commedia dell'arte* buffoonery and Fordism. Sordi lampooned the divide between the traditional indolence of a *commedia dell'arte* clown and the rigid expectations of various professions in films such as Mario Soldati's *Policarpo, official di scrittura* (1959), Luigi Zampa's *Il vigile/Traffic Policeman* (1960), Elio Petri's *Il maestro di Vigevano/Teacher from Vigevano* (1963), and Luigi Zampa's *Il Medico della mutua/The Family Doctor* (1968), *Il Prof. Dott. Guido Tersilli* (1969) by Luciano Salce, Monicelli's *Un borghese piccolo piccolo/An Average Man* (1977). In De Sica's *Il boom* (1963), a parody of the new consumer culture, a desperate Alberto Sordi decides to sell one of his eyes in order to keep his new consumer goods. Sordi also

Figure 6.3   Alberto Sordi in Antonio Pietrangeli's *It happened in Rome.*

used his comic talents in a foray into the mafia drama *Il mafioso* (1962) and in historical dramas like Mario Monicelli's WWI drama *La grande guerra/The Great War* (1959). Sordi also appeared in several films that deal with the plight of homesick Italian immigrants—*Un italiano in America/An Italian in America* (1967), *Bello, onesto, emigrato in Australia sposerebbe compaesana illibata/Girl in Australia* (1971)—themes later played to perfection in Franco Brusati's *Pane e cioccolato/Bread and Chocolate* (1973) starring Nino Manfredi as an Italian immigrant struggling in Switzerland.

Italian films of the 1960s also examined the peculiarities of the culturally and geographically separate south, in for example, like Pietro Germi's *Divorzio all'italiana Divorce Italian Style* (1961), *Sedotta e abandonata/Seduced and Abandoned* (1963), Monicelli's *La ragazza con la pistola/Girl with a Pistol* (1968), Lattuada's *Il mafioso* (1962), Visconti's *Rocco and His Brothers* and Antonioni's *L'avventura* (1959). These films displayed the contrasts between a modern industrial culture of a posteconomic boom Italy and the feudal social and economic codes of the Italian south.

The early 1960s also featured a current of films that revisited Fascist and wartime themes. This genre of films was the heir to the neorealist concentration on the war and the Resistance as an event that formed the essence of the postwar republic. But by the 1960s the heroic themes of films from the 1940s came to include more ironic and tragicomic depictions of Italy's struggles during and transition from Fascism. For example, the 1961 box office champion Luciano Salce's *Il federale/The Fascist* (1961) starring Ugo Tognazzi is the story of a committed Fascist who must ironically shed the layers of the virile Fascist rhetoric on which he based his personality as the regime falls. Other films in this current included *La lunga notte del '43/The Long Night of '43* (1960) by Florestano Vancini, *Anni ruggenti/Roaring Years* (1962) with Nino Manfredi, Giorgio Bianchi's *Il mio amico Benito* (1962) starring Peppino De Filippo, *La Marcia su Roma/The March on Rome* (1962) by Dino Risi, *Tutti a casa/Everybody Home* (1960) by Comencini in which Alberto Sordi plays an Italian soldier confused about which side the Italian army is on after September 8, 1943. More in the tradition of neorealism are *Il generale della Rovere/General Della Rovere* (1959) by Rossellini starring De Sica as a small time swindler who assumes the identity of a heroic imprisoned general during the Resistance or *Le quattro giornate di Napoli/The Four Days of Naples* (1962) by Nanni Loy about resistance to Nazi occupation in Naples with a title that refers to the struggles in Milan during 1848 nationalist revolts.

The Spaghetti Western of Sergio Leone

Italy's most accomplished director of westerns, Sergio Leone, came from a cinematic family. His father had worked as an assistant to Pastrone and discovered Bartolomeo Pagano, the actor who played Maciste in *Cabiria*. Leone had worked as an assistant director on De Sica's *The Bicycle Thief*, appearing in the film as an Austrian seminary student in a brief cameo role. Leone first made his mark as a director in the peplum genre with a remake of the sand and sword standard *Gli ultimi giorni di Pompeii/The Last Days of Pompeii* (1959) and *Il colosso di Rodi/The Colossus of Rhodes* (1960). But he truly found his calling with the western. In certain aspects Leone recalls the career of writer Emilio Salgari (1862–1911), who wrote popular adventure novels at the turn of the last century but reportedly never actually left Italy. Leone apparently did not speak adequate English, yet he seemed to have a visceral understanding for the storyline of a good western.

Leone's *A Fistful of Dollars* displays the diverse cultural influences running through Italy during the 1960s. The film is a remake of Akira Kurosawa's Samurai drama *Yojimbo* (1961) as a western starring American television star Clint Eastwood; however, Leone has insisted that the source for the film is a *commedia dell'arte* play by Carlo Goldoni *Arlecchino il servitore di due padroni/The Servant with Two Masters* (1745). In Leone's film Clint Eastwood plays the drifter Joe, a trickster figure like Harlequin from Goldoni's play who plays one powerful family against another to his advantage (figure 6.4). Another Italian source for the hero in the film, Joe, is Gian Piero Bonelli and Aurelio Galeppini's' still popular comic book series *Tex*, whose protagonist is an ordained Navajo chief, a government Indian agent, and a Texas Ranger.[8] With such credentials he has the backing of all opposing factions in the American West—the subjugated Indians, the local authorities, and the federal government. This polyvalence also gives Tex the ability to play one side against another in order to defend the oppressed.

Figure 6.4   Eastwood (Joe) and Marianne Koch (Marisol).

In *A Fistful of Dollars*, Joe liberates indigenous townsfolk from their Anglo (Baxters) and Iberian (Rojos) overlords. This outsider setup is a repeat from Leone's earlier film *The Colossus of Rhodes* (1961), where the hero is often a slave who champions a subjugated community against their overlords.[9] The *commedia dell'arte* roots of Joe's laconic nature in *A Fistful of Dollars* seem to parody the Protestant work ethic. George Steven's western hero in *Shane* (1953) as played by Alan Ladd mends fences for the pioneer family in his spare time. Leone's Joe in *A Fistful of Dollars* seems indolent but he is also highly skilled and cleverer than his adversaries. The theme of the lazy but clever male would reappear in the Italian western in the *Trinity* series starring Terence Hill, where the protagonist's skill with a gun is matched only by his desire to sleep.[10]

The success of Leone's westerns starring Clint Eastwood *A Fistful of Dollars* (1964), *For a Few Dollars More* (1965), *The Good the Bad and the Ugly* (1966), *C'era una volta il west/Once Upon a Time in the West* (1968) cowritten by Bernardo Bertolucci and Dario Argento, and *Giù la testa/A Fistfull of Dynamite* (1971) and their scores by Ennio Morricone spurred other Italian directors to display their talents. Tonino Valerii made the western spoof *Nobody Is My Name* (1973). Enzo Barboni directed the *They Call Me Trinity* (1970) series. Other Italian directors of westerns include Sergio Corbucci with *Django* (1966), Damiano Damiani's *A Bullet for the General* (1966). The profitability Italian western actually became central to the economic viability of the Italian film industry.

Leone's treatment of the foundational myth of American western, his use of graphic violence influenced Hollywood directors' approach to the genre. Leone had cast Henry Fonda, the hero of John Ford's *My Darling Clementine* (1946) as a child murdering outlaw in *Once Upon a Time in the West* (1968).[11] Films such as Sam Peckinpah's *The Wild Bunch* (1969) or Clint Eastwood's *Unforgiven* (1992) reviewed the ideological certainties of the American western. Leone's camera style and shot selection like his shot choice in the final shootout sequence of *A Fistful of Dollars* from the perspective of Clint Eastwood's right boot, or his minute attention to physical detail and extreme close-ups changed the style of popular cinematography brought the refinement of the long-shot style of art cinema to a popular genre. Critics have noted how Leone's attention to detail and reliance on Enrico Morricone's scores give his films an almost operatic tone. Other critics have noted that the spare and crude essence of Leone's film style and narrative is a result of his exposure to neorealism.[12]

7

The Later 1960s

1968   Student protests, labor unrest, Center–Left coalition governments
1969   Bombing of bank at Piazza Fontana in Milan opens autunno caldo protests
        and *anni di piombo* (leaden years) terrorist period in Italy

Not since the days of D'Annunzio's takeover of Fiume and Fascism's identification with songs of *Giovinezza* (Youth) during the 1920s had a youth movement so determined cultural and political change in Italy. In 1962 compulsory education was extended to age 14 and entrance restrictions to state universities were eased. With the demographic increase of the postwar baby boom, the result was overcrowding. Italian universities were built and designed to serve far fewer students than were attending by the 1960s. Furthermore, in the rebellious spirit of the times the education system in Italy was interpreted as having decreasing applications in the technical economy and a decreasing relevance within the context of consumer driven popular culture.

The student and youth rebellions centering on the year 1968 actually occurred throughout the West and should not be considered as national events but part of an international demographic phenomenon. In the West, by 1968, much of the offspring of the generation that had suffered through the 1930s economic depression and World War II reached physical and emotional adolescence with attitudes formed by the postwar peace ensured by a standing army in Europe from the United States. The idealism fostered by this protected environment came into contact with the realities of the shortcomings of a world that in the first half of the twentieth century had produced two world wars, a Holocaust, and was continuing to struggle with the legacy of colonialism.

The demographic changes were accompanied by changes in industrial working conditions. In northern Italy, waves of strikes and factory occupations by workers erupted in the fall of 1968, later referred to as the "Hot autumn" as Italian wages were still low by European standards. During this period, the radical leftist political parties such as *Autonomia Operaia* attempted to establish a constituency among Italy's working classes. The governing establishment reacted to the strife by granting concessions. Parliament proposed social legislation on pensions, healthcare, and workers rights laws, which anticipated demands from the Left. A divorce law was passed through popular referendum in 1975 in recognition of societal changes and a growing Italian feminist movement.

As in the rest of Europe and North America, the demographic boom was accompanied by a rise in youth culture perhaps best understood by the efforts of singers and songwriters influenced by Anglo-American pop music. Italian singer songwriters such as Adriano Celentano, Lucio Battisti, Fabrizio De Andre, Giorgio Gaber, and Lucio Dalla developed an indigenous Italian voice in popular culture. Part of the exuberance of the 1960s was a desire to break social, religious, and especially sexual boundaries taking advantage of the diffusion of oral contraception and decisive, if temporary, medical advances against venereal diseases. Irrationalism in art reached the point of Piero Manzoni's accurately entitled *Merda d'artista/Artist's Excrement* (1961) taking the technical achievements of world renowned masters such as Renato Guttuso and Piero Guccione to surrealistic hyperbole.

The Italian literary scene was still dominated by figures who had matured during the Fascist era and used their postwar freedoms to examine Italian life in a highly detached narrative style, as in the case of Natalia Ginzburg, or in a satirizing tone, as in the case of Alberto Moravia, Dacia Maraini, and Paolo Volponi. There were also writers who spoke the language of a rebellious era, for examples, Alberto Bevilacqua and Giuseppe Pontiggia. But literary influences were no longer limited to high literature but also extended to comic books such as the *Corto Maltese* series by internationally renowned Venetian author Hugo Pratt (1927–95). Other exponents of Italian comic art included Bonelli and Galeppini's *Tex Willer* series, Angela and Luciana Giussani's *Diabolik* (1962), Tiziano Sclavi's *Dylan Dog* (1986), and the erotically charged work of Manilo Manaro admired by Fellini. Although the most widely distributed newspaper in Italy in the postwar period has been the pink papered sports daily *Gazzetta dello sport*, there was a sustained influence of journalists such as Enzo Biagi, Giorgio Bocca, Oriana Fallaci, and Indro Montanelli who wrote books containing cultural and political commentary.

The cultural experimentation of the 1960s extended to the Italian theater with the rise of an experimental avant garde theater by Carmelo Bene or Luca Ronconi, although other figures for example, Giorgio Strehler (1921–97), worked to maintain the traditional formats of the *commedia dell'arte*. Influential theatrical performers of the period included Dario Fo (1926–) and his wife Franca Rame, who revived the tradition of the *giullare di piazza* (town square clown) with performances, at times censored on Italian television, which harkened back to the tradition of medieval improvisational performers who poked fun at official power. Fo's theatrical pieces *Morte accidentale di un anarchico/Accidental Death of an Anarchist* and *Non tutti i ladri vengono per nuocere/Not all Thieves Come to do harm*—expressed the iconoclastic spirit of the 1960s. Fo would continue his irreverent takes on Italian culture with one-man performances on the lives of Saint Francis, Leonardo da Vinci, and Caravaggio. Fo was awarded the Nobel Prize for literature in 1997.

The cinema club circuit that developed in countries, as in France as the informal educational setting for directors of the French New Wave, also appeared in Italy by the late 1960s and 1970s. Cinema clubs and *cineforum* became an important part of the development of a cinematic culture in Italy. Future directors

Roberto Benigni and Nanni Moretti, for example, gained ideas about cinema in the revival theaters of 1970s Rome. The development of a canon of films as required viewing also incited comic reactions. In the second of Luciano Salce's long-running *Fantozzi* comedy series featuring Paolo Villaggio *Il secondo tragico Fantozzi* (1976), the oppressed accountant Fantozzi expressed the divide between public tastes and art cinema by courageously standing up in a crowd of his coworkers at a forced viewing of Eisenstein's seminal *Battleship Potymkin* (1925), to announce in the best tradition of *commedia dell'arte* irreverence that the foundational film of formalist montage was actually "a *cagata pazzesca* (an insane bowel movement)."

Italian philosophers and intellectuals contributed to the cultural moment of what would become effimerally defined as postmodernism. University professor Umberto Eco (1932–) wrote on the differences between traditional readings and interpretations of art and the avant garde as open versus closed systems. Eco gave nontraditional subjects due respect as cultural phenomena. He wrote widely read semiotic analyses of the spy and television quiz shows. Eco's writings have been an important influence on contemporary media studies. Eco achieved worldwide fame with his first novel *The Name of the Rose* (1980) later adapted to film starring Sean Connery in 1986. Eco's novel combined his interest in popular forms like the detective novel with his training in medieval philosophy—Eco's university thesis had been on the scholastic philosophy of St. Thomas. Like Eco, novelist and cultural theoretician Italo Calvino (1923–85) gained fame through his novels first in the neorealist style *Il sentiero dei nidi di ragno/The Path to the Spiders' Nests* (1947) then in magic realism and fables *Cosmicomiche*.

Art Cinema

The commercial success of the Italian film industry in the 1960s extended to art cinema. French theorists, for example, Andrè Bazin and his disciples such as Francois Truffaut of the *Nouvelle Vague* (New Wave), arrived at the *auteur* theory of film appreciation, which interprets films as the work and the product of the artistic vision of a single author (*auteur* in French) or *cinema d'autore* in Italian. Certain directors (John Ford, Nicolas Ray, Jean Renoir, Roberto Rossellini, Orson Welles, etc.) were anointed as *auteurs* in recognition of their artistic abilities. Of course cinema is actually a collective enterprise of an entire industrial apparatus. Individual directors rarely enjoy enough financial production control in order to impose a single artistic vision. Nevertheless given European cultural heritage, film critics were able to advance the idea that cinema was an expression of the latest European avant garde. In 1958, French critic Andrè Bazin wrote about neorealism and films like Rossellini's *Paisan* in terms that inspired a generation of filmmakers to strive for the essential power of the neorealist style. However, by the mid-1960s, there was a reaction against the legacy of neorealism even by the directors who had made it famous. The films about the heroic resistance struggle of WWII gave way to films in which directors examined about more personal issues, reflective of a peacetime Europe with a growing economy.[1]

Roberto Rossellini

In the 1950s, Rossellini made films that had a somewhat quixotic and Catholic message such as *Francesco giullare di Dio/The Flowers of St. Francis* (1950) starring Aldo Fabrizi and *La macchina ammazzacattivi/The Machine that Kills Bad People* (1952), but both films performed poorly at the box office. He made more dramatically themed films with a similar message about spiritual realization with Hollywood star Ingrid Bergman—*Stromboli terra di Dio/Stromboli* (1948), *Europa '51*(1952), *Viaggio in Italia/Voyage to Italy* (1953), and *Giovanna d'Arco al rogo/Joan of Arc* (1954). Rossellini adapted the Catholic ideology of his early postwar films, *Roma città aperta/Open City* or *Germania anno zero/Germany Year Zero*, to the art cinema genre where moral questions were posed at a personal level, rather than in the context of the cataclysmic events of WWII. Rossellini had displayed a set of precise techniques that would become foundational to art cinema; long shots to induce spectator speculation about a character's psychological makeup and narratives without the sort of closure and happy ending that characterized Hollywood cinema in particular.

In the 1950s, public interest in Rossellini's personal life actually took precedence over his films. The already married Swedish actress Bergman reportedly wrote Rossellini a note after having seen *Open City*. The ensuing relationship between Rossellini and Bergman and their subsequent children, including actress Isabella Rossellini, made the couple a fixture in the tabloids during an era when divorce was not legal in Italy. The vicissitudes of Rossellini's personal life made for good press such as the furious reaction of his girlfriend Anna Magnani to the news of Bergman's arrival in Rome. Magnani jealously insisted on making an American produced film *Vulcano* (1949) directed by William Dieterle, near from Rossellini's production of *Stromboli* (1949) starring Ingrid Bergman.

Rossellini seemed to abandon the art cinema genre after his adaptation of a Stendhal novel *Vanina Vanini/The Betrayer* (1961) and his contribution to the multi-director episodic film *Ro.Go.Pag* (1963). In his later career Rossellini became increasingly interested in the educational possibility of films and made the documentaries *India* (1960) and dramatizations of moments in Italian history such as the Resistance drama starring Vittorio De Sica *Il Generale della Rovere/General Della Rovere* (1959) scripted by Indro Montanelli and *Viva Italia!/Garibaldi* (1960) about Garibaldi's campaigns of the *Risorgimento*. Rossellini also made educational films for television such as *Iron Age* (1964), *Rise of Louis XIV* (1966), *Acts of the Apostles* (1969), *Socrates* (1970), *Blaise Pascal* (1971), *Agostino Depretis d'Ippotona/Augustine of Hippo* (1972), *L'età di Cosimo de Medici/The Age of Cosimo de'Medici* (1973), *Cartesius* (1974). Toward the end of his life Rossellini held a brief appointment at the *Scuola Nazionale di Cinematografia* in Rome. Unfortunately, according to actor and director Carlo Verdone, then a student at the CSC, Rossellini, the master of neorealism whose style had inspired oppositional cinemas around the world, including the French New Wave, had difficulty conducting his courses due to the political exuberance of students during the 1960s counterculture protests.

Luchino Visconti

In 1960, Visconti made the emigration drama *Rocco e i suoi fratelli/Rocco and His Brothers* (1960), a film that combined the neorealist tone of common man stories with a sense of *avant garde* exploration of interpersonal relations. Visconti updates the story of Sicilian fishermen from *La terra trema/The Earth Trembles* (1948) to a tale of contemporary Lucanian immigrants alienated by industrial Milan in a film that has become a canonical example of Italian art cinema.

Visconti's next film, *Il Gattopardo/The Leopard* (1963), is an adaptation of the bestselling novel by Giuseppe Tomasi di Lampedusa (1896–57) about a Sicilian Prince who must relinquish power and status after Italian unification. In *The Leopard*, Visconti shows the dissolution of the aristocracy with sympathy and understanding for the aesthetic and intellectual qualities that he, as an aristocrat himself, so deeply appreciated. The Prince's demise is a metaphor for the decline of the aristocracy. Death images pervade the film as the Prince stoically witnesses the end of an era. The Prince, played by Burt Lancaster, summarizes the views of the fading aristocracy when he dismisses fears of revolution with his belief that the rising middle class is actually interested in becoming part of the system. The Prince offers a perfect definition of the fatalistic concept of *trasformismo* originally coined by one of the first prime ministers of unified Italy, Depretis, that the more things may change the more they actually remain the same. The film ends with a grand ball for the announcement that the Prince's nephew (Alain Delon) will marry Angelica (Claudia Cardinale), the beautiful and rich daughter of the *nouveau riche* social climber Don Calogero. The ball sequences show Visconti's extreme attention to historical detail and minutely lavish reconstruction of nineteenth-century artifacts. These scenes were reproduced with extravagance and self-indulgence in a complete departure from the neorealist style, and evidence Visconti's ability to give cinematography the same sort of high artistic power usually identified with painting or opera.

Visconti's *La caduta degli dei-Gotterdammerung/The Damned* (1969) with its Italian title referring to a Richard Wagner opera, chronicles the rise of Nazism in Germany through a study of the moral perversity of the Essenbeck clan, modeled after the Krupp family of armaments manufacturers. Visconti connects Nazism and sexual perversion, a point explicitly conveyed through a recreation of the *night of the long knives* when Hitler's SS purged the Nazi movement of its SA rivals. Visconti's *Morte a Venezia/Death in Venice* (1970) is based on the Thomas Mann short novel about a middle-aged man who remains in Venice during the cholera outbreak that will claim his life in order to ogle a Polish boy at the Lido beach. *Death in Venice* deals with the decadence of an individual, Whereas Visconti's next films deal's with the decadence of an entire family, *Gruppo di famiglia in un interno/Conversation Piece* (1974) and of an era, *L'innocente/The Innocent* (1976). *Conversation Piece* depicts the life of an Italian family in contemporary society and creates a rather bleak view of modern life, plagued by lack of communication, drug addiction, and political terrorism. Visconti's last film, *The Innocent,* is an adaptation of a story by Gabriele D'Annunzio in which a nobleman kills his wife's illegitimate newborn before committing suicide in a study of *fin-du-siecle* aristocratic society bound to self-destruction.

Federico Fellini

Fellini went from being Aldo Fabrizi's gagman and a screenwriter on Rossellini's neorealist film *Open City* (1945) to become an art cinema director. With its glamor kitsch and emphasis on contemporary consumerism, Fellini's *La dolce vita* (1960) is a sociological portrait of 1960s economic boom Italy. The film is divided into episodes that offer a journey through Roman society from the world of the jaded celebrity journalist Marcello, to the decadence of the Roman aristocracy and the banality of late night prostitution. *La dolce vita* caused scandal due to its striptease sequence, which heightened its box office appeal. In this vein the film is party to the erotic genre of the period, such as the Brigitte Bardot films directed by Roger Vadim in France or Alessandro Blasetti's *Europa di notte/Europe by Night* (1959) box office hit, which offered a glimpse into the world of European striptease parlors. *La dolce vita* is also remembered for the manner in which the stars Marcello Mastroianni and Swedish bombshell Anita Ekberg communicated a sense of Italian fashion to a world audience. The film contributed ot the English language through the reference to the scandal photographer Paparazzo whose name refers to celebrity photographers to the present day.

Fellini followed *La dolce vita* with one of his most autobiographical films, *8½* (1963). Fellini had previously made six feature length films and had contributed "half" segments to three others, so he considered *8½* as his eighth-and-a-half film. The protagonist is a film director who can no longer decide what films to make, a crisis connected to his problematic relationships with three different women: his wife, his mistress, and an angelic fantasy figure played by Claudia Cardinale. The story jumps rapidly from present to past, from reality to dream and fantasy as Fellini addresses the authoritarianism of the Roman Catholic Church and its effects on adolescents, the absurdity of the world of film production, and the paradox of living between reality and illusion. The film ends where it began; with a parade of characters performing at the director's whims.

Similar themes are present in Fellini's *Giulietta degli spiriti/Juliet of the Spirits* (1965), a film that puts the themes of middle-class alienation from Rossellini's *Europa '51* and Antonioni's *L'Avventura* into the style of spaghetti nightmare horror films. Giulietta is a middle-aged married woman faced with her husband's extramarital affair. She undergoes a series of traumatic experiences: spiritual séances, encounters with phony oriental prophets, outings with her oversexed, stunningly beautiful neighbor, and haunting by her inner ghosts. These latter include an overpowering mother figure, a beloved, rebellious grandfather, archaic figures, and Catholic martyr nightmares. Eventually, Giulietta chases away her ghosts to face the outside world.[2] Though Giulietta arrives at a certain sense of wisdom, there is a fatalistic realization that little will change for her.

Toby Dammit (1967) is Fellini's short film based upon Edgar Allan Poe's short story *Never Bet the Devil Your Head*, which appeared in the multi-director effort *Spirits of the Dead*. Fellini's contribution is a parody of many of the currents in film in the 1960s: horror, pornography, westerns, and art cinema. Fellini had already parodied the Italian film industry's reliance on the *maggiorata fisica* actresses such as Anita Ekberg and the Hercules series peplums starring American strongman

Steve Reeves in *La dolce vita*. In *Toby Dammit*, Terrence Stamp plays a dipsomaniac English actor suffering from visions of the Devil as a little blond girl chasing a large white ball. Toby has been cast as Jesus in the first Catholic western in which the Savior returns to the desolate, violent plains of the American west with a plot reminiscent of Fyodor Dostoevsky's short story, *The Grand Inquisitor*. Fellini takes aim at the world of film theory influential in the mid-1960s in the sequence when the producers' representative, Father Spagna (many so-called spaghetti westerns were filmed in Spain), introduces Toby to the directors who explain the theoretical basis for their film project as Fellini's camera scans his artificially re-created Roman streets. Fellini parodies film theory when the directors offer a quick synopsis of the theoretical grounding of their film: Roland Barthes's textual analysis, Georg Lukac's Marxist social determinism, the Hollywood montage style of Fred Zinneman—the director of the Gary Cooper western *High Noon* (1952). Toby finally performs the nihilistic soliloquy "Tomorrow, tomorrow, tomorrow" from *MacBeth* at Fellini's surrealistic re-creation of an Italian film award banquet.[3]

Fellini extended his parodies of popular genres to the peplum with *Satirycon* (1969), a disturbing, dreamlike vision of the fragmentary classical tale by classical author Petronius, which Fellini turns into a cautionary tale about the decline of ancient Roman society with the expressionistic style of a horror film. *Clowns* (1970) is a semi-documentary that discusses the disappearance of the clown as an entertainment phenomenon. With *Roma* (1971), Fellini repeated the autobiographical themes he had explored in *8 1/2* with an episodic film about the Italian capital that contrasts Fellini's memories of the city when he first arrived in the Fascist period with his impressions as a middle-aged director. For Fellini, Rome is not just a city, but a second home, a mother, a depository of ancient mysteries and current decadence, of filth, life, death, and renewal. After an enigmatic cameo of Anna Magnani, the film ends with an apocalyptic and ironic sequence about a new horde of scooter riding barbarians returning as if to sack Rome one more time.

Michelangelo Antonioni

Michelangelo Antonioni began as a critic in the Italian professional cinema of the 1940s and made neorealist style documentaries in the late 1940s including *Nettezze Urbane/N.U.* (1948), a faithful account of a day in the life of city garbage collectors. Antonioni brought the documentary long-shot camera style to his early feature films *Story of a Love Affair* (1950) and his docudrama about troubled youth in Europe *I vinti/The Vanquished* (1952). He gained international acclaim with *L'Avventura* (1959), the story of a group of wealthy vacationers who cannot find one of their party, Anna.[4] *L'Avventura* was censored in several countries and its projection suspended for six months in Milan for "obscenity" because of scenes of actresses undressing in front of the camera. In the film the only information that spectators have about Anna before her mysterious disappearance is that she is involved romantically with Sandro, and hers is the first female body seen undressing on screen. Otherwise she remains an enigmatic character whose disappearance offers an unanswerable philosophical parable regarding existence. The film became emblematic of art cinema for the manner in which Antonioni challenged the stylistic and narrative conventions of commercial cinema. His extended long shots and narrative without closure were in opposition to the Hollywood model.

Other Antonioni films include *La Notte/The Night* (1960), the story of a novelist suffering from writer's block who is also dissatisfied in his marriage. Antonioni expertly employs the setting of an all night party against the anonymous backdrop of industrial Milan as a metaphor for the estrangement between the film's protagonists. *L'Eclissi/The Eclipse* (1961) examines themes of alienation and separation from the natural world, a theme continued in *Deserto rosso/Red Desert* (1964). Antonioni has a reputation for being more sensitive to women's issues than Visconti or Fellini. His trilogy of solitude, however, and especially *L'Avventura* and *The Eclipse*, reveals an equally male-dominated handling of the female image. Yet Antonioni also made films that questioned the essence of reality with *Blow-Up* (1966) set in the London of the swinging 1960s, which features a cameo of rock guitarist Jimmy Page playing with rock group the Yardbirds. The film is a murder mystery in which the existence of a chance photograph of the murder scene by a callow English fashion photographer begs questions about the perception of reality. Antonioni continued to experiment with new narrative approaches with his film on youth rebellion in the Sam Shepard scripted *Zabrieskie Point* (1970) and the Peter Wollen scripted *Professione: Reporter/The Passenger* (1975) starring Jack Nicholson in an enigmatic story about a man who assumes the identity of another, filmed in a style that was the height of the long-shot art cinema style to reach commercial theaters. Antonioni has remained sporadically active in later years with the historical film *Il mistero di Oberwald/The Oberwald Mystery* (1980) as well as *Identificazione di una donna/Identification of a Woman* (1982) and *Beyond the Clouds/Al di là delle nuvole* (1995).

Vittorio De Sica

De Sica's career as an actor spans over 150 films from his appearance as a distinguished gentleman in the silent *The Clemenceau Affair* (1917) to his final role as the Greek god Zeus in *Ettore lo fusto/Hector the Mighty* (1975). De Sica's contributions as performer, composer, and director made him a foundational figure in Italian popular cinema from the 1930s until the 1970s. Despite his monumental contributions to world cinema with such masterpieces as *Ladri di biciclette/The Bicycle Thief* (1948) and *Umberto D.* (1952), De Sica's prestige as a director never fully recovered from the commentary of Italian critics such as Guido Aristarco who disdained De Sica's abandonment of the socially progressive themes of neorealism for the more commercial cinema of Sophia Loren vehicles in the 1950s and 1960s: *Ieri, oggi e domani/Yesterday, Today and Tomorrow* (1963).

Despite his abilities and popularity, De Sica struggled to find producers for his projects as he opted to participate in some unmemorable films in the 1960s and 1970s. De Sica once remarked that only the films he produced himself were worthy of his talents and, "Only my bad films made money. Money has been my ruin."[5] In this regard De Sica had a career similar to his American counterpart

Orson Welles, whose struggles with producers were legendary. Yet De Sica's later career included important literary adaptations such as the Alberto Moravia novel *Two Women* (1960), the Eduardo De Filippo play *Marriage, Italian Style* (1964), and the Giorgio Bassani story *Il giardino dei Finzi-Contini/The Garden of the Finzi Contini* (1970). De Sica also retained an eye for the pulse of his times with the popular films *Ieri oggi domani/Yesterday, Today and Tomorrow* (1963) and *I Girasoli/Sunflower* (1970), as well as attempts to understand the changing times of the 1960s with *Un mondo nuovo/A New World* (1965) or his quixotic comedy *Caccia alla volpe/After the Fox* (1966) starring Peter Sellers. This last film lovingly spoofs the fickle world of film coproductions and the pretensions of auteurism that had been treated in a more somber and pretentious manner by such directors as Jean Luc Godard in his Brigitte Bardot vehicle *Le Mépris/Contempt* (1963). At one point in *After the Fox* an aging Hollywood star played by Victor Mature asks, "What does 'neorealism' mean?" and De Sica answers "No money."[6]

Art Cinema Newcomers

The prestige afforded to Italian *cinema d'autore* directors, Fellini, Antonioni, Visconti, was adopted as a marketing strategy by producers to elevate a mass medium and attract an audience to art cinema houses around the world. The reputation of an *auteur* was dependent upon subtle interpretations and the critical reputation held by a director. Just as De Sica was somewhat held in suspicion by the critical tradition of *auteurism* developed in the New Wave period in France, other Italian showmen and actors who ventured behind he camera did not receive lasting critical acclaim as is the case with actor Nino Manfredi's undervalued auto-biographical film about Catholic education and flirtation with communism *Per grazia ricevuta/Between Miracles* (1971)or his last directorial effort *Nudo di donna/Portrait of a Nude Woman* (1981).

Yet other Italian directors were able to enter the ranks of the art director "club." The movement away from neorealism was a generational phenomenon and extended to a new generation of Italian filmmakers. Films including Marco Ferreri's *Dillinger è morto/Dillinger is Dead* (1969), *La grande abbuffata/The Grand Bouffe* (1973), *Non toccare la donna Bianca/Don't Touch the White Woman* (1974), or Bernardo Bertolucci's *Prima della rivoluzione/Before the Revolution* (1964), Marco Bellocchio's *La Cina è vicina/China Is Near* (1967) were heavily influenced by the theoretical and stylistic model of the French New Wave as well as the rebelliousness driven by the coming of age struggles of the youth of the 1960s. New Wave directors, Jean Luc Goddard or Francois Truffaut, had in turn been heavily influenced by Italian neorealism, especially Rossellini's *Paisan*, which New Wave critic/founding father saw as a primal example of effective filmmaking.[7] Truffaut's *The 400 Blows* (1959) arguably has elements that recall De Sica's *The Children and Watching Us*(1943).

In the cultural context of the late 1960s, films began not only to show a rebellious and iconoclastic attitude against society and standard narratives but also to challenge hygienic and sexual norms, for example, Liliana Cavani's *I cannibali/The*

Cannibals (1969), Pasolini's *Porcile/Pigpen* (1969), Ferreri's cannibalistic farce *La grande abbuffata* (1973), and Sergio Citti's *Il minestrone* (1981). Italian art cinema into the late 1960s even developed a current celebrating decandentism in the tradition of such turn-of-the-century figures as Gabriele D'Annunzio. Directors heavily influenced by Visconti even flirted with themes that recalled the writings of authors such as Nietzsche who championed an absolute reliance on instinct and an exaltation of the irrational to defeat bourgeois values. Themes of sexual rebellion or drug abuse brought a sense of apocalyptic pessimism expressed in aggressive language and shock values. Nietzchean themes appeared in *Al di la' del bene e del male/Beyond Good and Evil* (1977) by Liliana Cavani.

In hindsight, innovations in Italian filmmaking came not in the art cinema but also in popular genres such as the *commedia all'italiana*, the Italian horror film and the spaghetti western. This was recognized by Fellini who made his own versions of popular genres—the horror peplum mix of *Satirycon*, the satire of the Italian film industry's westerns in *Toby Damit*, and the sexy comedy in *Amarcord* (1974). Fellini's closeness to the style of the horror film in *Juliet of the Spirits* is particularly indicative of the genre's influence upon him. Like the peplum and the western, the Italian horror film appeared at a moment of retrenchment for the Hollywood film industry during the early 1960s. At times Italian horror films, like spaghetti westerns, could featured a multi-linguistic cast, which did not trouble Italian producers since most Italian productions were made with post-synchronous sound, a hold over from the neorealist days that continued to be a common practice. To cite one example, *Profondo rosso/Deep Red* (1975) is an Italian horror film by Dario Argento that became a stylistic harbinger of horror films both in Italy and abroad. Argento had first achieved success with *Il gatto a nove code/The Cat o' Nine Tails* (1971) and later with *Tenebre/Unsane* (1982). In *Deep Red*, Argento's camera work and sets recall the sterile cityscapes of famed Italian surrealist painter Giorgio De Chirico (1888–1978). The incessant and repetitive piano motifs in the film would become established as a signature of the horror genre including the later Hollywood *Halloween* (1978) series. Other directors enjoying success in the Italian horror genre include Mario Bava, Riccardo Freda, and Lucio Fulci.

A film indicative of the technical reach and unpredictability of the Italian film industry by the late 1960s was Mario Bava's adaptation of the Giussanis' long-running comic book series *Diabolik/Danger Diabolik* (1968) featuring a ruthless and invincible masked criminal/terrorist and his blond bombshell girlfriend (figure 7.1). The film was produced by Dino De Laurentiis, who like a number of Italian producers, Carlo Ponti, Angelo Rizzoli, or Goffredo Lombardo, was able to command a staff of Italian technicians. The set design was by Carlo Rimbaldi, probably best known for his work on Stephen Spielberg's *E.T. the Extra Terrestrial* (1982). The sound track by Ennio Morricone features the guitar work of Alessandro Alessandroni. Director Mario Bava brought his abilities as a cameraman to the production with technical trick photography with painted glass photomats giving the illusion of extensive and elaborate studio sets in scenes creating a sense of 1960s fashion and drug culture. In an ironic sense, the economic tradition of frugality and inventiveness from neorealism was repeated in camp productions such as

Figure 7.1   John Philip Law (Diabolik) and Marisa Mell (Eva Kant) in still from *Danger Diabolik!* (1968).

Danger Diabolik. The film was dismissed by critics due to its contrived plot, which has a thematic precedent in the French *Fantomas* silent series, also remade in the 1960s. But the frequent recursion to extreme violence and disdain by the main character, Diabolik, for anything beyond his immediate self-gratification or the whims of his stunning girlfriend is indicative of an anarchist current in Italian culture and politics, which would surface with virulence in the 1970s during the explosion of terrorism in Italy. In *Danger Diabolik*, the protagonist destroys the country's monetary system and blows up the entire government complex to the point that the minister of finance played by veteran English actor Terry Thomas makes a meek appeal to the public to pay their taxes according to the honor system since all their records have been destroyed. The anarchist/terrorist undercurrent and the technical ability of Bava and his collaborators give the film an importance particularly in light of the later development of Hollywood adaptations of comic book characters to cinema.

   Part of the appeal of art cinema directors was their willingness to experiment, to break narrative commonplaces, and to challenge censorship codes. However this iconoclastic urgency also propelled producers to cash in on the lower end of the market and attract spectators with a promise of taboo-breaking titillation not available on television. For every high brow film, such as the hugely successful *The Damned* by Visconti, the *Decameron* by Pasolini, or *Ultimo tango a Parigi/ Last Tango in Paris* by Bernardo Bertolucci, there were numerous films such as *Decamerotica* or the current of Nazi sadomasochistic movies inspired by the box office success of Liliana Cavani's sadomasochistic Nazi recollection film *Il portiere di notte/The Night Porter* (1974) or Pasolini's *Salò or the 120 Days of Sodom* (1975), which combined a Visconti like interest in decandentist historical settings with the shock effect of pornography and the horror film. Ultimately the inheritors of the art and auteurist film tradition in Italy, at least in terms of film distribution and marketing, have been such directors as Tinto Brass, who moved from making westerns to soft porn films.

Pier Paolo Pasolini

An important new voice in Italian art cinema was Pier Paolo Pasolini (1922–75), who began as a poet in the regional dialect of his mother's home in the Friuli region and then became a novelist before moving to the cinema with *Accattone!* (1961), a film about the brief career of a Roman thief. Pasolini also contributed to Fellini's *La dolce vita* (1960) and Bolognini's *La notte brava/Bad Girls Don't Cry* (1959), always taking inspiration from Pasolini's novels about the underbelly of Roman society, *Ragazzi di vita* (1955) and *Una vita violenta* (1959).[8] In *Accattone!* Pasolini mixes the sacred with the profane in a tale of a beggar/thief whose demise is accompanied by the high cultural signature of Bach's *St. Mathew's Passion* and framed by quotations from Dante's *Divine Comedy*. Pasolini was attracted by the cultural authenticity of poverty, whether in Italy or the Third World. Pasolini's nostalgia for archaic, pre-Enlightenment culture seems to recall French philosopher Jean Jacque Rousseau's (1712–78) idealization of the Natural Man or Noble Savage, themes he would develop in adaptations of sacred and classical texts such as *Il vangelo secondo Matteo/The Gospel According to St. Mathew* (1964), *Edipo re/Oedipus Rex* (1967), *Il decamerone/The Decameron* (1971), *I racconti di Canterbury/The Canterbury Tales* (1972), *Il fiore delle mille e una notte/A Thousand and One Nights* (1974), and a time travel film starring Totò, *Uccellacci e uccellini/Hawks and Sparrows* (1966).

Pasolini was also sort of a gadfly of Italian society at the time, a voice pointing out uncomfortable contradictions in contemporary culture. Yet he appealed to Italy's major political and cultural forces. He had claimed political alignment with the PCI, although he was eventually dismissed from the Party for his homosexuality. He also appealed to Catholic forces with his film version of *The Gospel According to St.Mathew* (1964), a spare and unadorned adaptation that remains on the Vatican's list of approved films, and publically announcing his opposition to abortion. In comments that echo the work of such media theorists as Marshall McLuhan, Pasolini pointed out the decline of regional dialects and culture, which he saw as being increasingly dominated by the homogenizing power of television and the technocratic influences of the industrial triangle in the north between Milan, Genoa, and Turin. These themes had a resonance among the Italian public in films such as Germi's top grossing, *Serafino* (1968), starring pop singer Adriano Celentano as a sheep herder who rejects modern life, or Monicelli's *La ragazza con la pistola/Girl with a Gun* (1968) starring Monica Vitti as a Sicilian girl who brings her code of honor to the swinging 1960s of London. Pasolini voiced environmental concerns by decrying the effects of industrialization on Italy's natural environment in a famous article about the disappearance of fireflies from the Italian hinterland, an insect quite sensitive to air pollution.[9] Part of Pasolini's legend was his ability to cut through ideology in his social commentary. When students occupied the University of Rome in 1968, Pasolini expressed more solidarity for the policemen than the students. Pasolini noted that the policemen desperately trying to maintain order were mostly the sons of working-class families with little chance of attending college. The students on the other hand had for the most part been raised in privileged environments.[10] The potential conspiracy theories surrounding Pasolini's violent death allegedly at the hands of male prostitutes on a Roman beach in 1975 are treated in Marco Tullio Giordana's *Pasolini, un delitto italiano/Pasolini, an Italian Crime* (1995).

The *Ricotta/Cream Cheese* episode of the multi-directed *Ro.Go.Pag.* (1963) offers a synthesis of many of Pasolini's favorite themes, in particular the contrast between archaic Catholicism and post–economic boom Italy (figure 7.2). With *Ricotta/Cream Cheese*, Pasolini invents a film about a film production of Christ's Passion directed by Orson Welles, during a period in which Welles was having trouble finding producers for his films. In *Cream Cheese*, an extra playing one of the thieves to be crucified with Jesus on Mount Calvary actually dies on the cross on the set, apparently of a stroke provoked by the fact that he had not eaten lunch. With this character, as with the protagonists of *Accattone* and *Mamma Roma*

Figure 7.2   Still from Pier Paolo Pasolini's *La ricotta/Cream Cheese.*

(1962), a melodrama starring Anna Magnani as a prostitute who aspires to middle-class stability by seeking a raise in class status for her indolent son, Pasolini presents an ironic martyr for the cultural authenticity and primitiveness of the lower-class inhabitants of the Roman periphery. *Cream Cheese* lampoons the contradiction between the baroque imagery of stills for the Passion produced by the film crew and the Gospel's actual message of poverty and spirituality. In ideological terms, another instructive example of the infiltration of 1960s iconoclastic ideology in a Pasolini film is *Teorema* (1968), in which Terence Stamp plays a mysterious stranger who destroys the paternal order of a Milanese industrialist's household by seducing each member of the family.

Bernardo Bertolucci

Bernardo Bertolucci (1940–) started his film career with *La commare secca/The Grim Reaper* (1962) based on a story by Pasolini.[11] He also contributed to the screenplay of Leone's re-reading of the western *Once Upon a Time in the West* (1968). But Bertolucci's breakthrough film was a re-examination of Rossellini's or Antonioni's middle-class alienation tales though the eyes of a male baby boomer in *Prima della rivoluzione/Before the Revolution* (1964). The film echoed the stylistic and narrative style of such French New Wave directors as Jean Luc Godard and established the young Bertolucci as an art film director. In the film a bourgeois youth considers rebellion and piddles with incest but eventually seems resigned to his heritage and destiny, a storyline Bertolucci would repeat in later films.

Initially Bertolucci seemed unable to move beyond the influences he took from this style of filmmaking. His next film *Partner* (1968) is based on a Fyodor Dostoevsky story, and *Amore e rabbia/Love and Anger* (1969) is an episodic film with contributions by Pasolini and Goddard, which exemplify the revolutionary and iconoclastic period in which they were made. Bertolucci's later films opt for a more expressionistic cinematography. He moved beyond the themes of rebellion, incest, and acceptance of class to examine Italy's Fascist past with an adaptation of Alberto Moravia's novel *Il conformista/The Conformist* (1970), *Spider Stratagem* (1972), *La Luna* (1979), *Novecento/1900* (1976), and the Oscar winning biopic of the last Chinese emperor Pu Yi, *L'ultimo imperatore/The Last Emperor* (1987). Bertolucci wisely relied upon the brilliant cinematography of Vittorio Storaro whose formalism extends to the point of using color-tinted lenses, a technique used in such Hollywood musicals as Vincent Minelli's *An American in Paris* (1951) and Joshua Logan's *South Pacific* (1958) later used by Storaro as cinematographer on *Apocalypse Now* (1979), Francis Ford Coppola's Vietnam-era adaptation of Joseph Conrad's novel *Heart of Darkness*.

Bertolucci's most acclaimed and controversial film was *Last Tango in Paris* (1972). Bertolucci ably filled the film with numerous metacinematic references such as the casting of Massimo Girotti, a leading man from Italian film of the 1940s in such films as Visconti's *Obsession* (1943) and Germi's *In the Name of the Law* (1949), as an aging neighbor obsessed with physical fitness, a metacinematic citation of the decline of the star system of which Girotti had been a part.

Figure 7.3 Marlon Brando (Paul) and Maria Schneider (Jeanne) in Bernardo Bertolucci's *Last Tango in Paris*.

Bertolucci also features French director Francois Truffaut's alter-ego Jean Pierre Leaud, an actor who Tuffaut had followed from adolescence in *The 400 Blows* to adulthood in *Day for Night* as a cuckolded filmmaker. The film's river dock references recall Jean Vigo's houseboat in *L'Atlante* (1934), a film about a barge ship owner who is consumed with jealousy for his attractive newlywed bride. Finally Bertolucci cast Marlon Brando, an actor with a rich history in Hollywood cinema playing individuals suited to a life of action who are faced with a moral dilemma: *Along the Waterfront* (1954), *One Eyed Jacks* (1960), *Mutiny on the Bounty* (1962), and *The Ugly American* (1963). Brando was fresh from a series of box office disappointments including Gillo Pontecorvo's anticolonial parable *Burn/Queimada* (1969). In *Ultimo tango a Parigi/Last Tango in Paris* (1972), Brando's character mourns the suicide of his wife by entering into a relationship with a Parisian girl with whom he insists on sex without emotional depth, leading to further tragedy (figure 7.3). The film received zealous critical acclaim, including the hyperbolic enthusiasm of Pauline Kael who called it the greatest film of all time.[12] The legacy of the film is that it demonstrated the degree of change in sexual mores in a public increasingly open (or numb) to sexually explicit imagery. The film received an X rating in the United States and the negatives of the film were ordered destroyed by an Italian court in 1976. But by 1988 it was shown on Italian television with less than seven minutes of cuts and a mere warning against viewing by anyone under the age of fourteen.[13] The Italian public acceptance of the explicit sexual imagery in Bertolucci's film was a watershed in Italian cultural history. It would remain Italy's all time top grossing domestic film until it was displaced by Roberto Benigni's *La vita è bella/Life Is Beautiful* (1997).

8

The 1970s

In the 1970s and 1980s terrorist attacks included bombings of buildings and transportation targets such as the Bologna train station bombing. There were shootings and assassinations of mid-level functionaries, university professors, even periodic sackings of regional headquarters of religious organizations such as Don Giussani's *Comunione e liberazione*. Anything remotely connected with the status quo was fair game for terrorist violence, topics treated in the Italian cinema in Francesco Rosi's *Tre fratelli/Three Brothers*, Gianni Amelio's *Colpire al cuore/Blow to the Heart* (1982), Mimmo Calopresti's *La seconda volta/The Second Time* (1996), Cristina Comencini's *La fine è nota/The End Is Known* (1993). If considered in the wider scope of Italian history, the 1970s terrorism seems to belong to a deeper current in Italian politics running from the anarchist assassin who killed King Humbert I in 1900, to the nationalist hyperbole promoted by D'Annunzio and the violence from rival political factions from both Left and Right until Mussolini's black shirt gangs prevailed in the civil strife of the early 1920s paving the way for the 20-year (1922–43) Fascist dictatorship.

In the 1970s the climate of violence of the *anni di piombo* (years of lead) came to be understood as part of a "strategy of tension" by which neo-Fascist groups or para-governmental entities were also responsible for terrorist acts attributed to anarchists as alluded to in Michele Placido's *Romanzo criminale/Crime Novel* (2005).[1]

The ultimate result of any terrorist act, whether originating from extreme left-wing groups like the Red Brigades or extreme right-wing neo-Fascist groups was the destabilization of republican institutions. Therefore any act of terrorism aided the extreme Left, which sought to impose a Communist totalitarian regime or the extreme Right nostalgic for Fascist totalitarianism. Both of the leading established political parties, the PCI and the DC, had an interest in maintaining the parliamentary republic, a fact parodied in Luciano Salce's *Il colpo di stato/Coup D'Etat* (1969). The country lived in a climate of apprehension not only due to the violence but also due to the rhetoric of such groups as the right-wing Black Order or the so-called "extraparlamentary left," an umbrella term to refer to left-wing, Communist groups including the Red Brigades. Radical leftist groups found common points of reference in the rhetoric of newspapers such as *Lotta Continua* (Continuing Struggle) and intellectual figures such as Toni Negri whose involvement with terrorist figures eventually led him to seek exile in France.

Later studies of communist terrorists such as the Red Brigades have offered the explanation that their members were often rebelling against strict Catholic upbringings or saw terrorist violence as a way to revive the Resistance factions active in WWII which had favored Communist revolution.[2] The *brigatisti* (Red Brigade members) were particularly perturbed by the "historic compromise" between the DC and the PCI, led respectively by Aldo Moro and Enrico Berlinguer (1922–84). Under Berlinguer, the PCI endorsed military cooperation with NATO and the European Common Market following Palmiro Togliatti's move toward an Italian PCI independent from the dictates of the Soviet Union.[3] The Italians joined the Spanish Communists in criticizing Soviet totalitarianism and asserting the viability of their "Euro-communist" model.

During the early 1970s, the PCI expanded its power base to include large sections of the middle class and Catholics. In the regions of Umbria, Tuscany, Piedmont, and Emilia-Romagna, the PCI had been in local government so long that they, not the DC, represented the status quo. In the 1976 parliamentary elections, the PCI polled just a few percentage points fewer than the DC, and by 1978 the Communists agreed to support some DC proposals in Parliament although without receiving commensurate ministerial appointments. As the PCI became more entrenched in the Italian political status quo, the extreme Left denounced what they considered the PCI's abandonment of revolutionary policy as the Party sought its ideological groundings in the years following the death of its postwar leader Palmiro Togliatti (1893–1964). Hard-line radicals saw much of their target constituency of factory workers controlled by powerful trade unions who negotiated deals with the government.

Tensions culminated in March 1978 when DC leader Aldo Moro was kidnapped by the Red Brigades. He was murdered 55 days later, his corpse left in the trunk of a car parked halfway between the party headquarters of the DC and the PCI in Rome, an act interpreted as symbolic of Moro's efforts to reach an accord between the two parties. After the Moro murder the Italian state redoubled its efforts to infiltrate and destroy terrorist groups like the Red Brigades through the creation of a unified command against terrorism under General Dalla Chiesa. By the time the Red Brigades kidnapped American army general Dozier in 1981, their organization had been infiltrated and compromised and much of their membership subsequently was imprisoned or fled to exile in France or South America. Red Brigade assassinations have continued sporadically past the turn of the millennium, often targeting government officials active in labor negotiations.

In the late 1960s and in the 1970s, political activism of feminist groups in Italy, as well as in other Western countries, stirred public opinion on the issue of women's rights. Traditional Italian society was based on Catholic and patriarchal values. In the 1970s, however, important laws were passed to improve the condition of women. A law passed permitted divorce after a waiting period for consenting parties. In 1975 the Christian Democrats challenged the law by a referendum, which upheld the law. In 1975 Parliament reformed laws regulating family rights (*riforma del diritto di famiglia*), which established the juridical equality of the couple. Parliament also passed an abortion law in 1978, upheld by referendum in 1981.

Polish cardinal Karol Wojtyla (1920–2005) was elected pope in 1978 as John Paul II after the shortlived 33-day papacy of John Paul I (1912–78). Wojtyla was the first non-Italian elected since Hadrian VI (1522–23).

Film and Television in the 1970s and 1980s

Since its inception in 1954, Italian state television and radio—RAI (*radioaudiovisioni italiane*) was aligned with the governing Christian Democrat Party. Changes in RAI programming came partly in response to the social changes that began in earnest in the late 1960s. In a 1976 decision, Italian courts opened the airwaves for private television stations, ending the state television monopoly. The Italian public gained increased access to films and serials broadcast from private television stations, including those owned by real estate developer and later Italian premier Silvio Berlusconi (1936–). In the Italian television industry, the period following the anti-monopoly court decision became known as *televisione selvaggia* (wild television).[4] As the term implies there were opportunities for experimentation and the breaking of social taboos and moral codes exemplified by Roberto Benigni's shortlived television show *Onda libera* (Free Wave). Benigni's break through program begins in the style of RAI state television with a close-up of a well-dressed female announcer, who in correct Italian invites the spectators to enjoy a light-hearted musical program ironically entitled *The Fabulous Years of the Pre-Boom*, which promises a nostalgic musical review of the years preceding the economic boom of 1957–62. A resonating, flatulent Bronx cheer interrupts this standard and predictable opening. Benigni, in his alter ego as Tuscan peasant Mario Cioni, appears in a barn filled with straw, cows, pigs, and chickens playing the guitar and shouting out a song called *La marcia degli incazzati/The March of the Pissed Off* in his heavy Tuscan accent.[5]

With the end of the RAI television monopoly, the politics of *lottizzazione*, an Italian version of the spoils system by which parties divide up political appointments, were applied to Italian state television. RAI 1 remained the network of the Christian Democrat Party and presented an evening news broadcast. RAI 2 became the domain of the Socialist Party, which entered into ruling coalitions in the 1980s under leader Bettino Craxi. RAI 3 came under the control of the Italian Communist Party. The system of political patronage and identification with Italian television networks remained in place until the early 1990s. The 1989 fall of the Berlin Wall, symbolically marking the end of the Cold War, would also change the Italian political landscape.

In 1971 the Italian film industry attained a historic market share of 65 percent compared to 27 percent for American films. Afterward the Italian cinema suffered a continued decline in spectatorship with attendance falling to around half a million cinema goers in 1975, then to 83,000 thousand by 1992 and rebounding to the low hundreds of thousands thereafter.[6] The Italian film industry, so vital in the early 1960s, finally felt the crisis that had hit Hollywood in the late 1950s. In the 1970s enough Italian households throughout the peninsula owned a television set for the new medium to offer a viable alternative to a trip to the neighborhood movie theater. The number of theaters have continued to decline in the new millennium. Italians preferred to stay at home and watch jazzman Renzo Arbore's television remake of the Italian vaudeville tradition with *L'altra domenica/The Other Sunday* or *Quelli della notte/The Night Guys* than an evening at the cinema. Italian cultural consensus began to be increasingly formed by such television personalities as Maurizio Costanzo, Mike Buongiorno, Gianni Minoli, Pippo Baudo, and by journalists Indro Montanelli, Enzo Biagi, Giorgio Bocca, and Oriana Fallaci. Even Umberto Eco, a noted intellectual figure, got a start as a national figure on television before becoming a bestselling author with *The Name of the Rose*, adapted to film in 1986 by Jean-Jacques Annaud starring Sean Connery.

Taking their cue from the success of Bertolucci's *Ultimo tango a Parigi/Last Tango in Paris* (1972), theater owners reacted to the decline in spectators by offering the only sort of product not available on television because of censorship codes. Italian theaters began to screen soft pornography films or sexy comedies. Actresses like Edwige Fenech, Barbara Bouchet, and Laura Antonelli who had begun their careers in the *commedia all'italiana*, 1960s slasher films, spy films, episodic films continued their careers in the sexy comedy genre in such movies as Salvatore Samperi's box office hit *Malizia/Malicious* (1973) or Dino Risi's *Sessomatto/How Funny Can Sex Be?* (1973). These films may seem tame by later standards but at the time the Italian public found them to be titillating. The actresses of the sexy comedy genre were the heirs of the *maggiorata fisica* (buxom actress) generation of the early postwar period. Major directors also made forays into the genre. Fellini's *Amarcord* (1974) may be about the director's memories of growing up in Rimini during Fascism, but the bodily humor and physical displays in the film also have much in common with the sexy comedy of the 1970s featuring a supporting role for actor Alvaro Vitali, who would also star in the *Pierino* naughty school boy series.

A successful director in this sexy film genre was Tinto Brass, who started his career as an assistant to Rossellini on *General della Rovere* (1959). Brass was heavily influenced by the exploration of sexuality in French New Wave films, for example, Godard's film about a callow prostitute, *Vivre sa vie/My Life to Live* (1962). In Italy he contributed to the sexy soft porn film with *Salon Kitty* (1976) and the later box office hit *La chiave/The Key* (1983), which featured a nude Stefania Sandrelli. These films made a requisite attempt to refer to the art cinema style of films like Visconti's *The Damned* (1969) or Bertolucci's *Last Tango in Paris* (1972), as well as appealing to the voyeuristic instincts of spectators.

Due to the decline in spectatorship, many Italian movie houses closed but not before some became outlets for *luci rosse* (red lights) pornography films when laws permitted in 1977. The arrival of hard core pornography in centrally situated cinemas in large Italian cities eventually led to the diffusion of the genre as videocassettes of hard core pornography became available at any neighborhood Italian newsstand. Porn actresses—Moana Pozzi (1961–94) and Cicciolina (Ilona Staller) (1951–)—became national figures with Shahler even occupying a parliamentary seat.

Comedies and Popular Cinema in the 1970s

The 1970s has a reputation for marking the beginning of a decline of Italian cinema. Yet the prevalence of serials and the consistent production of low-brow comedy points to resilience in the Italian cinema not often noted by critics more attuned to trends in art cinema, but of vitality nonetheless. In fact, 37 of the top 100 grossing films between 1945 and 1999 were produced in the 1970s. The Italian film industry of the 1970s, as in the 1920s, relied on serials in a time of retrenchment. There were the slapstick adventures of the comedy team Ciccio Ingrassia and Franco Franchi; also, sexy school comedies and military farces with Lino Banfi, police man comedies directed by E.B. Clucher (Enzo Barboni) starring Terrence Hill and Bud Spencer: *E poi... (il magnifico)/A Man from the East* (1972), *Anche gli angeli mangiano/Even Angels Eat Beans* (1973), *I due superpiedi quasi piatti/Crime Busters*. Comedy director Stefano Vanzina produced six high grossing comedies in the series between 1973 and 1991. Pop star and Elvis impersonator Adriano Celentano took his laidback persona to the screen in a number of comedies including Pietro Germi's box office hit *Serafino* (1968), *Il bestione/The Beast* (1974) by Sergio Corbucci, *Di che segno sei?/What's Your Sign* (1975), *Bluff storia di truffe e... /The Con Artists* (1976), *Er Più Storia d'amore...* (1971), *Ecco noi per esempio...* (1977). Comedies continued to offer examinations of Italian mores—*Venga a prendere il caffè/Come for Coffee* (1970) by Alberto Lattuada, or Valerio Zurlini's coming of age story in Rimini recalling Fellini's *Vitelloni/The Young and the Passioante* (1953), *La prima notte di quiete/The Professor* (1972), or Marco Vicario's coming of age story based on the Brancati novel *Paolo il caldo/The Sensual Man* (1973).

Old hands at *commedia all'italiana* such as Dino Risi made films that increasingly bordered on soft porn—*Straziami, ma di baci saziami/Kill Me with Kisses* (1968) and *Vedo nudo* (1969). The changes in Italian culture and the exposés on traditional Catholicism brought two films about married priests into the domestic top 10 of 1970—*Il prete sposato/The Married Priest* (1970) by Marco Vicario and *La moglie del prete/The Priest's Wife* (1970) starring Marcello Mastroianni and Sophia Loren. Swan songs of the *commedia all'italiana* genre were offered by

Mario Monicelli with *Romanzo popolare/Come Home and Meet My Wife* (1974) starring Ugo Tognazzi and Ornella Muti and the *Amici miei/My Friends* (1975, 1982, 1985) series, a Boccaccian farce about a group of middle aged men trying to exorcise fears of death.

In the mid-1970s, Italian filmmakers outside the circle of the recognized directors began to make important films. Giuseppe Bertolucci's undervalued *Berlinguer ti voglio bene/Berlinguer I Love You* (1977) was also Roberto Benigni's first film as actor and scriptwriter. The film is a study of the malaise of rural Italian youth of the 1970s in which Benigni adapted his appearances in the Roman avant garde theater from his monologue *Cioni Mario di Gaspare fu Giulia/Mario Cioni Son of Gaspare and the late Giulia* (1975) to feature film. In the film version, Benigni's Mario Cioni alter ego expresses the alienation of a generation that reached physical maturity estranged from the centuries old peasant economy of subsistence farming.[7] Like the Taviani brothers' *Padre padrone/Father and Master* (1977), *Berlinguer ti voglio bene* displays the tensions between preliterate society and postindustrial society. The theme of alienation from *Berlinguer ti voglio bene* is shared by another film now cited as a watershed in Italian cinema, Nanni Moretti's *Ecce Bombo* (1978), a study of the problems and attitudes of urban youth in the 1970s. The film portrays the alienation of the urban, middle-class youth who try to create a vital cultural life in their urban existence. However, in the final sequence of the film when the protagonist Michele, played by Nanni Moretti, and friends plan to greet the sunrise they face the wrong direction because they are so unacquainted with natural world of their ancestors.

Political Film/Instant Movie

In the 1960s and 1970s some directors tried to continue a commitment to social criticism and political expose in the tradition of neorealism. However, they injected increased complexity in the psychological make-up of the characters, which reflected the heritage of art cinema of the late 1950s. The Italian political films of the 1960s and 1970s were a forum for political expression often in contrast to the Catholic ideological mindset that had dominated Italy since reconstruction, instead reflecting a more progressive, liberal worldview with particular attention to the often shady realities of Italian political life, which surfaced as scandals and disasters. In the same vein, the term *instant movie* refers to films produced soon after an important current event. The often murky backdrops of events in Italian history provided a forum for conspiracy theories from the underbelly of public and intellectual dissatisfaction about Italian politics.[8]

Key figures in this Italian political film include the Taviani brothers—Vittorio (1929–) and Paolo (1931–)—with their *Uomo da bruciare/A Man Is Burning* (1962) about a man who returns to Sicily and attempts o organize peasants against the mafia. In *San Michele aveva un gallo/St. Michael Had a Rooster* (1971), Mastroianni plays an imprisoned rebel who realizes that he is out of touch with reality and commits suicide. Elio Petri's (1929–82) *Indagine su un cittadino al di sopra di ogni sospetto/Investigation of a Private Citizen* (1970) and *La classe operaiaia va in paradiso/The Working Class Goes to Heaven* (1971) featured such actors as Gian Maria Volontè and Flavio Bucci voicing political viewpoints of open distrust and suspicion of the status quo. Pasquale Squittieri (1938–) has shown a preference for stories connected with the south and its problems in *Camorra* (1972) and *Corleone/Father of the Godfathers* (1978) and thinly veiled dramatization of mafia intrigues from the 1970s and 1980s featuring figures involved in the *pentito* witness protection program, for example, Tommaso Buscetta and Michele Sindona in *Il Pentito/The Repenter* (1985). His other films, however, have concentrated on historical biographies—his dramatization of the experiences of Mussolini's antimafia minister Cesare Mori in *Prefetto di ferro/The Ironclad Prefect* (1977) or the biopic of Mussolini's mistress *Claretta/Claretta Petacci* (1984).

The tradition of the Italian political film continued in this period in the work of a number of directors—Giuseppe Ferrara (1932–) with his film about the strategy of tension *Faccia di spia/Spy Face* (1975) or the Moro assassination in *Il caso Moro/The Moro Case* (1986). In Marco Tullio Giordana's *Maledetti vi amerò/To Love the Damned* (1980) an ex-terrorist returns to Italy and experiences difficulty reintegrating into post-leaden years. Other directors not immediately identified with the political film genre also ventured into the field. Mario Monicelli made *I compagni/The Organizer* (1963) starring Marcello Mastroianni as an early union organizer. Ettore Scola made *Trevico Torino* (1973) about southern Italian emigration to Turin. Fellini continued to make films in diverse genres by offering a political film originally intended for television, *Prova d'orchestra/Orchestra Rehearsal* (1979), a political allegory of the terrorist years in Italy, in which an orchestra in rehearsal argues with its conductor mimicking the chaos of the 1970s. Fellini considered the film a response to the kidnapping and murder of Aldo Moro in 1978. Other directors active in the political film mode include Carlo Lizzani, Francesco Maselli, Giuliano Montaldo, Antonio Pietrangeli, and Florestano Vancini, whose films are a testament to the vitality of the Italian industry even into the 1970s.

Francesco Rosi

One of the main exponents of the Italian political film, Francesco Rosi (1922–), began as an assistant to Visconti on *The Earth Trembles, Bellissima* and *Senso/Livia.* Rosi's films include *Salvatore Giuliano* (1962), a film about the famous Sicilian bandit (1922–56) that probes the mysterious interrelation of crime, political interests, and mafia power. The film was important for bringing the "Southern question" to a widespread audience. Rosi approached the topic of organized crime in *Le mani sulla città/Hands on the City* (1963) and *Dimenticare Palermo/The Palermo Connection* (1991). Rosi's *Cadaveri eccellenti/Excellent Corpses* (1976) is based on the novel *Equal Danger/Il contesto* by Leonardo Sciascia with its sharp insights into Sicilian mentality in a story much in the vein of conspiracy films of the time like Alan J. Pakula's *The Paralax View* (1974), in which an omniscient state engineers the elimination of a political rival. In the case of Rosi's film *Excellent Cadavers*, the police commissioner investigating a series of murders of Sicilian judges is framed for the murder of the Italian Communist Party secretary. Rosi's *Todo modo* (1976), also based upon a Sciascia book, features Gian Maria Volontè as Christian Democrat Premier Aldo Moro during a secret conclave of DC leaders, in which the infighting leads to a series of murders and eventually the suicide by the Volonté character. In hindsight, some of these films have become somewhat dated. The criticism of Italian political filmmakers of the Italian Communist Party for not demanding a measure of power in accordance with its electoral performance could be reinterpreted in light of the eventual fall of the Soviet empire. Criticism of the Christian Democrat party elite in films like *Todo modo* lost quota in light of the subsequent kidnapping and murder of former DC premier Aldo Moro in 1978. The underlying theme of these movies is the idea of shadow forces controlling the destiny of Italian politics with the political film providing a forum for conspiracy theories in such films as Rosi's study of the career and mysterious death in an airplane crash of Italian energy minister Enrico Mattei with *Il caso Mattei/The Mattei Affair* (1972). Rosi's other examinations of historical themes have included an adaptation of Carlo Levi's *Christ Stopped at Eboli* (1972) and an adaptation of Primo Levi's post-Holocaust memoir *La tregua/The Truce* (1997).

Rosi made an important allegory of the terrorist years of the 1970s with *Three Brothers* (1981). The film is an adaptation of "The Third Son" by Andrei Platonov, a story set in the Soviet Union in the 1930s during a period when religious ceremonies were strictly forbidden by the Stalinist regime. In the Platonov story when the family decides to include a priest at their mother's funeral, the third son, an ideologically fanatical communist, remains silent throughout the entire affair and the threat of reprisal hangs heavily in the air upon his departure. Rosi's film takes the Platonov story as a starting point for a depiction of commonplaces about Italian culture, politics, and society of the 1970s during the terrorist attacks that destabilized the Italian Republic and continue sporadically to the present day. As in the Platonov story, the family patriarch calls his three sons to the family home for the wake and funeral of their mother. However, in contrast to the Platanov story, the point of contention between the brothers is not religious. Rosi makes each son a stereotype for the years when political violence dominated Italian political life. Each son is presented with a flashback or dream sequence, which is indicative of the different social realities facing 1970s Italy. Rocco is a teacher in a reform school for minors in Naples. His dream sequence indicated the incendiary idealism that inspired terrorists of the period. Nicola has emigrated north to work in the auto industry and periodically engages in labor disputes in Turin. The eldest son, Raffaele, is a judge in Rome who lives in constant fear of assassination. Despite this violent climate, Raffaele remains committed to the ideals of republican legalism and is determined not to surrender to intimidation. This determination mirrors the attitude of much of the Italian ruling elite in the 1970s on both the Right and Left in the face of terrorism. In fact, the 1970s was characterized by attempts by status quo from Left and Right to calm the political climate.

When Raffaele visits the town bar, locals recognize him from appearances on television, and the film reverts to a flashback in which his wife accuses him of finding a perverse thrill in a celebrity of danger. Raffaele meets a former schoolmate, now a teacher, who refers to the constancy of Italian political life: violence, blood, and upheavals. The teacher refers to the essence of *trasformismo* in a cynical vein and cites Alessandro Manzoni's nineteenth-century novel *The Betrothed* to prove his idea of the traditional strife and violence in Italian politics. The mother's death had temporarily reunited the three brothers but as the film ends there is a return to the familial separation that opened the film. Nothing is resolved and the pessimistic warning of Raffaele's school teacher friend that Italy is as it has always been "violent, bloody, corrupt" as in Manzoni's *The Betrothed* echoes as the only conclusion the filmmaker provides.

Gillo Pontecorvo

An Italian political filmmaker with wide international resonance is Gillo Pontecorvo (1919–2006). After wartime experience as a leader in the Resistance, Gillo Pontecorvo appeared in an autobiographical role as partisan fighter Pietro in Aldo Vergano's neorealist WWII drama *Il sole sorge ancora/Outcry* (1946). Like the French critics and directors of the New Wave, Pontecorvo was profoundly influenced by Rossellini's *Paisan* and decided to become a filmmaker after viewing the episode in Rossellini's film that depicted the struggle of American OSS (the forerunner of the CIA) commandos and Italian partisans in the Po river valley.

Pontecorvo's early documentaries were firmly in the neorealist documentary style of stark portrayals of common man stories as is his first contribution to a multi-director feature by Joris Ivens about women's rights, *Giovanna* (1956). Pontecorvo's first feature film *La grande strada azzurra/The Wide Blue Road* (1957) was a pink neorealist drama about a dynamite fisherman played by Yves Montand with a plot recalling Visconti's *La terra trema/The Earth Trembles* (1948). Pontecorvo's next film, the Oscar nominated *Kapò*, is a Holocaust drama with noted historical and plot inconsistencies such as the love story between the Russian prisoner and the deportee.

Pontecorvo's *La battaglia di Algeri/The Battle of Algiers* (1966), also nominated for an Oscar, is a film that Pontecorvo financed himself with the backing of an Algerian government that gained independence from France in 1962 (figure 8.1). The film depicts the Algerian resistance against French occupation in the late 1950s. The strength of *Battle of Algiers* is that Pontecorvo ably presents the rationale for all sides in the conflict in a manner that recalls Rossellini's *Open City*. In fact Pontecorvo's somewhat sympathetic portrayal of the military leader of the French colonialists did not please the film's Algerian coproducers. Nor did the film please the French, as it was banned in France until 1971. *The Battle of Algiers* harkens back to the finest moments of neorealism with a cast of nonprofessionals and a filmic artificial recreation of the neorealist documentary black and white style using the reexposure of film stock to create a dupe negative to give the film a documentary hue. The result of this artificial attempt to recreate the neorealist style was so effective that the film had to be advertised as not containing any documentary footage as Pontecorvo's recreation of events in the city and Casbah of Algiers were so riveting that audiences assumed it was a documentary.

Figure 8.1   Still from Gillo Pontecorvo's *The Battle of Algiers*.

Although *The Battle of Algiers* was made during the years of worldwide anticolonial struggles in the 1960s, it has gained a new relevance at the turn of the millenium with the rise of worldwide Islamic terrorism and has been used as a training film by both terrorist and anti-insurgent groups.[9] A possible explanation for the enduring popularity of *The Battle of Algiers* among both insurgent and anti-insurgent groups may be that the film actually has two endings. One ending highlights the success of the French paratroopers' campaign against the rebellion in the city of Algiers in the late 1950s. Pontecorvo also added a coda depicting a popular, spontaneous uprising in Algiers in the early 1960s, which led to the ultimate achievement of Algerian independence from France. With this coda Pontecorvo hoped to communicate how the attacks and general strikes organized by the Algerian independence movement of the Algerian National Liberation Front (FLN) successfully created a sense of national consciousness among the Algerian populace, a point in common with Pontecorvo's own experiences in the Italian Resistance during WWII. Particularly in consideration of the film's current popularity on both the political Left and Right, the two endings and matter-of-fact depiction of the use of violence as a political tool by French anti-insurgents and Algerian insurgents impart a more basic and troubling message—that violence is the key method by which political forces seek to establish and retain legitimacy.[10]

After *The Battle of Algiers*, Pontecorvo made *Queimada/Burn!* (1969), financed by United Artists, set in the mid-nineteenth-century starring Marlon Brando as a

British agent whose protégé is a rebel island leader, whom Brando's character eventually must hunt down and destroy. The film mixed influences from the nineteenth-century novels of Joseph Conrad and aspired to be a parable for the manner in which Third World resources and indigenous communities have been exploited first by colonial powers and later by multinational corporations. The film's depiction of a fictional Caribbean island nation provides a vision of the transition from slave-based colonialism to corporate-based postcolonialism. *Burn!* has a vast resonance not only for the experiences of former colonies in Africa and South America, but for any country burdened with legacies of human slavery and racism.[11]

The planned release of Pontecorvo's last feature film, *Ogro/Operation Ogre* (1979), about a Basque terrorist assassination of a Spanish general, coincided with the kidnapping/murder of former Italian premier Aldo Moro by Red Brigade Communist terrorists. By the time of the release of the film the idea of ideologically driven violent struggle simply lost currency in an Italy reeling from the backlash of the Moro murder. Pontecorvo rewrote the ending of *Ogro* to condemn acts of terrorism in the context of representative institutions, as would be the case in post-Franco Spain. The film ends with a flash forward to the hospital deathbed of one of the Basque terrorists, who asks his comrades to confirm the idea that terrorism is a just form of political struggle, but they refuse. *Ogro* would prove to be Pontecorvo's last feature film. The projects that Pontecorvo completed after 1979—the documentary *Ritorno in Algeri/Return to Algiers* (1992) or the short *Danza della fata confetto Nostalgia di protezione/Protection Nostalgia Dance of the Sugar Plum Fairy* (1997)—confirm the uncertainty that Pontecorvo felt about the use of violence expressed in *Ogro*.

The *Poliziesco* Crime Genre

Like the spaghetti western, the sexy comedy and the Italian horror film, the Italian film industry also developed a strain of crime thrillers known as the *poliziesco*.[12] Early examples of the genre appear in the *neorealismo nero* tone: De Santis's *Bitter Rice* and Luigi Zampa's *Il bandito/The Bandit*. More traditional detective stories include Pietro Germi's *Un maledetto imbroglio/The Facts of the Murder* (1959) or films referring to the historical plague of mafia, such as *Il brigante Mussolino/Outlaw Girl* (1950), *La banda Casaroli/The Casaroli Gang* (1962) by Florestano Vancini, *Banditi a Milano/Bandits in Milan* (1968) by Lizzani, Germi's *In the Name of the Law*, Rosi's *Salvatore Giuliano*, Elio Petri's *Indagine su un cittadino al di sopra di ogni sospetto/Investigation of a Private Citizen* (1970), and Ettore Scola's *Il commisario Pepe/Police Chief Pepe* (1969). By the 1970s the *poliziesco* genre developed with urban settings and featuring a level of violence familiar from the Italian western with world weary police officers played by actors such as Tomas Milian, Ray Lovelock, Maurizio Merli, and Mario Adorf in films by directors including Riccardo Freda, Emilio Miraglia, and Fernando Di Leo (1932–2003), whose films include *I ragazzi del massacro/Naked Violence* (1969), *Roma a mano armata/Brutal Justice* (1976), *La mala ordine/Hit Men* (1972),

Milano calibro 9/Caliber 9 (1972) an adaptation of a Scerbanenco novel, and *Il boss/Wipeout!* (1973).

Revisiting Fascism

In the early 1960s, a number of films reexamined Italy's Fascist past. Films such as Lizzani's *Cronache di poveri amanti/Chronicle of Poor Lovers* (1954), *L'oro di Roma/The Gold of Rome* (1961), Nanni Loy's *Le quattro giornate di Napoli/The Four Days of Naples* (1962), Luigi Comencini's *La ragazza di Bube/Bebo's Girl* (1963) reemphasized the values of collectivism and political cooperation against Nazi–Fascism.[13] These films came after the neorealist period, but still had a sense of the idealism of neorealism in their presentation. By the mid-1970s, films about the same period tended to be less heroic with microcosmic examinations of how Fascist culture and mentality turned characters into servile hypocrites. Examples include Bertolucci's adaptation of a Moravia novel *Il conformista/The Conformist* (1970) in which a man is sent to visit his former anti-Fascist professor in Paris as a cover for his assassination. In Bertolucci's *Strategia del ragno/Spider Stratagem* (1972), the heritage of the Resistance is challenged when a young man discovers unexpected truths behind the death of his father, an anti-Fascist martyr. Bertolucci scored a box office hit with *Novecento/1900* (1976), a film that covers the entire spectrum of Italian history from the death of composer Giuseppe Verdi at the turn of the century through both world wars in a highly politicized vision of revolutionary triumph over Fascism with an international cast including Robert De Niro and Gerard Depardieu.

An important film revisiting the Fascist era was Fellini's *Amarcord* (dialect for "I remember," 1974). The film is a nod to the sexy comedies that were prevalent as the Italian film industry attempted to compete with more openly *luci rosse* pornographic films. In *Amarcord*, Fellini recreated the climate of his youth in the provincial town of Rimini where any representation of the outside world was awe-inspiring and legendary. In *Amarcord*, magic passageways outside Rimini include: the resort hotel with its wealthy exotic guests including a parody of Crown Prince Humbert; the ocean liner Rex or the *mille miglia* car rally recalling the machine myths of the Futurists; sexual fantasies about prostitutes or a Sultan's harem; the comic arrogance of Fascist officials from Rome; the attempts by Rimini locals to act and dress like Hollywood movie stars like Ronald Coleman or Greta Garbo.

Fellini also ably lampoons the Fascist educational system.[14] During the city's celebration of the anniversary of the founding of Rome and the corresponding visit of the Fascist prefect, the town's teachers are among the most visible of the regime's supporters. Inside *Amarcord's* school, Fellini's camera pans over the three portraits of the powers that presided over the sort of education he received: King, Duce, and Pope. But the regime's official education is always countered by the sophomoric or Rabelaisian impulses of the students. They react to a lesson about Galileo's pendulum experiment by joking about an elephant's balls. A lesson about the medieval painter Giotto's invention of perspective elicits a similar lower-body response. When the principal teaches a lesson on history and the peace treaty signed by Lombard King Alboin, he is interrupted by animal sounds. The Greek teacher's attempt to impart a lesson on pronunciation is an opportunity for a joke about flatulence. When the math teacher upbraids a faltering student, his classmates lead her to believe this student has urinated on the floor. In Fellini's school, the sciences, history, and languages are all given common lower-body denominators: flatulence, urine, or barnyard choruses in a strong carnevalesque parody of Fascist-era education.[15]

The Heirs to Italian Art Cinema

With the aging of directors Rossellini and De Sica, some Italian directors—Bertolucci and Pasolini—were promoted as heirs to the Italian art cinema *cinema d'autore* tradition. Among these directors, Ettore Scola began his career with contributions to Italian episodic films in the tradition of the *commedia all'italiana*. His film *C'eravamo tanto amati/We All Loved Each Other so Much* (1974) connects the protagonists' lives to Italian film and television history through the rise and fall of neorealism, the television quiz show phenomenon of the 1950s, the filming of Fellini's Trevi fountain scene in *La dolce vita*, and art cinema against the backdrop of the social and political changes in Rome and Italy from the partisan resistance to the building boom in postwar Rome. The film is a brilliant mixture of the political film and the *commedia all'italiana* genres starring Stefania Sandrelli, Vittorio Gassman, and Nino Manfredi, which not only expresses the cultural changes from the Resistance period to the mid-1970s, but its inherent fatalism and narrative circularity is part of a cultural imprint of the Italian cinema. Scola's later adaptation of the Carlo Castellaneta story *Passion/Passione d'amore* (1981) is an unlikely love story staged just after the unification that evokes the irreverent themes of the *scapigliatura* movement of the late nineteenth-century. The film chronicles the unlikely relationship between a sickly woman and a dashing army officer. Many of Scola's films seem to concentrate on a specific space, usually an interior, and inquire into the connections between that space and the individuals. The story of *La famiglia/The Family* (1987) takes place in the apartment where a family has been living from the beginning of the century to the present. Scola's *Una giornata particolare/A Special Day* (1977) features Marcello Mastroanni and Sophia Loren as a homosexual and a bored Roman housewife who find themselves together on the day of Hitler's visit to Rome. The film visits themes of the personal microcosms suffocated by the regime and features Alessandra Mussolini, the real life granddaughter of the deposed *Duce*, and later right-wing parliamentarian, as Loren's daughter.

Lina Wertmüller (1928–) began her career as an assistant to Federico Fellini where she developed an interest in grotesque political comedy in such films as *The Seduction of Mimi* (1971) and particularly the Academy Award nominated Holocaust tragicomedy *Pasqualino settebellezze/7 Beauties* (1976). Like Benigni's later *La vita è bella* (1997), *7 Beauties* was criticized for profaning the Holocaust in the scenes in which an Italian deportee played by Giancarlo Giannini performs a grotesque copulation with the camp commandant and upon his return to Naples champions procreation as the only means to ensure survival in the face of the inevitable horrors of the world. Wertmüller would continue examinations of the Fascist period in *Film d'amore e anarchia/Love and Anarchy* (1973) about an aborted assassination attempt on Mussolini by a naïve country lad again played by Giannini and a prostitute played by Mariangela Melato. Wertmüller, applied her eye for grotesque comedy, very much in the tradition of the *commedia all'italiana*, to Italy's north–south cultural divide in films featuring Melato and Giannini: *Fatto di sangue . . . /The Blood Feud* (1978) and *Travolti da un insolito destino nell'az-zurro mare d'agosto/Swept Away* (1974). *Swept Away*, the story of an upper-class northern lady and a southern sailor marooned on a Mediterranean island. The film has echoes of the examination of class tensions and social satire from the days of the *telefono bianco* period with subject matter expected of an adult comedy in the 1970s.

The Taviani brothers began directing political films like the mafia drama *Un uomo da bruciare* (1962) but by the 1980s they gained international acclaim with *La notte di San Lorenzo/Night of the Shooting Stars* (1982), a film that relates how the Resistance and the *de facto* civil war in WWII temporarily broke class bound-aries. Later films include *Kaos* (1986), a cinematic adaptation of some short stories of Luigi Pirandello and *Il sole anche la notte/The Sun Shines also at Night* (1990), which is based on a story by Tolstoy. *Good Morning, Babylon!* (1987) tells the story of two Italian artisan brothers who built the sets for the Babylonian episode of D.W. Griffith's silent film *Intolerance* (1916).

A director from Bergamo, Ermanno Olmi (1931–) gained international acclaim for his realistic portrayal of the lives of the Lombard peasantry with *L'albero degli zoccoli/The Tree of the Wooden Clogs* (1978). Olmi has also tried his hand at religious allegory in *Cammina, cammina/Walking on* (1983). In the 1980s he made *Lunga vita alla signora/Long Live the Lady* (1987) and *La leggenda del santo bevitore/The Legend of the Holy Drinker* (1988).

9

The 1980s and 1990s: A Changing Society

1985–92	Public debt increases to record levels
1987	Lombard League separatist party first appears in elections, Large scale trials against Sicilian Mafia
1989	Fall of the Berlin Wall, beginning of dissolution of Soviet communist empire with reprocussions for post war Italian political party system
1990	Operation Gladio: anti-Communist organization formed by NATO in the 1950s exposed
	PCI changes name to PDS (Democratic Party of the Left) *Rifondazione comunista* neo-Communist party formed
	Tangentopoli political scandal involving postwar political parties and *Mani pulite* (clean hands) investigation
1991	Italy sends forces to aid the United Nations liberation of Kuwait Intensification of mafia violence
1992	Treaty of Maastrict established European Community as an economic and political entity with abolition of intra-European border controls and a timetable for monetary union under a single currency—the Euro
1993	Terrorist bombings in in Milan, Rome and Florence
	Lombard league electoral gains
	Neo-Fascist party MSI becomes *Alleanza Nazionale* (National Alliance) Premier Bettino Craxi resigns as leader of Socialist Party and flees Italy to avoid corruption charges
1994	Italian birth rate ranked among the lowest in the world
	Media tycoon Silvio Berlusconi founds and leads Forza Italia and Liberty Pole Coalition to victory with Northern League and National Alliance
1996	Olive Tree alliance wins election with Romano Prodi as premier with PDS and Rifondazione Communista parites

In the1980s, cabinets were formed with a non-Christian Democrat presidency for the first time since the advent of the postwar Republic. After the republican Giovanni Spadolini's government in 1981–82, the Socialist Bettino Craxi held the position of premier intermittently in the late 1980s. There was a rise of new political forces such as the environmentalist Green Party and the separatist Northern League, led by Umberto Bossi, which proposed a secessionist program for northern Italy taking advantage of anti-immigrant and anti-taxation sentiment.

After WWII Italian politics had been dominated by the competition between the pro-Western Christian Democrat party and the historically pro-Soviet Italian Communist Party. After the fall of the Berlin Wall in 1989 and the implosion of the Soviet empire that followed, Italy's postwar political parties became embroiled in a political corruption scandal known as *tangentopoli* (city of kick-backs). These bribery scandals targeted the leaders of the last coalition governments led by the Socialist Party and Bettino Craxi in particular, who fled prosecution and died in exile in Tunisia in 2000. The end of the Cold War bipolarity that had divided Italian politics between the pro-Soviet communist party and the pro-Western Christian Democrats resulted in what some commentators have referred to as the end of the first postwar Italian Republic. The Italian Communist Party changed its name to the PDS (*Partitio Democratico della Sinistra*—Democratic Party of the Left), causing a split with its most fervent members who formed the *Rifondazione comunista* (communist refoundation) party. The Christian Democrats also split into rival factions—the Left-leaning UDC, United Christian Democrats and the conservative CCD, Democratic Christian Center Party.

The conservative forces of parties like the CCD were eventually marshaled not by Catholic parties but by media magnate Silvio Berlusconi whose party *Forza Italia* (Go Italy) took its color (blue) and name from the slogan that reminded voters of the Italian national soccer team that won the 1982 World Cup. Berlusconi's center–right coalition, the *Polo delle Libertà* (Liberty Pole later the *Casa delle Libertà*—Freedom house), became one branch of a new bipolarism in Italian politics with the opposing Center-Left Olive Tree Coalition led by the post-Communist PDS leader, university professor, and government functionary Romano Prodi. The first *Forza Italia*–led government fell in 1994 due to a falling out with the North League members of its coalition. In 1996, a PDS-led government fell due to the withdrawal of support from *Rifondazione Comunista* delegates.

Berlusconi's entrance into the Italian media market had come after Italian courts ended the state monopoly on television broadcasts. Berlusconi's Finninvest media corporation founded several private Italian television stations: *Canale 5* in 1980, *Italia Uno* in 1982, *Rete Quattro* in 1984. In 1991, Berlusconi also acquired the Mondadori publishing network, which includes book, magazine, and newspaper interests. The combination of these printing and television holdings would give Berlusconi an unprecedented stake in the Italian media, particularly when combined with the political influence he could exert over RAI state television as premier through appointments in the state agency. The duality between RAI state television and Berlusconi's private television networks was put into law by the Mammì statute (1990). The concentration of media control under Berlusconi caused concern among opposition politicians who lobbied unsuccessfully for a law to establish conflict of interest laws to limit the ability of a single source to control both private and public television.

Organized crime, and more specifically the *Mafia* in Sicily, the *Camorra* in Naples and Campania, and the *'ndrangheta* in Calabria, continued to be serious problems facing the government as depicted in Pasquale Squittieri's films such in *Camorra* (1972), Rosi's *Le mani sulla città/Hands on the City* (1963), *Dimenticare Palermo/The Palermo Connection* (1991), or Alessandro Di Robilant's *Il giudice ragazzino* (1994). The depth of mafia power became evident with the 1982 assassination of General Dalla Chiesa (1920–82), an event dramatized in Giuseppe Ferrara's *Cento Giorni a Palermo/One Hundred Days in Palermo* (1984). Dalla Chiesa, who was credited with infiltrating and breaking up the Red Brigade terrorists, was murdered in Palermo where he had been directing anti-mafia operations. In 1980, the *legge sui pentiti* (penitent law) had offered reductions in sentencing in exchange for information on terrorist or mafia activities. In the early 1990s some terrorists and mafia bosses including Totò Riina were arrested and brought to trial in high-security courtrooms, and several actually received life sentences. Terrorist activities still continued sporadically in the 1980s, often aimed at labor dispute negotiators. In 1992, organized crime forces murdered Giovanni Falcone and Paolo Borsellino, two magistrates in charge of anti-mafia operations in Sicily and Rome—events depicted in Giuseppe Ferrara's *Giovanni Falcone* (1993) or Michele Placido's *Un eroe borghese/Ordinary Hero* (1995). The murder of these two high-profile anti-mafia state prosecutors was an act of defiance and provocation by the mafia against the Italian state. In this climate there was a spate of deadly terrorist attacks in 1993 in Milan, Rome and in Florence attributed to the mafia. By the turn of the millennium, some of the criminal activity that had traditionally been the turf of indigenous clans was increasingly taken over by immigrant groups who would appear in the Italian cinema as new antagonists in films.[1]

Another prominent scandal was the *gladio* affair (from the Latin for sword—*gladius*), which broke in the 1980s and centered on the establishment of stay behind military organizations and potential shadow governmental agencies established by American and Italian secret services in the mid-1950s in anticipation of a Soviet invasion. There were also revelations about the Masonic Lodge (P2), which involved leaders of the political, economic, and social establishment events evoked in Giuseppe Ferrara's film starring Massimo Ghini, *Segreto di stato/Sate Secret* (1995).

The "New Italian Cinema"

Ever since the decline of neorealism in the 1950s, critics have periodically attempted to identify a revival in the Italian cinema—a *nuovo cinema italiano* (new Italian cinema). But by the 1980s and 1990s the hopes for a revival dimmed because of the continuing decline of the Italian theater system. After the late 1970s, many young directors did not have the same opportunities for the domestic distribution of their films as previous generations.

Despite difficulties, some directors were able to gain public and critical attention, aided by laws that subsidized films by Italian directors. Francesca Archibugi has been recognized as one of the most original voices of the "new cinema". Her first film, *Mignon è partita/Mignon Has Left* (1988), is a delicately handled story of love among young people and adults, with the backdrop of busy family life. Archibugi's second film *Verso sera/In the Evening* (1990) tells the story of a young widow and her father-in-law who belong to two different generations, and classes, but eventually find a way to communicate and interact. *Il grande cocomero/The Great Pumpkin* (1993) focuses again on family life with the illness and solitude of an adolescent girl.

Pupi Avati came to cinema with a biopic of the 1920s jazz musician Bix Beiderbecke. In *Noi tre/The Three of Us* (1984), he tells the story of Mozart to counterbalance Forman's Oscar winning *Amadeus* (1984). In his following films, he uses music as an integral part of his stories of love, triumph, or despair at all levels of society, from *Aiutami a sognare/Help Me Keep on Dreaming* (1981), where the heroine is a ballet teacher, to his latter *Storie di ragazzi e ragazze/Stories of Boys and Girls* (1989) centered on the love story between a city boy and a country girl contrasted by their respective families.

One of the most innovative of the "new cinema" directors is Nanni Moretti. His early films *Sono un autarchico/I'm an Authartic* (1977) and *Ecce Bombo* (1978) are set among the disillusioned and hyper political youth of the 1970s. In *Bianca/Sweet Body of Bianca* (1984), Moretti defines his alter ego Michele Apicichella, a neurotic figure unable to accept the difference between his desires and the reality he faces. *La messa è finita/The Mass Is Over* (1985) is about a delusional young priest and the crisis of spirituality in Italy. *La palombella rossa/Red Wood Pigeon* (1989) anticipated of the decline of the Italian Communist Party in the year of the fall of the Berlin Wall with a scene in which Moretti must deliver a penalty shot in a water polo match and, like the PCI, he is symbolically paralyzed by whether he should aim to the right or to the left.

Gabriella Rosaleva has delved into the question of magic and witchcraft, focusing on the repressive power of superstition, ignorance, and intimidation, to tell the story of a woman accused of witchcraft in *Il processo a Caterina Ross/The Trial of Caterina Ross* (1982).

Gabriele Salvatores gained international acclaim with his film *Mediterraneo* (1991) awarded an Oscar for Best Foreign Film in 1991. *Mediterraneo* (1991) is the story of a group of Italian soldiers stationed on a Greek island during WWII and left without any further contact with their commanders or country until they are finally rescued at the end of the war by a British war ship. The story is handled with humor and sympathy for antiheroes who have little in common with the militaristic regime of Mussolini in an echo of De Santis's *Italiani brava gente/Attack and Retreat* (1964). Salvatores's earlier films, *Marrakesch Express* (1989) and *Turné* (1990) scripted with Paolo Virzì placed him among the most promising directors of his generation.

Many performers who had gained popularity on television made the transition to cinema. Like comedians of previous generations, such as Totò (Naples), Aldo Fabrizi, and Alberto Sordi (Rome), these new comedians are often identifiable with a specific region. Paolo Villaggio of the *Fantozzi* series directed by Luciano Salce is identified with Genoa. Carlo Verdone (1950–) the director of *Un sacco bello/Fun Is Beautiful* (1980) and *Bianco, rosso e Verdone* (1981) is identified with the dialect and stereotypes of Rome like his mentor Alberto Sordi. The Neapolitan comedian Massimo Troisi (1954–94) made *Ricomincio da tre/I'm Starting from Three* (1981) and starred with Tuscan comedian Roberto Benigni in *Non ci resta che piangere/Nothing Left to Do but Cry* (1985) (figure 9.1). Troisi gained international celebrity status shortly before his death for his codirection with Michael Radford of the Academy Award winning *Il postino* (1994).

Roberto Benigni's (1952–) cultural origins are in the rural Tuscany where he developed abilities in the *poeta a braccio* (improvising poet) tradition. The authenticity of Benigni's abilities, as a clown and performer able to recite large swaths of the Italian literary canon of Dante and Ariosto by memory, make him a throwback to the premodern era. Benigni's career blossomed when he brought the voices from his upbringing in the Tuscan hinterland to the *avant garde* stage in Rome with his scandal provoking monologue *Cioni Mario di Gaspare fu Giulia/Mario Cioni Son of Gaspare and the Late Giulia* (1975). His first starring role in a feature film was in Giuseppe Bertolucci's undervalued film *Berlinguer ti voglio bene/Berlinguer I Love You* (1977), based on Benigni's theatrical monologue *Cioni Mario di Gaspare fu Giulia*. The film brought Italian audiences in contact with the earthy reality of the foul-mouthed peasants from the Tuscan boondocks. Benigni later reprised material from the *Cioni Mario* monologue for Jim Jarmusch's episodic film *Night on Earth* (1991) as a taxi driver in Rome.

Benigni's formation in the Italian cinema extended to a period under the tutelage of Cesare Zavattini, the chief theorist of neorealism who singled out Benigni to star in what was to be Zavattini's last film, *La veritàààà/The Truth* (1982). The experience gave Benigni a crash-course on Zavattini's ideas on the cinema and was an important influence on Benigni's future work. Because of tight narrative structure and planned sight gags in Benigni's films, he may seem far from Cesare Zavattini's neorealist school of cinema. Yet a spirit of jocularity is part of the Zavattini/De Sica repertoire in films such as *Miracle at Milan* (1951) and *Il giudizio universale/The Last Judgement* (1961).

Benigni had been a rising star of Italian cinema since the mid-1980s after his film with Massimo Troisi *Nothing Left to Do but Cry* (1985) and *Il piccolo diavolo/The Little Devil* (1988), with Walter Mathau and Benigni's wife Nicoletta Braschi in one of her many roles as the love interest in Benigni a film. One of the first films to bring Benigni to the attention of an international audience was Fellini's last film *La voce della luna/The Voice of the Moon* (1990) based on the novel *Il poema dei lunatici* by Ermanno Cavazzoni. In *The Voice of the Moon*, Fellini criticizes the dehumanizing confusion of the modern lifestyle with a focus on the interior, spiritual life of characters who are isolated from the noise of contemporary culture and society.[2] The protagonists of the film are marginal figures who live a life of poetic mystery and memory. Benigni plays Ivo, a recently discharged mental hospital patient who hears voices in wells, among which are many quotes from Giacomo Leopardi, whose verses are also featured in *Amarcord*. The other main character is a paranoid ex-prefect Adolfo Gonella, played by Paolo Villaggio, who, like Ivo, has become a marginal figure after losing his job due to mental instability. In *The Voice of the Moon* Fellini questions the contemporary definition of normality under the yoke and cacophony of modern consumer culture. For Fellini these characters that society labels as insane have retained a connection to the natural world and local culture, which is dissipating among "normal" people.[3] The experience with Fellini would be an important step in Benigni's development as a director.

Benigni's first international success was the mafia spoof *Johnny Stecchino* (1991); a timely topic given the concurrent events of mafia prosecution trials that dominated Italian front pages in the early 1990s. Through the common-place of mistaken identity central to classical comedy, the innocent if mischievous bus driver, Dante, enters the double-dealing upper echelons of Italian political power. He meets government ministers and is paraded at the Palermo opera house before the flower of Sicilian society. In Benigni's parallel between Dante and Johnny Stecchino, small-time criminality and lack of civic standards among the Italian people explain the larger picture of corruption and organized criminality.[4] After Dante steals a banana, a judge who mistakenly recognizes him as the mafia boss advises Dante not to collaborate with the police. Dante, misinterpreting this advice, returns to the police station and finds the reporting officer eating the stolen banana in a parody of the *pentito* (penitent) witness protection program. The final statement on the mafia is anything but conciliatory. In one of the last scenes, Dante leads a grotesque chorus of mafia hit men in the same barnyard song sung by handicapped students at the beginning of the film, the inference being that the mafia is an organization for the mentally retarded.

In *Il mostro/The Monster* (1994), Benigni's character, Loris, is mistaken for a serial killer and the genre spoofed is the slasher film. The title of the film caused the Italian public to think immediately of the serial killer near Florence whose crimes remained unsolved into the 1990s. *Mostro* in Italian means "monster" but may also refer to a serial killer. In *The Monster* the impersonal world of urban Italy is juxtaposed with Benigni's character, the nonconformist Loris. In *The Monster* the president of the condominium who tries to evict Loris has been widely identified with Silvio Berlusconi. The television broadcast of Loris's police composite photograph depicting him as a serial killer unleashes mass hysteria allowing Benigni to stage chase scenes echoing the silent Hollywood slapstick films of Buster Keaton and Charlie Chaplin. Hints in the plot lead the spectator to believe that the serial killer will be one of the police investigators in what would have been a comic version of the political commentary of Petri's *Investigation of a Citizen above Suspicion* (1970). The ending of the film evokes classic slasher films. In Fritz Lang's *M* (1931), the serial killer is given away by a tune he whistles. In *The Monster* the guilt of the Chinese professor is revealed by the jingle of a Chinese charm doll.

The tradition of Italian popular comedy was continued by the Vanzina brothers Carlo and Enrico, sons of Steno (Stefano Vanzina) with commercial success in genres which fulfilled audience expectations of light humor in the vacation and beach movie genres with *Vacanze di Natale* (1990, 1991, 1995, 1999), *Sapore di mare/Time for Loving* (1983), and the road movie series *Viaggio nel Tempo* (1996, 1997) starring Christian De Sica, son of Vittorio De Sica, and the comedian Massimo Boldi. The success of the Vanzinas' films has been credited with saving many Italian theaters from bankruptcy. Like the Vanzinas, Neri Parenti made a large number of well-received comedies (30) from 1979 to 2003. The Tuscan director and actor Leonardo Pieraccioni triumphed on the Italian market with *I laureati/Graduates* (1995), *Il ciclone/The Cyclone* (1996), and *Fuochi d'artificio/Fireworks* (1997), romantic comedies that echoed the 1950s *maggiorata fisica* physicality with actresses including Maria Grazia Cucinotta and Manuela Arcuri. In the 1990s, with comedies the Italian film industry maintained a solid presence in the domestic market.

Along with the arrival of new voices in the Italian cinema, Lina Wertmüller continued to produce films that deal with contemporary political problems in a satirical and grotesque style. Her films include an adaptation of Marcello D'Orta's novel *Io speriamo che me la cavo* as the comedy *Ciao Professore!* (1993) starring Paolo Villaggio, with themes treated previously in Elio Petri's *Il maestro di Vigevano/The Teacher from Vigevano* (1963) starring Alberto Sordi. Some of the masters of comedy Italian style from the 1960s remained active into the 1980s. Monicelli's *Bertoldo, Bertoldino and Cacasenno* (1984) and *Los Picaros/I Picari* (1987) revisits the comic adventures of his *Brancaleone* series (1966, 1970). Dino Risi's production in the 1980s conveys the same entertaining and biting humor of his late 1970s works in different types of films: from *Fantasma d'amore/Love Ghost* (1981) and *Dagobert* (1984) to *Scemo di Guerra/War Fool* (1985) and *Tolgo il disturbo/I Am Leaving* (1990). But attempts to revive the *commedia all'italiana* were never truly successful despite attempts at such episodic films as *Qua la mano/Give Me Five* (1980) or *Culo e camicia* (1981) directed by Pasquale Festa Campanile or Alberto Sordi's attempt to pass the baton of Roman comedy to Carlo Verdone with the father/son road movie *In viaggio con papà/Journey with Papa* (1982).

Although he was never able to break out of the Italian market, pop singer Adriano Celentano continued his film career with costar Ornella Muti in popular films directed by Castellano and Moccia: *Mani di velluto/Velvet Hands* (1979), *Il bisbetico domato/The Taming of the Scoundrel* (1980), *Innamorato pazzo/Madly in Love* (1981), *Grand Hotel Excelsior* (1982), and *Segni particolari: bellissimo* (1983).

The political film/instant movie genres have also remained vital with Gianni Amelio's *Porte aperte/Open Doors* (1990) from a story by Sciascia, set in 1937 Sicily during the Fascist period. The main character is a judge (played by Gian Maria Volonté) presiding over a multiple murder involving a Palermo man, himself a convinced Fascist, who had methodically murdered the boss who fired him, the man who replaced him at work, and even his wife. The film deals with how a totalitarian regime exploits its citizens and makes a case against capital punishment, a penalty abolished throughout Western Europe after its abuse by Europe's totalitarian regimes during WWII. Gianni Amelio's tragic *Il ladro di bambini/The Stolen Children* (1992) recalled the best moments of the neorealist period's emphasis on children. Amelio's *Lamerica* (1994) is about the appearance of Albanian boat refugees in Italy after the fall of that country's Stalinist regime. Amelio treats the theme of historical memory immigration, since Italy, which had long been a supplier of emigrants, had become a destination country in the last decades of the millennium.

Daniele Lucchetti's *Il portaborse/The Yes Man* (1991) was released during the height of the *tangentopoli* corruption scandals that accompanied the end of the so-called first republic of political parties which had ruled Italy from the end of WWII. The film stars Silvio Orlando as an idealistic school teacher turned idealistic party functionary working for an Italian politician played by Nanni Moretti. The former teacher decides to work within the system if he can realize personal goals such as attaining subsidies and recognition for a poet he considers the greatest voice in Italian culture of his day.

Ricky Tognazzi's *La scorta/The Bodyguards* (1993) is about the trials of the policemen who guard judges and politicians under the threat of assassination. Tognazzi's *Vite strozzate/Strangled Lives* (1996) deals with the scourge of usury. Marco Risi's *Mery per sempre/Forever Mary* (1989) stars Michele Placido as a school teacher attempting to reform troubled youths. Risi's *Il muro di gomma/The Invisible Wall* (1991), a so-called *instant movie*, is about the mysterious downing of a passenger jet near the island of Ustica, *Giovanni Falcone* (1993) was made soon after the mafia murder of the Sicilian prosecutor.

There was a continuation of examination of the terrorist years with Giuseppe Ferrara's *Segreto di stato/State Secret* (1995) with references to the Milan, Florence and Rome bombings. Giordana's *Pasolini un delitto italiano/Pasolini an Italian Crime* (1995) is about the murder of Pasolini with an interest in conspiracy theories. Cristina Comencini's *La fine è nota/The End Is Known* (1993) brought the years of terrorist violence to a personal level in which the moral ramifications of the extremist violence took a secondary role to their actual affect on people's personal lives. In the film a mysterious suicide leads a prosecutor to former Red Brigade terrorists in exile in France and the brutal discovery that the prosecutor's own wife was a former terrorist about whose true identity and past he knew nothing. The film is a chilling metaphor for the legacy of the terrorist years in Italy. Similar themes are explored in Mimmo Calopresti's *La seconda volta/The Second Time* (1996) starring Nanni Moretti as a victim of terrorism who recognizes his attacker years after the event. Their confrontation leads the former terrorist to abandon the work release program which would have meant her gradual reintegration into society, choosing to remain in the safety of her prison.

A Nostalgic Narrative

In the 1990s, a major contribution of the Italian cinema was in films about the cinema itself and promoted the idea of a national collective memory dominated by the cultural commonplaces of the years from the late 1930s to the early 1950s. The Italian film set in the Fascist or WWII era is a genre that had gone through different periods from the heroic films of the early neorealist period such as *Roma città aperta/Open City* to the ironic films of the early 1960s such as *Il federale/The Fascist* (1961) or *Tutti a casa/Everybody Home* (1960) to the more politically motivated films of the 1970s like Bertolucci's *Il conformista/The Conformist* (1970) and *Novecento/1900* (1976).

In the past, international validation brought welcome recognition to the Italian cinema. *Open City* (1945) and *Ladri di biciclette/The Bicycle Thief* (1948) received their due domestically after being screened and praised by audiences abroad, a trend that continued with the reception for films such as De Sica's *La ciociara/Two Women* (1960). Italian films seemed to be more exportable if set with the cultural stereotypes of the pre- and post-WWII period.[5] The stylistic elements of an Italian film set between the 1930s and the 1950s reaffirm Italian cultural identify and solve the challenge of expressing Italian cultural uniqueness apart from international postwar consumer culture with an undertone of a nostalgic yearning for the predominantly agricultural and Catholic Italy of centuries past. Some Italian films from the late 1980s and 1990s with elements of this nostalgic or *retro* mode received wide international awards and distribution. Giuseppe Tornatore's *Il nuovo Cinema Paradiso/Cinema Paradiso* (1988), Gabriele Salvatore's *Mediterraneo* (1991), Benigni's *La vita è bella/Life is Beautiful* (1997) are all set in the Nazi/Fascist period from 1936 to 1945. Radford and Troisi's *Il postino/The Postman* (1994), which also had echoes of the *maggiorata* period with costar Maria Grazia Cucinotta tapped into the international audience's romantic vision of a picturesque, traditional Italy. Set in 1952, the film depicts an innocent communism that predates the revelations that followed the Soviet invasion of Hungary and Khruschev's admissions about Stalinist atrocities. The main character, Mario, inspired by the exiled Chilean poet Pablo Neruda, is accidentally killed in a crowd stampede at a Party rally where he came not to incite revolution but to read a poem.

Part of this *retro* mode were films that examined Italian cinema history as a cultural phenomenon, a topic arguably inspired by the decline of the Italian theater system, which began in earnest in the late 1970s. Scola's *Splendor* (1989) starring Marcello Mastroianni and Massimo Troisi recounts events in a small town cinema hall, which is the focus of town life until it closes. Maurizio Nichetti's *Ladri di saponette/Icicle Thieves* (1989) ironically portrays the transformation of Italian society from the poverty of De Sica's *The Bicycle Thief* (1948) to the consumerism of the 1990s. In Nichetti's film, the dutiful wife from De Sica's original is trapped in a netherworld of television commercials with never-ending jingles. When she finally escapes, she demands labor saving appliances. Tornatore's *L'uomo delle stelle/The Star Maker* (1995) contrasts the dreams of consumer culture with a setting in postwar, rural Sicily. Marco Ferreri's *Nitrato d'argento/Nitrate Base* (1996) connects the lives of the spectators of a theater with the films they viewed. *Celluloide* (1996) is Carlo Lizzani's fictionalization of the making of Rossellini's *Open City* (1945) with the Italo-Finnish actress Anna

Falchi. Maurizio's Ponzi's *A luci spente* is a fictionalization of the making of Marcello Albani's *Redenzione* (1943) with references to De Sica's *La porta del cielo/The Gate of Heaven* (1945).

Perhaps the most indicative example of this metacinematic nostalgic mode in Italian cinema comes from Giuseppe Tornatore's Oscar winning *ll nuovo Cinema Paradiso/Cinema Paradiso* (1988). Born in Bagheria, near Palermo, Giuseppe Tornatore (1956–) is a self-taught camera man who started working for television and eventually collaborated on the script and the filming of Giuseppe Ferrara's *Cento giorni a Palermo/100 Days in Palermo* (1984), a docudrama on the mafia assassination of General Dalla Chiesa in 1982. His first feature film was *The Professor/Il camorrista* (1986) about a Neapolitan gangster and his criminal activities and connections. Tornatore's *Cinema Paradiso* recounts how the cinema influenced a small Sicilian town since the end of WWII. The film opens with the form of public spectacle most often repeated in a small town in Sicily: the Catholic Mass. Then the film depicts the cultural changes in Italy as reflected by a media-dominated culture. The cinematic imagery of the larger global culture actually poses a metaphorical threat to the familial iconography of the protagonist Totò. A a pre war photo of Totò's parents burns after chemical reaction with the flammable film stock the boy had hidden under his bed. The film points out the boy's confusion between cinematic culture and his identity, expressed by the mature Toto's eventual admission after the funeral of Alfredo, his mentor, that it is illusory to run away from one's roots. The film has a circular narrative, frequent in Italian film, where life experiences impart a lesson of fatalism of the unchanging nature of life.

Besides its emotional power, the film is an interesting document of the types of films that appeared in Tornatore's memories of Sicilian theaters of his youth, creating a parallel between the life of a small Sicilian town and film history. The film opens with homage to Jean Renoir's *Le bas-fonds/The Lower Depths* (1936) starring Jean Gabin. Renoir's mentorship of Luchino Visconti's *Toni* (1935) is often mentioned as an important influence on Visconti's brand of cinema. In *Cinema Paradiso* the American cinema is a constant point of reference, from the cameo of John Ford's seminal western *Stagecoach* (1939) starring John Wayne to the silent-era slapstick of Fatty Arbuckle and Charlie Chaplin. Tornatore emphasizes the importance of newsreels, such as the *Settimana Incom*, which brought news to the provinces with a cameo of Italian Resistance leader and later president of the Republic Sandro Pertini (1896–1990), and the news that soldiers from the Russian front, including Totò's father, will never return. The film shows a sequence from Pietro Germi's *In nome della legge/In the Name of the Law* (1949), which adapted the narrative structure of the American western, to the mafia film. Another sequence features Riccardo Freda's *Aquila nera/Black Eagle* (1946), an adaptation of a Pushkin adventure tale, one of the highest grossing domestic films in 1946. The Hollywood cinema makes a determined impression with Spenser Tracey in *Dr. Jekyll and Mr. Hyde* (1941), the Civil War epic *Gone with the Wind* (1939), and stills of American sex symbol Rita Hayworth in Alfredo's projectionist cabin, a poster that recalls the poster of

Hayworth pasted up before the protagonist's bicycle was stolen in De Sica's *The Bicycle Thief* (1948). There is a near riot over the lack of seating for a screening of Mario Mattoli's Totò vehicle, *I pompieri di Viggiù/The Firemen of Viggiù* (1949), resulting in a fire that blinds Totò's mentor, the projectionist Alfredo. Silvana Mangano appears in De Santis's *Riso amaro/Bitter Rice* (1949) and in a dance sequence from Lattuada's *Anna* (1952), a film that mixes the sexual power of Mangano's screen presence with melodramatic elements apparent in the *strappalacrime* (weepie) genre films such as Raffaele Matarazzo's *Catene/Chains* (1949). Totò must carry the only print of *Chains* back and forth from two neighboring cinemas due to public demand. Pink neorealism makes an appearance with Risi's *Poveri ma belli/Poor but Beautiful* (1956) with Marisa Allasio. De Sica's performance as the aging gambler in *L'oro di Napoli/The Gold of Naples* (1954) is the only direct cameo of De Sica in the film. Tornatore also shows Fellini's *I vitelloni/The Young and the Passionate* (1952) starring Alberto Sordi. The peplum appears with a scene of Kirk Douglas in Mario Camerini's peplum *Ulysses* (1954).

For Tornatore, cinema is a popular art and the theater is the center of a town's social life. A mafia murder in the balcony is cut with a publicity still of Paul Muni and a scene of machine gun fire seemingly from Howard Hawks *Scarface* (1932). Upper middle-class patrons in the balcony seats spit on the patrons below them. There are allusions to sex in the aisles, breast feeding, boys masturbating to Brigitte Bardot in Roger Vadim's *And God Created Woman* (1956). Italian cultural life from previous centuries was reflected in the public square performances of the *commedia dell'arte* or on the operatic stage. Tornatore shows how twentieth-century audiences' lives were reflected on the screen at the cinema. A final montage of scenes censored by the village priest played by Leopoldo Trieste and saved by Totò's mentor Alfredo offers a history of the cinema. Tornatore appears as the camera operator rolling a montage of kisses from De Santis's *Bitter Rice*, Hawks/Hughes's *His Girl Friday* (1940), *The Outlaw* (1943), Frank Capra's *It's a Wonderful Life* (1946), and the first exposed breast in Italian commercial cinema history in Blasetti's *La cena delle beffe* (1942). Tornatore pays particular homage to Visconti with kisses from *Ossessione/Obsession* (1943), *Senso/Livia* (1954), *The Earth Trembles*, and finally the Jean Renoir film that opened the film, *The Lower Depths*.

When Totò returns to the town in early middle age as a successful film director to attend Alfredo's funeral, the owner of the *Cinema Paradiso* relates the slow decline of the theater due to the rise of television and videocassettes. The abandoned building is set for destruction and conversion to a parking lot. The placards of famous films from Totò's youth have been replaced with torn adverts for the pornographic films that owners attempted to use to keep their theaters open. The film celebrates the vibrancy of the cinema as a popular art, but also chronicles its decline.

Tornatore's next film *Stanno tutti bene/Everybody's Fine* (1990) is the story of a Sicilian retiree, played by Marcello Mastroianni, who decides to visit his children scattered throughout northern Italy. *Everybody's Fine* treats the themes of nostalgia for Italy's pre-industrial past with a devastating condemnation of the impersonality of the consumerist culture that developed out of the economic boom of the 1960s as foretold by Pasolini. The film reveals a profound generational gap between father and children. The Sicilian patriarch discovers that all of his children have abandoned the traditional codes that stressed not only family ties but also local regional identity. One son is a flunky for a political boss, one daughter is ashamed to admit her divorce, and another has an illegitimate child and works precariously as a fashion model. None of the siblings have the courage to reveal that the father's favorite son has apparently committed suicide. The patriarch's ventures from his Sicilian abode into contemporary Italy where the natural world is under threat. In Rome, birds kill themselves, disoriented by the city lights and smog. A confused elk blocks traffic on the freeway. The patriarch's grandson creates a firefly virtual reality, a reference to Pasolini's famous statements about the disappearance of the fireflies from Italy.

Like *Cinema paradise*, Nanni Moretti's (1953–) *Caro diario/Dear Diary* (1993) is about film history. Moretti opens with a running joke about American celebrity culture with the protagonist's search for Jennifer Beals the star of Adrian Lyne's Hollywood musical *Flashdance* (1983) among his chance encounters in Rome. Then the film refers to the crisis of the Italian theaters and the lack of spectators. The only films Moretti can find playing in theaters in the Roman summer are self-deprecating films about the 1960s generation along the lines of Andrea Barzini's *Italia Germania 4-3* (1990), or pornographic and slasher films such as John McNaughton's *Henry Portrait of a Serial Killer* (1990). In disgust Moretti visits an insomniac film critic played by director Carlo Mazzacurati to berate him for having praised the films of directors like David Lynch and Jonathan Demme. A long-shot homage to the decaying monument at Pier Paolo Pasolini's murder site at the beach outside Rome brings up questions about the depth of Pasolini's legacy. Moretti's trip to the Eolian islands in the second episode of the film is a further voyage through Italian cinema history. There is a cameo of Silvana Mangano dancing in Alberto Lattuada's *Anna* (1952), an Italian melodrama of the 1950s. A sequence on the volcanic island of Stromboli is an ironic homage to Roberto Rossellini's film *Stromboli* (1949). Moretti wryly replaces Ingrid Bergman's quest for God and the meaning of existence in Rossellini's film with a television-addicted intellectual's search for future plot summaries of American soap operas from passing tourists. Stromboli's mayor fantasizes about converting the island into an international environmental art zone with lighting by Bernardo Bertolucci's cinematographer Vittorio Storaro and music similar to Ennio Morricone's "Sean Sean" sound track from Sergio Leone's *Giù la testa/A Fistful of Dynamite* (1971). The last segment of Moretti's film, *Medici/Doctors*, could be read as a homage to the Cesare Zavattini documentary style of neo realism. The episode recreates day to day life with non professional actors and a social message, in this case criticism of the medical profession. The documentary depiction of Moretti's suffering with cancer effectively removes the Pirandellian mask of the actor—an essence of the appeal of neo-realism.

Benigni's *La vita è bella/Life is Beautiful*[6]

A film that belongs to the nostalgia current in the Italian cinema is Roberto Benigni's *La vita é bella*, co written with Vincenzo Cerami, the top grossing Italian domestic film of all time, finally dislodging Bertolucci's *Ultimo tango a Parigi/Last Tango in Paris* (1972). *La vita é bella* triumphed at the Cannes Film Festival and at the Academy Awards where it was recognized as Best Foreign Film (figure 9.2). Benigni also took home the Oscar for best actor, achieving recognition for the Italian cinema unseen since Sophia Loren won similar recognition for her starring role in Vittorio De Sica's *Two Women* (1960). However the film also stirred a great deal of controversy particularly over the delicate question of the suitability of using comedy to depict the Jewish Holocaust by Nazi Germany.

In his previous films the contrast between Benigni's jocular or giullaresque approach and the underlying terror of topics like the mafia or serial killer was apparent. Guido in *La vita è bella* subverts societal order with a carnival-like suspension of the rules, a reversal of power relationships. However, with the Holocaust Benigni tackled a subject whose aura of historical defeat and pessimistic resignation to evil was much more profound than the topics he had chosen before. The simple Rabelaisian contrast between lower and upper body, between unofficial and official society, would not seem to be effective to deconstruct a subject of such inherent horror and collective guilt as the Holocaust.[7] Benigni and screenwriter Vincenzo Cerami's approach was to apply the fabulous current in the Italian cinema in the works of Zavattini with whom Benigni had an extended apprenticeship. By contrasting the violence and evil of the Holocaust with a father's attempt to preserve the innocence of a child, Benigni and Cerami hark back to the greatest films in the Italian canon. Benigni's film was partly inspired by the stories of his father, Luigi, who was an Italian soldier interned in a Nazi work camp after the Italian monarchy switched sides on September 8, 1943, following the Allied invasion of Sicily. Benigni recalled that his father never retold the story of his internment in a way that would frighten or depress his children. This respect and protection of innocence made a profound impact on Benigni, who sought to apply his father's approach to the topic in the film (figure 9.3).

With neorealism the Italian cinema offered a canon of films that placed Italian national identity in the postwar period on the memory of the defeat of Nazi/Fascism.[8] Just as the western genre has come to represent the essence of American nation building, the Italian film such as *Open City* even if set in the period of Fascism represents characters that embody the essence of the Italian political consciousness of the first postwar Italian Republic (1948–93).[9] However, unlike some recent nostalgically themed Italian films such as Salvatores's *Mediterraneo*, *Life is Beautiful* confronts Italian audiences with the image of Fascist Italy as an arrogant and aggressive nation, not the country defeated and torn by the civil war that followed the Allied invasion of 1943.

The film offers the character of Dr. Lessing representing German intellectuals to explain the Nazi's destruction of less barbaric traditions of German civilization. In the

Figure 9.1   Nicoletta Braschi (Dora) and Roberto Benigni (Guido) in *La vita è bella*.

Figure 9.2 Roberto Benigni in *La vita è bella*.

first half of the film, Dr. Lessing is a guest at the Grand Hotel who plays word games with Guido. Benigni and Cerami give this failed German intellectual the same last name as one of the greatest exponents of the German Enlightenment, Gotthold Ephraim Lessing (1729–81). Due to his previous friendship with Guido, when Lessing reappears in the second half of the film as the concentration camp doctor there is the expectation that he might reject the insanity of the Nazi system. The final riddle that Lessing asks Guido to solve seems like a metaphor for the cowardice and failure of the better angels of German civilization to resist the Nazis. Lessing asks Guido to find a solution for something that is fat, ugly, yellow, and walks about defecating.[10] Lessing claims that the expected answer "duck" is incorrect. The solution to the riddle is something that is "fat, ugly, and yellow" which could be a physical color, perhaps blond. The answer to the riddle seems to be the German people or German intellectuals like Lessing. These fat (rich), ugly, yellow (blond) people march like duck or geese, the Nazi army parade step, producing waste. Benigni has explained the riddle as a "nonsense" that appears at a point of great tension in the plots since Guido expects a more rational response from Lessing. The emphasis on Lessing points out how many Germans reacted to the Holocaust by retreating into their personal microcosms, as symbolized by Lessing's retreat into his fantasy world of riddles.

The film's wise man, Guido's Uncle Eliseo, voices whatever points Benigni and Cerami wish to make about God and free will. While admonishing Guido that a waiter should not behave like a sycophant, uncle Eliseo insists that, like God, a waiter must maintain his dignity. Uncle Eliseo explains that God is the first servant. God serves man but he is not man's servant. According to uncle Eliseo's instructions, God's place is not to do everything for man, but to aid man in the struggle to behave according to God's instructions. Therefore the crimes by the film's Nazi–Fascist villains are the result of their individual choices of behavior and should not be attributed to God's negligence. The statement is a quick synthesis of the differences in philosophical and religious traditions between free will and determinism and points to a Catholic undertone in the film. A Catholic undertone is confirmed by elements in the film's plot line. A holy family hides their child from an infanticidal regime.

Most criticism of Life is Beautiful focused on the film's lack of historical realism. Benigni's screenwriter Vincenzo Cerami warned of the capability of contemporary film to remove all barriers of representation as a factor in reducing film's expressive quality. Material that was previously deemed obscene and required evocation due to moralistic sensibilities or technical limitations is now readily depictable. The decision to limit realistic displays and story lines in Life is Beautiful was a conscious effort to avoid what Cerami has called the sense of "hyper-reality" in contemporary cinema that has led to a lessening of its poetic power.[11] In previous films, Benigni introduced elements of the grotesque and even the horrible, such as the severed hand at the serial killer's table in The Monster. But in Life is Beautiful this is reversed. Benigni and screenwriter Vincenzo Cerami riskily trust the audience to understand that the film is not historically accurate.

The essence of Benigni's appeal has been his ability to use his comedic talents in tragic settings. He has been compared to a fescennino, the ancient Etruscan rodeo clowns who distracted crowds at the Coliseum while seconds removed fallen gladiators.[12] Like a fescennino, Benigni's works are dependent on public approval and reflect currents in popular culture. In fact Benigni films have consistently reflected larger trends/events in Italy—the decline of peasant culture in Berlinguer I Love You (1977), debates about the American military in places like Comiso in Nothing Left to Do but Cry (1984), the new Concordat and decline of Catholic adhesion in The Little Devil (1988), the anti-mafia struggles of the early 1990s in Johnny Stecchino (1991), serial killing and Berlusconi spoofing in The Monster (1994). The case of Life is Beautiful (1997) was not helped by subsequent events in a Europe, where a candidate from the National Front came in the second in French presidential elections of 2002 or a European Union report about anti-Semitism in 2003 revealed the persistence of unsettling attitudes.[13]

10

The Next Millennium

1999   Italy supports US military action against Serbia (Yugoslavia) and sends forces to Kosovo

2001   Silvio Berlusconi's Forza Italia party wins elections and forms coalition government with Gianfranco Fini (National Alliance) and Umberto Bossi (Northern League)

2002   European Union currency Euro replaces the Italian Lira
Lower house of parliament passes controversial criminal reform bill *Legittimo sospetto* (legitimate suspicion) allowing change of venue due to suspicion of judges' political affiliations

2003   Parliament passes laws granting immunity from prosecution to top government officeholders
Italian sends peace keeping troops to Iraq in the aftermath of the US led invasion
Parmalat financial crack

2005   Election of German cardinal Joseph Ratzinger as Pope Benedict XVI

2006   Romano Prodi's Olive coalition defeats Silvio Berlusconi's Liberty coalition in elections decided by absentee ballots
Ammendments increasing federalist nature of Italian constitution rejected in general referendum
Italian national soccer team wins fourth World Cup title

In 2002 Italian government's statistical and census institutes warned that in the last decades of the twentieth century Italy had birth rates among the lowest on Earth.[1] The educational and research level of the country was also at levels lower than other Western nations. Historians of contemporary Italy have even written in almost moralistic tones about the decline of ideological and religious traditions and challenges to the nation's families.[2] The country also faced economic challenges as stalworths of Italian industry such as Fiat, the automaker centered in Turin, experienced increased competition for the Italian market.

In the 1980s and 1990s a symbiosis developed between soccer and politics in a manner recalling the *panem et circenses* (bread and circus) policies of the later Roman Empire as ownership of high-profile soccer teams became a means for the wealthy to attain renown. The Agnelli family, which owned the Fiat automobile factories, ran the Juventus club of Turin, the major beneficiary of favors revealed in the referee fixing scandal of 2006. Italian premier and media magnate Silvio Berlusconi owned the Milan soccer club. The Moratti family continued its ownership of the Inter soccer team. On occasion, salaries paid to individual soccer players approached the figures for the entire gate revenue earned by the club, a financial situation clubs temporarily masked by exchanging player contracts at ever higher face values. In Rome the Cragnotti family of the Cirio food product company owned the Lazio football team before collapsing in 2002. The Tanzi family controlled the Parma soccer club until their Parmalat milk empire collapsed following a run on junk bonds in 2003. The Florentine film producer Mario Cecchi Gori lost his the Fiorentina soccer team following bankruptcy hearings.

In the opening years of the new millennium, the Italian Republic faced tensions between media magnate turned premier Silvio Berlusconi and the Italian judiciary, which attempted to try Berlusconi on corruption charges dating back to the *tangentopoli* corruption scandal leveled mainly against the Socialist Party of the late 1980s, events alluded to in Daniele Lucchetti's *Il portaborse/The Yes Man* (1991). There was protracted battling between the courts and the parliament controlled by Berlusconi's *Forza Italia* party, and the Liberty coalition passed laws granting high government officials immunity or allowing defendants to change venue because of the political affiliation of particular judges with the *legittimo sospetto* (legitimate suspicion) law. The year 2006 saw the defeat of Berlusconi's Liberty coalition by Romano Prodi's Olive coalition in close elections decided by votes cast by Italian citizens residing abroad. The Liberty coalition's defeat was foreshadowed by Nanni Moretti's bitter film satire on Berlusconi, *Il caimano/The Caiman* (2006), released weeks before the elections and winner of the majority of awards at Italy's Oscar equivalent, the Donatello competition. Berlusconi's Liberty coalition and particularly the Northern League of Umberto Bossi also suffered a referendum defeat when Italian voters rejected amendments to the Italian constitution, which would have purportedly granted more authority to Italy's regional governments.

The Cultural Scene

Important authors of the period include Antonio Tabucchi who wrote psychological studies of moral dilemmas such as *Sostiene Pereira/According to Pereira* (1985) adapted for the cinema by Roberto Faenza starring Marcello Mastroianni as *According to Periera* (1996). Susanna Tamaro wrote a nostalgic memoir *Va' dove ti porta il cuore/Follow Your Heart* (1994), which became a bestseller and was adapted for the cinema by Cristina Comencini in 1996. There was also the unexpected popularity of a serial killer mystery thriller by comedian and singer turned author Giorgio Faletti and the continuing popularity of detective novelist Andrea Camilleri who has taken up the mantle of such Sicilian authors as Leonardo Sciascia and Tomasi de Lampedusi. Andrea Camilleri's Montalbano crime series was adapted into a popular detective television miniseries. Journalists continued to publish popular and revealing books, for example, Beppe Severgnini's attempts to explain Italian mores or Oriana Fallaci's apocalyptic warnings about the decline of the West in the face of theocratic influences from the Middle East.

The availability of films from cable outlets and satellite dishes brought further competition for traditional cinema houses. By the 1980s the Italian film industry was increasingly dependent on government subsidies and concentrated on themes with reasonable hope of international distribution in what remained of the ever-diminishing art film theater network. These subsidies would be reduced in 2005 leading to a drop in Italian feature film production to levels unseen since the 1930s and 1940s.

In response to the decline of the theatrical system Italian producers such as Titanus or Taodue interested in popular entertainment increasingly moved toward developing television miniseries, known as *fiction* in Italian, instead of venturing into the traditional theatrically released cinema. Some of the Italian *fiction* productions were of high quality, including those on RAI Italian state television. Damiano Damiani's dark and fatalistic mafia drama *La piovra/The Beast* (1985) series had already established a high level of quality for Italian miniseries viewers. In the 1960s and 1970s Italian television had already adapted novels and offered biopics about subjects like Italian unification hero Giuseppe Garibaldi. But with the closing of domestic theaters, the entrance into *fiction* and television became more sustained and reached a higher level of production value. The Titanus production house that had produced popular Italian films such as *Catene/Chains* (1949) or *Il Gattopardo/The Leopard* (1963) developed the successful *Orgoglio* melodrama series set in pre WWI Italy as well as a television remake of the Bolognini film about Fascist Italy, *Il Bell'Antonio*. The goodhearted police officer played by De Sica in the *Pane, amore . . .* series of the 1950s has become the territory of Gigi Parietti and Stefania Sandrelli in the *Il maresciallo Rocca* miniseries. Television also offered Andrea Camilleri's Montalbano detective series starring Luca Zingaretti. Former sexy comedy actress Edwige Fenech has become a television producer offering series such as *La omicidi* starring Massimo Ghini and Luisa Ranieri, a tale written by prolific screenwriter Sandro Petraglia, in which the mystery hinges on uncovering clues form the murder's interpretation of Dante's *Inferno*. Italian television has even ventured into examination of subjects never fully examined by the Italian cinema. The forced deportations and mass executions suffered by Italian resisdents on the Istrian coast in the waning days of WWII are depicted in the compelling miniseries directed by Alberto Negrin, *Il cuore nel pozzo/Heart in the Well* (2005). A dramatization of the efforts of an Italian diplomat who fought the Holocaust is offered by *Perlasca. Un eroe italiano/Perlasca: An Italian Hero* (2002). Italian television has also produced a number of religious miniseries featuring international casts such as the biopic about Pope John Paul II, *Carol, un uomo diventato Papa/Karol, A Man who Became Pope* (2005), the most watched program on Berlusconi's private television stations in that year. Such programs have taken advantage of the Italian tradition for craftsmanship and have been distributed worldwide.

The development of the television *fiction* in Italian media culture may be understood by Marco Tullio Giordana's revocation of the *film impegnato* (political film) with *La meglio gioventù/The Best of Youth* (2003). This television miniseries for RAI chronicles the struggle for maturity of the baby boom generation between 1966 and 2003 with depictions of the student protests and growth of the Red Brigades in the Turin of the 1970s, and references to the *mani pulite* (clean hands) corruption investigations of the 1990s, all framed by pivotal games of the Italian national soccer team—the defeat at the hands of North Korea in 1966 and the World Cup championship of 1982. The protagonist, Nicola, played by Luigi Lo Cascio, becomes a psychiatrist who eventually achieves familial and emotional stability after the suppression of his Red Brigade terrorist wife, the suicide of his alienated policeman brother Matteo, played by Alessio Boni, and his seeming cure of a mentally ill woman his brother had sought to rescue from a mental ward in 1966. The miniseries is ripe with literary references. The miniseries' title is taken from a Pasolini poem. The two main characters work to salvage rare manuscripts from the 1966 flood of the Arno River in Florence. In the first episode Matteo iconoclastically responds to a university oral exam question about the love poems of Senuccio del Bene (1275–1349) by citing the hedonistic poetry of Cecco Angolieri (1260–1313) before announcing that he intends to abandon his studies. He later checks out Sherwood Anderson's novel *Winesburg Ohio* before committing suicide. The series ends with a call for the appreciation of beauty with images of the midnight sun in Scandinavia and the refurbished Tuscan villa of Nicola's brother-in-law, as a response to generational angst and violence of the 1960s generation and the acceptance of the corruption and disappointments of an Italy still tied to the cultural and political immobility of *trasformismo*.

Roberto Benigni returned to television to reach a mass audience with his nationally televised *L'ultimo del Paradiso/The Last of Paradise* (2002) monologue, in which the Tuscan comedian followed a politically satirical monologue with a brilliant recitation and commentary of Dante's declaration of faith in the last canto of *Paradise* from the *Divine Comedy*. Benigni would appear on television again on Adriano Celentano's television program *Rockpolitic* (2005) in which the Tuscan comic recited the last words of Socrates after reprising the letter-writing scene from *Totò, Peppino e la malafemmina/Totò, Peppino and the Hussy* (1956) with a mocking letter to Berlusconi, a scene Benigni and Troisi had redone in *Non ci rest ache piangere/Nothing Left But Tears* (1994) with a letter to the fundamentalist friar of the Renaissance, Girolamo Savonarola.

Italian Cinema in the New Millennium

Outside of television in recent years several historical genres with a rich tradition in Italian filmmaking have declined. For example, films depicting Roman antiquity had been a constant presence in Italian production since the silent period, from *Cabiria* (1914) and the ensuing Maciste or Hercules series that ran from the 1920s into the 1960s. The Italian western has also all but disappeared. A perhaps final attempt, Giovanni Veronesi's *Il mio West/Gunslinger's Revenge* (1998), starring Leonardo Pieraccioni as a pacifist doctor in conflict with his aging gunfighter father played by Harvey Keitel, was unable to rekindle international public interest in the Italian-produced western. There have been periodic Italian horror films such as efforts by Dario Argento with *The Phantom of the Opera* (1998), *L'imbalsamatore/The Embalmer* (2002) by Matteo Garrone, or a revival of the zombie film with *Dellamorte dellamore/Cemetery Man* (1994) by Michele Soavi.

Another staple in Italian production, the Renaissance costume drama, has also nearly disappeared. Exceptions include Olmi's *Il mestiere delle armi/Profession of Arms* (2001)—a dramatization of the grueling if unexpected death of Renaissance military leader and knight Giovani dale Bande Nere (1498–1526) from small arms fire. The film has an epic pictorial sweep, evoking imagery from Renaissance painting and conveying the pace, attitudes, and threat to a patriarchal and aristocratic society from the technological change that gave a lowly foot soldier armed with an archbusier an advantage over a mounted knight. Pupi Avati made a film about the history of the holy shroud of Turin: *I cavallieri che fecero l'impresa/The Knights of the Quest* (2001).

Another period of Italian history that has long been a staple of Italian production was the *Risorgimento* Italian unification film. Films in this vein includes Blasetti's *1860* (1933) and important films from the postwar period such as Visconti's *Senso* (1854), *The Leopard* (1963), and Rossellini's *Viva l'Italia/Garibaldi* (1960). But after the 1960s, films on the period of Italian nation building became more infrequent, although there was an current of films depicting the pre-*Risorgimento* period such as Luigi Magni's *Nell'anno del signore . . . /The Conspirators* (1969), Monicelli's *Il marchese del grillo* (1981), *In nome del papa re/ In the Name of the Pope King* (1977), and *Fiorile/Wild Flower* (1993).

An attempt at a resuscitation of the Italian operatic biopic was Monicelli's box office disappointment, *Rossini! Rossini!* (1991). Other films in this vein include *Stradivari* (1989), *Artemesia* (1997), a French coproduction about Cremonese artist Artemesia Gentileschi (1593–1652), as well as a biopic about a castrato opera singer *Farinelli* (1994), and Zeffirelli's *Callas Forever* (2002). Despite mixed reception for these films, there have been incredibly vibrant Italian musicals that have more regional than national cultural focus such as Roberta Torre's grotesque Sicilian-set mafia satire with a soundtrack of Nino D'Angelo songs, *Tano da morire/To Die for Tano* (1997), which may be one of the most undervalued films in modern Italian cinema history. Torre treats the topic of the mafia with an irreverence and irony worthy of Fellini or Wertmüller. Torre returned to the musical with an immigration update of the Broadway musical *West Side Story* (1961) (and Shakespeare tragedy) *Sud Side Story* (2000) and the mafia drama *Angela* (2002).

The Italian *retro* film has remained a steady presence with Emanuele Crialese's *Respiro/Grazia's Island* (2002) starring Valeria Golino in an update of Rossellini's *Stromboli* (1949). Guido Chiesa offered an adaptation of a Beppe Fenoglio resistance novel, *Il partigiano Johnny/Johnny the Partisan* (2000). Giuseppe Tornatore evoked the *maggiorata fisica* period with *Malena* (2000) starring Monica Bellucci. Ferzan Ozpetek's *La finestra di fronte/Facing Windows* (2003) features Massimo Girotti as Holocaust survivor whose memory loss brings him into contact with a troubled Roman family. Enzo Monteleone reexamined the story of defeated Italian armies in North Africa in WWII in *El Alamein the Line of Fire* (2002), themes seen previously in Giuliano Montaldo's *Tempo di uccidere/A Time to Kill* (1990) or even Alessandrini's *Giarabub* (1942).

The Italian *retro* film no longer relied exclusively on the WWII period to evoke a sense of nostalgia for Italian cultural identity. Davide Ferrario's *Dopo mezzanotte/After Midnight* (2004) is about the night watchman in Turin's landmark building, the Mole Antonielliana, which houses the city's cinema museum. Ferrario presents montages of stills from turn-of-the-century Turin juxtaposed with images through the decades to the present in which the vibrant shots of old Turin have a ghostly hold over the modern, empty cityscape of the present day. There is a love triangle between a fast food employee, a car thief, and a night watchman, a change from Turin's reputation as an industrial city.

The Italian *retro* film has extended its reach beyond the WWII period to the 1970s with Renato De Maria's grotesque *Paz* (2002), an adaptation of the comic strip by Andrea Pazienza about stoners at a dysfunctional university of Bologna humanities department in the 1970s. There were also 1970s radio movies—Mario Tullio Giordana's *I cento passi/One Hundred Steps* (2000) about an anti-mafia radio station in Sicily, which retains the essence and vitality of Italian culture in scenes such as the protagonist's radio address, which puts his criticism of the mafia in the poetic meter of the opening verses of Dante's *Divine Comedy*. Guido Chiesa made *Lavorare con lentezza* (2004) about 1970s Bologna radio, and rock singer Luciano Ligabue ventured into filmmaking with *Radio Freccia/Radio Arrow* starring Stefano Accorsi in a film about 1970s drug addiction and radio broadcasts in the lower Po valley.

Gabriele Salvatore's critically acclaimed film *Io non ho paura/I'm not Scared* (2003) is an adaptation of a Niccolò Ammaniti novel set in 1978 about a ten-year-old boy who discovers that his father is part of a gang that has kidnapped another ten-year-old boy and chained him in a hole in the field of rural southern Italy. Nostalgia elements of the 1970s creep in with stills of Italian footballer Paolo Rossi or the solo dance of one of the kidnappers to Mina singing *Parole, parole, parole* (Words, words, words). The northern Italian leader of the kidnapping gang played by Diego Abbantuono, a frequent actor in Savatores's film, has a whose brutal and selfish worldview that complements the impatient dissatisfaction of the bewildered boy's father. There is a parallel between the numb and mindless cruelty that the children display in their games and the bumbling efforts of the adults to collect a ransom. Yet the children are glorified riding their bicycles through lush long-shot cinematography of grain fields by Italo Petriccione and a score by perennial master Ennio Morricone. The idea of demasking the hypocrisy of the adult world and the loving depiction of bicycles harkens back to the greatest moments of the Italian cinema as the film's young protagonist achieves a moral victory, saving the kidnapped boy from the murderous intentions of his father and his gang.

Hollywood productions portraying Italian themes have continued to rely on the cultural stereotypes of Italy as the country of the mafia and Latin lovers not only in films such as *The Godfather* (1972) or *Moonstruck* (1987) but also in the sense of Nordic romanticism about Italy, which pervades films such as *A Room with a View* (1985), Franco Zeffirelli's autobiographical *Tea with Mussolini* (1999), or the dramatization of the massacre of Italian army units at Cefalonia in *Captain Corelli's Mandolin* (2001) and the American tourist fantasy *Under the Tuscan Sun* (2003).

The tradition of Italian art cinema continued in the work of the diminishing cadre of established directors who have often made their films in English at times with little reference to Italy. After the international success of *The Last Emperor*

Figure 10.1   Roberto Benigni (Atillio) in *La tigre e la neve.*

(1987), which won the Oscar for best film, Bernardo Bertolucci continued to make films in English geared toward an international market such as his adaptation of the Paul Bowles's novel *The Sheltering Sky/Tè nel deserto* (1990) starring John Malkovich, *Little Buddha* (1993) with Keanu Reeves, or *Stealing Beauty* (1996) with Jeremy Irons and Liv Tyler. In *Besieged* (1998), Bertolucci returned to an Italian setting with a long-shot examination of an African woman wooed by an English pianist in Rome. *The Dreamers* (2003) could be read as a baby boomer's elogy to the excesses of his generation. The film is set during the student revolts in 1968 Paris and features incestuous, privileged, mixed twins who live a hermetic fortnight of fornication and neglect of household chores with a naïve American student in their posh apartment. The American eventually reveals the hypocrisy of the siblings' glorification of Maoist communist rhetoric by citing the ideals of nonviolence. *The Dreamers* is in the tradition of Tornatore's *Cinema Paradiso* with incessant cameos of the films lionized in the critical opinions of the French New Wave.

Other Italian directors making films in English include Visconti's disciple Franco Zeffirelli (1923–) who had specialized in Shakespeare adaptations in the 1960s and 1970s. Giuseppe Tornatore ventured into the English-language film with *The Legend of the Pianist on the Ocean* (1998). The panel for Italy's 2005 Oscar candidate, which eventually chose Cristina Comencini's child abuse drama *La bestia nel cuore/Don't Tell* (2005), considered selecting *Private* (2005) by Saverio Costanzo, a film in English depicting the Israeli—Palestinian conflict.

With his latest feature film, *La tigre e la neve/The Tiger and the Snow* (2005) Roberto Benigni leaves behind the examination of his Tuscan roots in *Pinocchio*

(2003). His clown persona takes the role of Atillio De Giovanni, a university professor/poet in Rome estranged from his wife Vittoria, after his affair with an English colleague. Atillio ventures to Iraq at the beginning of the American invasion to rescue Vittoria played expectedly by Nicoletta Braschi as she lay near death in an Iraqi hospital.

If Benigni's previous efforts contained references to the films of Fellini and Chaplin, in *The Tiger and the Snow* the point of departure is Sergio Leone's western, *Il buono, il brutto e il cattivo/The Good, the Bad and the Ugly* (1966), whose last sequences are featured in a cameo. In Leone's film, three competing gunslingers enter the treacherous no-man's land between Union and Confederate armies in the American Civil War. The Good/Blondie (Clint Eastwood) and the Ugly/Tuco (Eli Wallach) take risks to help the common soldier on both sides of the conflict, although the film defers any real comment on the larger issues of the Civil War or its backdrops such as slavery. In Benigni's film the connection to the common suffering in the war is not expressed through the sort of anonymous but powerfully emblematic figures as in Leone's western. Instead the insurmountable issues of war and ethnic conflict are expressed through the character of an elite Iraqi poet, Fuad, a friend of Atillio who is recognized and celebrated in the West. Fuad, played by French actor Jean Reno, is an enigmatic figure who enters a mosque for prayers before his suicide, perhaps Benigni and screenwriter Vincenzo Cerami's attempt to express the contradictions and attraction between (self) destruction and religion in certain Islamic cultures. The film ends with the oft-repeated refrain of the Tom Waits's graveley song, "You can never Hold back Spring," as if the power of love and goodwill were sufficient to overcome the tragedy of the Iraqi War and its backdrops of Baathist authoritarianism, American invasion, and Islamic terrorism.

Leone commented that the narratives of his westerns recalled Carlo Goldoni's *commedia dell'arte* plays, which placed the clown Harlequin in predicaments between opposing masters. In Benigni's previous films comedic situations were created when his character was a victim of mistaken identity and insane societal assumptions. In *The Tiger and the Snow* the efficacy of carnivalesque reversals and oppositions changes as Atillio is not a victim as much as a *furbo*, a crafty opportunist, whose ingenuity helps him save Vittoria. Atillio improvises Harlinquin-like solutions: impersonating an Italian Red Cross doctor, looting a Bagdad bazaar, and running medical supplies through an American army checkpoint. Like Leone's characters in *The Good, the Bad and the Ugly*, Atillio overcomes the chaos of the conflict to reach his goal without taking sides. Whenever he is cornered, Atillio repeats the line, "I am Italian," in English, as if a declaration of Italian identity were a protective charm and an excuse for his escapdes at the expense of Arabic straightmen. Yet Atillio's feeble claim for preferential treatment as an Italian is ignored. He gains release from a prisoner-of-war camp only when he is recognized as a innocuous poet. Ironically, when Atillio finally returns to Italy and presents himself as an Italian to an Italian customs agent, he is taken directly to jail, a consequence of his long-standing troubles within the Italian legal system, a setting where his comic persona has more relevance.

Literary adaptations constitute a trend that has continued to the present in the Italian cinema. Francesca Archibugi offered *Con gli occhi chiusi/With Closed Eyes* (1994) based upon the Federico Tozzi novel. Francesca Comencini directed an adaptation of a Italo Svevo novel *The Confessions of Zeno* with *Le parole di mio padre* (2002) as well as adaptations of her own novels including the Oscar candidate *La bestia nel cuore/Don't Tell* (2005). Mario Martone adapted an Elena Ferrante novel *L'amore molesto/Nasty Love* (1995). Perhaps the most important recent literary adaptation is Roberto Andò's *Il manoscritto del Principe/The Prince's Manuscript* (2000), a brilliant film in the best tradition of serious art cinema, which examines the backdrops of the composition of Tomasi de Lampedusa's novel *The Leopard.* Marco Risi adapted a Niccola Ammaniti novel with the apocalyptic film *L'ultmo capodanno/Humanity's Last New Years* (1998) starring Monica Bellucci. Gabriele Salvatores made an attempt to revive the *poliziesco* with an adaptation of Grazia Verasani's crime novel *Quo Vadis Baby?* (2005).

The *film politico* also remained a vibrant genre with the overlooked mafia film *La vita degli altri* (2002) by Nicola de Rinaldo or Roberto Faenza's *Alla luce del sole* (2005) about the efforts of the anti-mafia priest Don Giuseppe Puglisi starring Luca Zingaretti. Renzo Martinelli's *Vajont* (2001) deals with the political corruption leading to a tragic damburst in 1963. Michele Placido offered a story about a criminal gang in Rome with political undertones, *Romanzo Criminale/Crime Novel* (2005). Tulio Giordana turned to issues of immigration *Quando sei nato non puoi più nasconderti/Once You're Born You Can No Longer Hide* (2005). Marco Bellocchio resuscitated the seemingly defunct Catholic conspiracy movie of decades past such as Rosi's *Todo modo*, with *L'ora di religione Il sorriso di mia madre/The Religion Hour* (2002) starring Sergio Castellitto.

Perhaps the most compelling recent political film is Bellocchio's *Buon giorno notte/Good Morning Night* (2003), a paradoxical dramatization of the 1978 Aldo Moro kidnapping from the point of view of a female Red Brigade terrorist. After participating in the minute planning for the kidnapping, the female terrorist indulges herself in the moral dilemma regarding Moro's inevitable murder. Yet she chooses to suppress her doubts, pervert her conscience, ignore the objections of coworkers in her day job and help murder the lucid and ghostly Aldo Moro despite editing his plaintive letters to his family, political leaders, and the pope. Rather than putting a human face on the terrorist, the film becomes a metaphor for the power of an ideology, in this case the hyperbolic quest of the Red Brigades to foment a class-based civil war, to trap the human spirit. Similar themes are examined in *Attacco allo stato/Attack Against the State* (2006), a television miniseries starring Raul Bova in the tradition of the Italian political film. The miniseries convincingly examines the assassinations organized by a Red Brigade terrorist cell in late 1990s from the points of view of both the tenacious terrorists and the hardpressed police unit trying to stop them.

The Italian cinema evidenced a surprisingly vitality of directors working in the tradition of the *commedia all'italiana*. The slapstick comedy trio, Aldo Baglio, Giovanni Storti, and Giacomo Poretti, known as Aldo, Giovanni an Giacomo made the box office hit: *Tre uomini e una gamba/Three Men and A Leg* (1997). The film is a road movie that treats Italian society with due irreverence even spoofing the neorealist tradition with a ridiculous black and white retro sequence about the struggle between a man who does not want to pay his tram fare and the ticket collector. In the film the narrative aura of neorealist films about common man stories is transferred to a trio of brothers whose status as *mantenuti* (freeloaders) is an ironic homage to neorealist aspirations about social justice. The film also pokes fun at elite culture. The "Leg" in the title refers to a modernist sculpture of a mannequin leg that the trio must transport to their uncouth but extremely wealthy father-in-law. The comic trio followed the success of *Three Man and a Leg* with further box office hits *Chiedimi se sono felice/Ask Me if I'm Happy* (2000), *La leggenda di Al, John and Jack/The Legend of Al, John and Jack* (2002) and *Tu conosci la Claudia?/Do you Know Claudia?* (2005). These films offer a grotesque slapstick ride through contemporary Italy as did Antonio Albanese's *L'uomo di acqua dolce* and Carlo Mazzacurati's *La lingua del santo/Holy Tongue* (2000).

Veteran comedian and director Carlo Verdone's (1950–) consistently made well-received films such as *Sono pazzo di Iris Blond/I'm Crazy about Iris Blond* (1996), *C'era un cinese in coma/A Chinese in a Coma* (2000), or *L'amore è eterno finche dura/Love Is Eternal while It Lasts* (2004), which have reached a level of social satire that compares favorably with the golden years of the *commedia all'italiana* in the 1960s. Verdone also acted in Giovanni Veronesi's resuscitation of the Italian episodic film with the box office hit *Manuale d'amore/Love Manual* (2005) from a Vincenzo Cerami story. These comedies and their warm reception by Italian audiences point to the vitality of the comedy genre in the Italian cinema.

Some directors, for example, Gabriele Muccino, Marco Ponti, and Paolo Virzì, and Fausto Brizzi with the box office hit *La notte prima degli esami/The Night Before the Exams* (2006) have offered coming of age stories in the tradition of the *commedia all'italiana* treating themes relevant to contemporary Italy with heavy irony. The extra peninsular validation of the Italian nostalgia or *retro* film has not helped these Italian directors to find an international audience for their films depicting a contemporary Italy. The film style of new directors evidences apprenticeships or technical influences from the style of television commercials with rapid tracking shots and frenetic handheld montages familiar from quick paced advertising spots. The themes of their films seem to confirm Pasolini's warnings (with a debt to McLuhan), about the power of mass media and consumer culture to envelope Italian cultural identity. The work of these directors reveals the level of cultural homogenization in turn-of-the-millennium Italy as if the country has ironically achieved a national culture based upon the shared media experience derived from television watching, a goal of cultural identity that had been seemingly unachievable despite attempts by nationalist, Communist, and Catholic cultural and political forces in generations past. Yet the style of these films is so reminiscent of advertising spots that the ultimate result is a cheapening of both characters and themes as just other examples of the mundane alienation produced in a society where the populations' primary concern is not survival, but entertainment. Some of the films by the latest generation of Italian directors combine great technical ability with deep concentration on themes of personal reality in particular in coming of age stories that have constituted a current in turn-of-the-millennium Italian cinema. Coming of age stories, even for adults, have been a steady theme in the

Italian cinema from Risi's *Il sorpasso/The Easy Life* (1962), Fellini's *La dolce vita* (1960), or *I vitelloni/The Young and the Passionate* (1953) and many, many others. But given the statistical data regarding Italy's extremely low birth rate and the continuing trend for Italians to delay parenthood, the coming of age stories in the tradition of the *commedia all'italiana* so frequent among the works of the latest generation of Italian directors take on added importance as a reflection for a country whose inhabitants struggle to match emotional with physical maturity.[3]

Gabriele Muccino (1967–) has made films with a regional focus, set in contemporary Rome. His brother Silvio Muccino stars in *Come te nessuno mai/But Forever in My Mind* (1999), a juvenile love story in the setting of political protests in a Roman high school. Muccino's concentration on Roman settings makes him an example of the regional aspect of the latest Italian cinema. His seeming remake of Fellini's *The Young and the Passionate* with the wealthy, affected Roman youth struggling with adulthood of the turn of the millennium in *Ultimo bacio/The Last Kiss* (2001) would apply coming of age issues not just to adolescents but to most of the characters in the film. There are the marital tensions of the main character's future mother-in-law played by Stefania Sandrelli and her ex-lover played by Sergio Castellitto or the desire of the protagonist played by Stefano Accorsi and his friends to delay marriage and fatherhood in favor of high school sex, road trips, and dope smoking.

Muccino would repeat the coming of age theme in *Ricordati di me/Remember Me My Love* (2003), where again the difficulty in accepting maturity extends to an entire Roman nuclear family. The desire to be relevant to the media culture world threatens familial unity. In scenes that offer an update of Visconti's *Bellissima*, the sixteen-year-old daughter is callowly eager to trade sex for a short-run stint as a television dancing girl. The commodity of a young actor is not innocence or unaffected photogenic emotivity but a willingness to be sexually available to television producers. The father (Fabrizio Bentivoglio) is tormented by encounters with a former girlfriend (Monica Bellucci) who encourages his youthful aspirations to become a novelist. The mother (Laura Morante) regrets giving up an acting career for her family. The son (Silvio Muccino) is so desperate to make friends among his peers that he bribes his classmates with drugs so they will attend his birthday party. When the daughter achieves her goal and becomes a *velina* dancing girl on a television game show, her family and friends watch her fleeting appearances on television with solemn reverence. To break into the world of television is the achievement of ultimate status in contemporary culture. These characters from Muccino's film could exist in any developed nation. Their desires and identities are common to any society where mass media consumer culture has heavily influenced earlier ethnic identities not only in terms of religion and mores but also in language and even culture.

The Livornese director Paolo Virzì (1964–) teamed up with his brother the composer, Carlo, and coauthor Francesco Bruni to make a number of films with a regional focus set in contemporary Tuscany. *La bella vita/Living It Up* (1994) features Sabrina Ferilli, an actress with *maggiorata fisica* appeal, in the milieu of the decline of large industry in Italy in the late 1980s. The protagonist loses his job in a steel mill and then his wife to a television emcee before starting over by running

Figure 10.2   Sergio Castellitto (Giancarlo Iacovoni) and Alice Teghil (Caterina Iacovoni) in Paolo Virzì's *Caterina va in città*.

a campground on the Tuscan coast. With *Ferie d'agosto* (1996), Virzi again featured Sabrina Ferilli, in a vacation/beach movie featuring two families from opposite ends of the political/class spectrum who find themselves living in close quarters during a summer vacation. With *Ovosodo/Hardboiled Egg* (1997), Virzì repeated themes of class and political strife with another story set in Tuscany about a talented high school boy whose encounter with the spoiled son of an industrialist leads him to abandon hopes of social climbing through education. The ironic result is that his rebellious friend returns to his privileges of his class leaving the boy to work in a factory.

Virzì seemed to hit his stride as a director with *Caterina va in città/Caterina in the Big City* (2003), a film about an adolescent girl from the provinces who moves to Rome (figure 10.1). The film is in the tradition of Italian films that present the reactions of children or adolescents in order to criticize the assumptions and hypocrisies of the adult world. Caterina finds herself in a school attended by the children of the country's political and cultural elite where she is courted by two opposing gangs in a school—the leftist 1960s nostalgics and rightist fashion conscious girls. Each faction is led by the daughter of a rich and powerful father. One father (Claudio Amendola) is a Gianfranco Fini-like right-wing member of parliament, who enjoys his status in the political mainstream and seeks to distance himself from the Fascist nostalgics in his party. The other father is played by Flavio Bucci, a face familiar from the political films of the 1970s such as Elio Petri's *La classe operaia va in paradise/The Working Class Goes to Heaven* (1971) and *La proprietà non è un furto/Property is no longer Theft* (1973), as a revered leftist cultural figure who in the film is enthralled by the excrement produced by his infant son. Caterina's father (Sergio Castellitto) yearns to enter the cultural and political elite and attempts to use his daughter's friendships to gain favor among their parents whom he recognizes from television talk shows. When Caterina's father finally gets a chance to appear on television, he embarrasses himself on the long-running nationally televised talk show, the *Maurizio Costanzo Show*. Caterina's father realizes that the cultural and political elite is beyond his reach and falls into debilitating depression. Ironically Caterina also has a television cameo at a party for the city's in-crowd. Her mundane answer to the celebrity reporter's question of whether she has anything to say, "Ciao," reveals the ubiquity and inanity of the world dominated by the mass media, a point driven home by cameos of Michele Placido, Roberto Benigni, and Maurizio Costanzo, and a passing scene of a Berlusconi-like figure hounded by reporters. Like Muccino's films, Virzì's *Caterina in the Big City* seems to confirm the struggle between indigenous cultural identity in the face of the power of consumer and mass media driven culture. Virzì also has a film style influenced by the television commercials. Some scenes in *Caterina in the Big City* were shot with two cameras to capture the improvisations of a roomful of nonprofessional actors, a technique now common in television commercials and reality television. Yet Virzì adds an improvisational verve and thematic depth that ironically recalls the ability of the neorealist period to create a documentary essence. The film also imparts a lesson, repeated from *Hard Boiled Egg* and *August Vacation*, about the importance of economic class in a Rome that is both Italy's cultural and political capital. When Caterina encounters the studious son of a wealthy family with whom she shares a passion for classical music, his patrician mother forces the son to reject Caterina after she mentions her lower-middle-class status. Although the fathers of Caterina's friends are seemingly from diametrically opposite ends of the political spectrum, upon meeting they demonstrate an elitist solidarity that deepens Caterina's father's alienation and depression. In a central scene, Caterina's teacher asks a student to describe the difference between those on the political Left and Right. He ironically answers in an almost carnival-like reversal of traditional political identity that the rich and privileged are of the Left and the common working people are of the Right.

To escape this media driven society, Caterina's mother played by Margherita Buy seeks to recreate in Rome the same sort of microcosm of local friendships and relations that she enjoyed in the provinces. She has an affair with a neighbor who is connected to life in their apartment block. Caterina dreams of escaping her Italian identity by dating an Australian boy next door who seems unencumbered by the ambitions of Caterina's father. In one of the last scenes a game of charades at the beach results in the answer *La dolce vita*, Fellini's film about 1960s Rome, in which Marcello Mastroianni played a reporter whose aspirations for literary recognition are ironically shared by Caterina's defeated father. In *Caterina in the Big City*, Caterina and her father retrace the steps of Matroianni's character in turn-of-the-millennium Rome, although Virzì's film, unlike Fellini's, avoids much reference to the city's underclasses. The film ends with a cameo of a popular television show about missing persons, *Chi l'ha visto/Who's Seen Him*, where

Caterina's father's disappearance on his motorcycle becomes more relevant as a media moment than to his own family, who no longer miss him.

In 1948, Vittorio De Sica's *Ladri di biciclette/The Bicycle Thief* had chronicled a protagonist's struggle to reclaim his stolen bicycle as a symbol reaffirming his position as the head of a humble reconstruction-era Roman family after the humiliations of the war. Antonio's goals were stable employment and the health and sustenance of his family. In *Caterina in the Big City*, Caterina's father lovingly restores a flashy Moto Guzzi motorcycle in turn-of-the-millennium Rome. Caterina's father does not face the same basic threat for survival as the protagonist in *The Bicycle Thief*. The Moto Guzzi motorcycle is irrelevant to his ability to earn a living as a teacher. Yet the motorcycle is important for his self-image of independence and vitality, traits vaunted by the mass media consumer culture. The goal of Caterina's father is not simple sustenance, health, family, and work but the additional charge of media-driven fame.

The centrality of coming of age issues examined in the films of Muccino and Virzì in turn-of-the-millennium Italy was not lost on Roberto Benigni whose *Pinocchio* (2002) anticipated many of the themes in Muccino's and Virzì's films by offering a faithful adaptation of Collodi's foundational coming of age fable. The film was heavily influenced by the participation of the former staff of Federico Fellini, which gave the film its cinematic and stylistic imprint. It was also a top domestic box office film, relatively well received by Italian audiences who brought their children to the theater. The ability of Italian audiences to accept Benigni (1952–) in the leading role as a boy puppet is a telling indication of the nationwide attitudes about delaying adulthood. However, the film also created controversy, receiving criticism that included a political undertone whereby critics sought to distance themselves from the Mazzinian, republican precepts of Collodi's cautionary tale. The film elicits comparison with an earlier adaptation of Collodi's fable for Italian television by Luigi Comencini, *Le avventure di Pinocchio/The Adventures of Pinocchio* (1972), starring Nino Manfredi as Geppetto and featuring a brilliant musical score by Fiorenzo Carpi. Comencini's adaptation ably communicates the misery and poverty of nineteenth-century Italy. The struggle for survival depicted in Comencini's film at the heart of Collodi's fable and perhaps still in the collective memory of spectators in the 1970s, but was problematic for Benigni to evoke and represent for an Italian audience in the 2000s.

Gianni Amelio also made a film about trouble accepting maturity with *Le chiavi di casa/The Keys to the Houose* (2004) in which Kim Rossi Stuart (who appeared as Lucignolo—Lampwick in Benigni's *Pinocchio*) portrays a man who abandoned his mentally retarded son at birth and tries to reenter his life 15 years later. The film recalls Rossi Stuart's earlier role as a mentally disturbed young man in Alessandro D'Alatri's *Senza pelle/No Skin* (1994). Coming of age issues were also relevant to Nanni Moretti who continued to work in a personal microcosm in such films as *Aprile* (1998) about baby boomer angst due to the birth of his son, an event arguably singular enough for a member of Moretti's generation in an Italy with historically low birth rates to be considered material for a feature film. In the critically successful *La stanza del figlio/The Son's Room* (2001), Moretti offers a look at a family that must grieve the accidental death of their teenage son, gaining the maturity to deal with the inevitable tragedies of life. Asia Argento, daughter of Italian horror film director Dario Argento, followed acting roles in Hollywood with the direction of the autobiographical *Scarlet Diva* (2000), yet another film about a protagonist attempting to achieve maturity and even parenthood, in which Argento seems to play an aged version of one of Caterina's priviledged and debauched adolescent friends in *Caterina in the Big City*. Marco Ponti's (1967–) *Santa Maradona* (2001), filmed in the frenetic tracking shot and handheld camera style familiar from television commercials, chronicles the struggle of a college graduate played by Stefano Accorsi to find employment that will allow him to remain in the middle class. Pupi Avati offered two films on a similar theme: *Il cuore altrove/The Heart is Elsewhere* (2003) about a 35-year-old virginal Latin teacher's struggle to establish independence and *Ma quando arrivano le ragazze* (2005) about a young man's flirtation with a career as a jazz musician, a passion inspired by his father. The preponderance of coming of age stories in the Italian cinema, which not only examine the course to maturity for youths but also for adults, demonstrated how cinema has the ability to reflect larger issues over a specific time period; in the case of Italian cinema, the Italian population's demographic challenges at the turn of the millennium.

Despite often warm domestic and critical reception, most of the works above did not attract wide international distribution in the increasingly fierce competition for foreign-language and art house cinemas. An effort like Giuseppe Piccioni's (1953–) *Luce dei miei occhi/Light of My Eyes* (2001), mixes a tale of a single mother and an underachieving limousine driver with the underworld of organized crime and illegal immigration, recalls the long-shot style of art cinema of decades past, and offers an unsettlingly vibrant vision of contemporary Italy. Piccioni's follow-up, *La vita che vorrei/The Life I Would Like* (2005) cast the same romantic pair, Sandra Ceccarelli and Luigi Lo Cascio, as self-absorbed actors in a remake of William Wellman's *A Star Is Born* (1937), which concludes with actors' acceptance of parenthood rather than Fredric March's suicide as in Wellman's original.

Perhaps more than any other director Silvio Soldini's (1958–) career exemplifies the difficulties faced by directors interested in contemporary Italian themes. Soldini's efforts—*L'aria serena dell'ovest/The Peaceful Air of the West* (1990)—featured a concentration on the microcosm of Italian interpersonal relationships despite the changes in global culture and history. In the case of *The Peaceful Air of the West*, the fall of the Berlin Wall and the change to the Italian and world political landscape did not seem to have a direct effect on the lives of the protagonists. Soldini has also cast his eye on the actual cultural transformations in Italy and Europe with films that deal specifically with immigration with a unlikely but tender love story between a Gypsy girl and an Italian man in *Un anima divisa in due/Brucio nel vento/Burning in the Wind* (2002).

With *Pane e tulipani/Bread and Tulips* (2000), Soldini made a film that plays on the limitations of contemporary Italian cultural identity with an echo to the film *retro*. The film tapped into the sense of Nordic romanticism about southern Europe, which appears in the work of the Finnish Kaurismaki brothers like *Arvottomat/The Worthless* (1982) or in Danish director Lone Scherfig's *Italian for Beginners* (2000). Soldini's film was rewarded with international distribution and recognition. *Bread and Tulips* is the tale of a contemporary Italian housewife who goes to Venice after she is forgotten at a truck stop by the tour group after a visit to the archeological site at Paestum. Instead of returning straight home to Pescara, she hitchhikes to Venice and meets an Icelander actually in touch with the beauty of Italian culture in contrast to her husband and son so immersed in the banalities of contemporary life. The Icelander delights in the delicacies of traditional Venetian cuisine and is able to recite Italian poetry including Ludivico Ariosto's verses describing the unlikely love story between the humble servant Medoro and Lady Angelica from *Orlando furioso* that leads the knight Orlando to madness. The housewife finds an accordion, the traditional instrument of popular culture, in the Icelander's closet and becomes reacquainted with her own cultural identity.[4]

Italy, like other European countries, relied upon government subsidies in order to maintain a film industry in an era of declining distribution possibilities, a situation that would reverse in 2005 with the reduction of these state subsidies. The irony with the dependence on government funding is that Italian cinema has long been a popular cinema. At the high points of film production in the early 1960s, the works of critically lauded directors were also popular with the Italian public such as the top three box office films of 1960: Fellini's *La dolce vita*, De Sica's *La ciociara/Two Women* (1960), Visconti's *Rocco e I suoi fratelli/Rocco and His Brothers* (1960). There was a similar public interest in the 1970s in Bertolucci's *Novecento/1900* (1976) and Pasolini's *Decameron* (1971), Scola's *C'eravamo tanto amati/We Loved Each Other So Much* (1974) and Wertmüller's *Pasquallino Settebellezze/Seven Beauties* (1975). Massimo Troisi and Roberto Benigni continued the connection between popular and critically recognized cinema into the 1980s 1990s with *Nothig Left But Tears, Il postino/The Postman* (1994), and *La vita è bella/Life is Beautiful* (1997).

If considered objectively in terms of box office production and market share, the Italian cinema is not in a situation that is dramatically different from previous periods of difficulty in the 1920s, 1940s, or 1980s. What has changed for the Italian cinema is the level of continued international recognition and sustained distribution for its products abroad. The films from the Italian cinema in 2003 that finished in the domestic top ten—Ferzan Ozpetek's *Facing windows*, Gabriele Muccino's *Remember Me, My Love*, Carlo Verdone's *Ma che colpa abbiamo noi/What Fault is it of Ours*, Bernardo Bertolucci's *The Dreamers*, Gabriele Salvatores's *I'm not Scared*, Paolo Virzì's *Caterina in the Big City*, and Marco Bellocchio's *Good Morning, Night*—compare well with the Italian canon and received a commercial consensus from the Italian public. Yet these latest efforts by Italian directors did not break out of domestic distribution to attain the sort of international recognition and awards historically vital to the Italian cinema. Despite the quality of its products, the lack of possibility for international distribuutiuon and the structural changes to the domestic film distribution theatrical network have challenged the Italian cinema's ability to remain a vital force in the nation's culture, a prospect shared by many national cinemas.

The cinema was introduced in Italy, as in much of the world, by the early 1900s. Television arrived in Italy, again as in much of the world, in the mid-1950s, an event that brought dramatic changes to the Hollywood film industry and later to the Italian film industry. Some 100 years after the introduction of cinema and 50 years after the introduction of television, there is further competition from new forms of entertainment media such as video games, the Internet, satellite and cable television, even television and film broadcasts via cellular telephone. Maverick directors Barbara Seghezzi and Marcello Mencarini shot a 93-minute film *Nuovi comizi d'amore* (2006) entirely on a Nokia N90 cell phone. The title is a homage to Pasolini's documentary *Comizi d'amore/Assembly of Love* (1963) about the sexual attitudes of Italians. Such new formats will undoubtedly have further impact on the number of theaters available for the traditional market release of a film, and will continue to contribute to changes in the Italian cinema and the distribution of visual entertainment media in the future.

Appendix 1: Short Introduction to Film Study

The next few pages offer an alphabetical list of topics often used in the critical evaluation of film with sample questions to aid in the critical discussion.[1]

Acting/Actors/Stars

The cinema has long been driven by the visual appeal of its actors. Acting styles have changed since the silent days from the pantomime of the *diva* to the preference for nonprofessionals in the neorealist period to the present close connection between television, new media, and film. Silent-era actors in particular were universally popular because of the lack of linguistic barriers in their performances. Over the decades the personas of certain actors has even become identified with national, cultural, and class identities as well as with the style of living and attitudes in various time periods. In Italy, actors such as Alberto Sordi and Marcello Mastroianni were widely identified with the basic character traits of the Italian populace as were female stars such as Sophia Loren, Monica Vitti, or Anna Magnani.

What type of acting style is used (nonprofessionals, method acting, theatrical, star persona)?

Audience

Film industries, including Italy, have periodically changed the type of films they produce in response to changes in target audiences. In the United States for example, Hollywood film production was targeted toward a female audience until the 1960s when the target audience became increasingly younger and male. In Italy, production in the 1960s and 1970s and thereafter introduced entertainment (art cinema, erotically charged cinema) not available on television because of censorship codes.

What was the intended audience of the film?

How was the film received when released?

How has the film aged?

Camera techniques

Film theorists such as Christian Metz and Pier Paolo Pasolini wrote of the ability of shot selection to provide a language for film.[2] The image on the screen has been filmed through the eye of a camera, which approaches its subject from certain angles and movements. Techniques used with a camera **lens** can include **zoom** or **telephoto** variations that will increase the size of an object in relation to the frame, or a **wide angle** which conversely pulls the camera frame back. An **anamorphic lens** may be used for making films for wide screen projection. Cameras may also have a **filter** of glass or gelatin in order to change the color and hue of the image that is exposed onto the **film stock** which may also be manipulated to change the final image. For example the use of a **dupe negative** may give a rough documentary tone. The photographic image is limited by its **framing**, which allows for the reduction, deletion, or magnification of images. There are established standards for frame ratios or the **aspect ration** of a frame's width to height.

Decisions about **lighting** are essential, especially in black-and-white film. The proportion of light to dark in a scene is called **tonality** and is important in creating mood and atmosphere. A **low-key tonality** is achieved when more than half the image on the screen is devoted to darks and half-tone values, so as to give an aura of ominous foreboding, fear, or the mystery of romance. A scene is in **high-key tonality**, instead, when more than half the image is committed to light bright values to suggest cheerfulness and gaiety. An extremely bright white hue, however, may suggest coldness, lack of human values, and alienation. In color film certain colors may be used to portray emotions or in relation to specific character and plot elements.

A director's and cinematographer's choices are evident in the kinds of shots used. Sequences are presented with what may be called either an **objective** or **subjective camera**. The objective camera style usually consists of a technique that aims at reproducing the narrative in the most realistic way possible, close to a documentary technique. According to Bazin, De Sica and Zavattini's *Ladri di biciclette/The Bicycle Thief* (1948) is a clear example of such a style, and most neorealist films have a reputation for being shot accordingly. The story, however, or part of it, may also be presented in such a way that the audience feels that they are seeing it through the **point of view** of one of the characters. This subjective camera style is a technique also found in neorealist films, usually to underline the emotional connections between the film characters and the audience. Even in what is considered a paradigm of Neorealist film, Rossellini's *Roma città aperta/Open City* (1945), we have a powerful subjective camera shot whereby when Francesco, Pina's fiancé, is being taken away by the Nazis in a truck, the sequence of Pina running after the truck and being shot, is filmed by a camera on the truck, that is, it is projected as if seen through Francesco' s perspective.

Sometimes the camera is fixed and its movements are exclusively from a pivotal point. A **pan** is the image produced when the camera films its subject horizontally from a fixed position by simply turning on its axis. But a camera may also be in motion with a **crane shot**, a **dolly** or **tracking shot**, moving forward, backward, or diagonally, which create angles to heighten or emphasize the interests of the director. The camera can perform other movements from a fixed position such as the **tilt**, an up or down movement of the camera from a pivotal point. Some other interesting shots are marked by a progressive approach or retreat of the camera eye from its filming subject. In a **zoom-in**, the camera eye approaches its subject, magnifying the details on which it concentrates, while reducing at the same time the area being filmed. With a **zoom-out**, instead, the camera progressively moves away from its subject, connecting it with the surroundings that are being included in the shot. An excellent example of both zoom-in and zoom-out shots is included in the central sequence of Scola's *C'eravamo tanto amati/We All Loved Each Other So Much* (1974). An initial zoom-out includes all three important male characters on a piazza that they exit from three different streets—signaling the different ways of life that each of them will choose from then on. At this point, the camera zooms-in to the center of the piazza onto a chalk-drawing on the pavement, which slowly turns into color with the progressive approaching of the camera eye—signaling the film time change from black-and-white to color.

As with painting where works may be classified as a still life, portrait, or landscape, the camera presents different perspectives. Sometimes characters are presented in **close-up**, a shot that focuses on the head of a person, which may become an **extreme close-up** of facial features, for example, for dramatic concentration. Antonioni often uses close-ups of objects to dramatize their importance in the narrative, as in the opening sequence of *L'eclisse/The Eclipse* (1962). Other figure shots are the **medium shot** waist-up view of a character, the **three quarters shot** (known in Italy as the *piano americano*, the American shot) and the **full shot**, which presents an actor's entire body and is often used to introduce new characters. In the **following shot** the frame shifts to follow the movement of a character or object. The **long shot** frames figures within a wider landscape. With these different size variations are definitions for the amount of time that a shot is held such as the **long take** which is an extended shot of a character or image, often with the intent of communicating a psychological state. An **establishing shot** may be used at the beginning of a film or at the start of a sequence usually to reveal the setting for events may be revoked in a **reestablishing shot**. Sometimes an establishing shot prepares the scene for the general mood of the story or for the type of characters that will be introduced. The Salina estate shown at the opening of Visconti's *Il gattopardo/The Leopard* (1963) in all its imposing grandeur and beauty, and yet only partially cultivated and parched, establishes the right atmosphere for the story of the downfall of the House of Salina conveyed through a melancholic and static narrative mood and the complex and pessimistic character of the Prince. For example, in Visconti' s *The Leopard*, during most of the credits sequence, the camera dwells on the country estate of the Prince of Salina, first from a far away panoramic view, then slowly zooming in on the facade of the villa until it enters through one of the terrace door into the chapel where the family is reciting the evening rosary. These shots clearly establish the social and historical background of the story as well as the upbringing of the members of the Prince's family.

Part of camera techniques involves trick photography where images are photographed in a foreground or background of **photomats** of painted glass or sets with the intention of creating an illusion about a setting. Such special effects as the **process shot** or **matte shots** have given way to entirely digital computer-generated imagery or the use of backgrounds such as **bluescreens** onto which generated imagery may be applied through the use of computer graphics.

Editing

Shot assembling (*mise en scène* in French and *messa in scena* in Italian) is an essential function in constructing the narrative of the films. Single shots are connected together through what in Europe is called **montage** (from the French *monter*, to mount, like in a frame), the process of assembling selected shots into coherent sequences that will form the scenes and episodes of the film narrative. The assembling of the shots is accomplished through **cuts** or transitions when two different shots are joined together so that the second replaces the first. The most common is the **straight cut**, by which one shot is replaced abruptly by a completely different one. A **parallel cut**, or **crosscut**, is narratively significant, as it connects two actions, by presenting them as occurring at the same time. Another common cut is what is called a **jump cut**, which shows a break of continuity in the action. This is especially clear in what is called a **shot-counter shot** sequence, whereby the screen alternatively presents character views. These shots are typical of conversation sequences that create the illusion of natural conversation. A **transition** provides what cannot be found in a cut, that is, a way to smooth over the differences between two shots. A **fade-in** is used to open a film or to start up a new sequence of a film with the gradual appearance of a scene from the black darkened screen. A **fade-out**, on the other hand, is often used to end a scene, a sequence, or the film itself, with the gradual disappearance of a scene to a black, darkened screen. A **dissolve** is an effective device for connecting scenes combining simultaneously the fade-out of an outgoing scene with the fade-in of an incoming one. A **graphic match** or **graphic transition** is when a director ends one sequence on an image with geometrical spatial characteristics that are repeated in a different image with the same characteristics to start the next scene or sequence. Another similar connecting device is provided by **super-imposition**, the simultaneous printing of one over the other of two or more scenes, often to connote   stream-of-consciousness. In the sequence from Scola's *We All Loved Each Other So Much* previously mentioned, the image of the color drawing on the pavement of the piazza in which the zoom-in ends, gradually fades-out through dissolve into a fade-in scene, also in color, that starts a totally new sequence about Gianni, one of the main characters of the story.

Similar devices that stress psychological or emotional connections, while showing, however, a clear difference in time dimension, are the **flash-back** or **flash-forward** devices. They are important filmic elements, in as much as they provide a way by which film can show either past or future, that is, a time dimension different from the present. A flash-back, in facts, portrays events that occurred before the action happening on the screen in the present, whereas a flash-forward portrays events that will occur in the future. Flash-forwards may be used to project events simply imagined or fantasized by a character, as in the case of the flash-forward projected by the youngest of Rosi's *Three Brothers* about his relationship with his wife. Both flash-backs and flash forwards provide a crutch to compensate for the inability of cinema—a perceptual form—to change its time dimension from present to past or future.

Is there a particular pattern of camera movements in the film? For example—close up, extreme close-up, medium shot, full shot, three-quarters shot, pan shot, shot reverse shot pattern, cuts (jump, continuity, match, cross), long take, crane shot, tracking shot, zoom, low angle, high angle, eye line matching?

Are there patterns to the editing of the film? Are there occasions when the director prefers editing (montage) versus long shots?

Where is the story presented by objective versus subjective camera shots?

Do important events occur off camera?

How does the camera work create or reinforce the point of view of characters?

Are there patterns in the theatrical composition of the sets in the film?

Are the sets realistic or do they seem artificial?

Is the lighting and tinting of scenes overtly artificial or does it seem natural?

Cultural Influences (National, Literary, Foreign)

National cinemas have been defined by the various movements that critics have created, which are often identified with certain periods of film production and specific directors who seem to work in a certain style. Examples include French poetic realism (1930s), French New Wave (1950s and 1960s), German Expressionism (1920s and 1930s), Soviet formalism (silent period to 1940s), cinéma vérité (1950s and 1960s), Brazilian *cinema novo* (1960s and 1970s). The most dominant of these schools has been provided by the Hollywood commercial model as well as so-called independent Hollywood film. The most recognized school of Italian filmmaking is the Italian neorealist movement (1940s and 1950s), but Italy has also offered models in genres such as the *telefono bianco* (white telephone) film of the 1930s and *commedia all'italiana* (Italian style comedy) of the 1950s and 1960s, the spaghetti western of the 1960s, and the art cinema of the 1950s, 1960s and 1970s. A national cinema can be examined from the manner in which it may be identified with certain genres, such as the western for Hollywood cinema and the manner in which certain national cinemas echo deeper cultural traditions. Critics have noted, for example, that the cinema of India has narrative roots in the epic cycles the *Mahabharata* and the *Ramayana*.[3] Hollywood cinema often feature films with a three-act structure (boy meets girl, boy loses girl, chase to resolution). Other national cinemas have more tragic narratives such as the French cinema's narratives which echo the country's often traditions in tragic Romantic literature or the often circular plot structure of Italian cinema.[4]

National cinemas may also be identified for the manner in which they continue literary or visual art traditions or as a reflection of the historic essence of a national experience such as the similarity between the *commedia all'italiana* films and the theatrical tradition of the *commedia dell'arte*. Often the difficulty a film may have with censorship is a good indication of an occasion in which a film touches upon themes that offend or threaten a political establishment's concept of national cultural identity.

Italy also offers a unique case for the study of ethnic issues, since the country has been a multiethnic collection of languages and ethnic groups due to the periodic invasions of the peninsula. Italy also offers a case of a country that was a supplier of emigrants in the nineteenth and early twentieth centuries to a country that is a destination for immigration. Ethnic issues in an Italian context in the twentieth century were largely limited to the antagonism between northern and southern Italians, a societal dynamic that has evolved with immigration from outside of Europe to Italy.

What cultural influences are at work in this film?

How does the film fit or break with its national tradition?

Did the film have trouble with censorship?

Are there connections to other art forms (painting, literature) or historical processes and traditions?

Does the film treat issues of ethnic, religious, sexual or geographic discrimination and difference?

How are these issues resolved and how do they reflect the period in which the film was made?

Film Theory

A popular method for the academic analysis of film is to apply a theoretical paradigm to a certain film or the work of a filmmaker. Theories in vogue with critics have changed just as artistic preferences over the course of time. The traditional aesthetic approach is for a film or work of art to be judged or understood by its ability to provoke reaction due to its aesthetic qualities.[5] Another foundational method of film analysis is the model whereby the work of a director or period is examined for how it mimicks and replicates the larger cultural influences that produced it. This idea is as ancient as Aristotle's concept of *mimesis* and the realist tradition in the arts. In film theory, Siegfried Kracauer in the late 1940s wrote a history of the German cinema of the interwar period as a reflection of the mass consciousness of the German people. One of the most influential critical theories has been the idea of *auteurism* (from the French for "author"). The *auteur* theory studied the works of selected directors (for example, John Ford, Nicolas Ray, Jean Renoir, Roberto Rossellini) as an expression of the personality or vision of the director. This method has a long history in Italian culture. In the high

Renaissance, the painter Giorgio Vasari (1511–74) wrote accounts of the lives of important Italian artists by finding (often inventing) a story with a didactic moralizing lesson, as was popular among historians of his day for artists such as Michelangelo Buonarroti—"the universal genius," Leonardo Da Vinci—"the tortured soul unable to complete his projects," and Rafaello Sanzio—"the talent extinguished too soon."[6] In the study of film this tradition of examining a work as an expression of the personality and genius of an individual artist was developed by French critic and theoretical patron of the French New Wave, André Bazin.[7]

By the 1960s, film theory began to adopt other approaches, often borrowed from disciplines such as the social sciences and literary studies. Formalist theories study narrative according to basic plot formats as in fairy tales. Structuralism is a term borrowed from the social sciences that applied the data gathering methods of the hard sciences to the social sciences. Attempts to mimick so-called structuralist methods to film study were undertaken by Metz's *Grand synthematique*, Pasolini, Roland Barthes with his textual analysis, and the semiotic approaches of Ferdinand Saussure, Umberto Eco, and Peter Wollen.[8]

Much of the attention of film theorists has centered on the influence of avant garde movements or counter or oppositional cinema, for the manner in which certain directors or films challenge the status quo and reveal the plot and cultural assumptions made by classical Hollywood cinema so dominant from the early sound period until the decline of the Hollywood studio system in the late 1950s. For example, feminist theory has examined the way in which film opposes or confirms patriarchal structures in the writings of theorists such as Teresa De Lauretiis and Laura Mulvey, who developed an interpretation of the cinema as an extension of the "male gaze" with a reading of Alfred Hitchcock's film *Rear Window* (1954).[9]

Another influence has been from the Marxist theories of critics such as Antonio Gramsci and in particular his concept of hegemony, which indicates how the power of a dominant class is not limited to economic power but extends to the tendency of subordinates to interpret reality and act in accordance with the dominant mindset. Louis Althusser identified some cultural production as the result of industrial apparatuses, which promote the dominant hegemony and emphasize economic and class-based realities. Marxist theory ascribes to the idea that cultural output is a superstructure, which is the result of deeper economic forces resulting from the economic and class structure of society.

In the early postwar period, the psychoanalytical theories of Sigmund Freud gained increasing diffusion and reached the level of mass entertainment with the many psychologically laced *noir* films produced in Hollywood, in particular. The *noir* has not been a particularly frequent object of films by Italian directors, nevertheless the influence of psychoanalytical theories, which discern a sexual basis for human interaction (the Oedipal trajectory) or at the basis of visual culture (Jacque Lacan's mirror stage theories), were widely used by film academics, particularly into the 1980s. These theories did influence Italian art cinema directors such as Fellini, Antonioni and Visconti.

Which theoretical model is applicable to the film (Marxism, psychoanalysis, textual analysis, semiotics, the reflectivist model, auteurism, feminism)?

Industry History/Marketing

In Italy the vicissitudes of the film industry have had a strong effect on the type and number of films made. The economic history of the Italian film industry may arguably be divided into six periods.

(1) The silent era of international distribution.
(2) Decline in the 1920s after WWI and the influx of competition from Hollywood.

(3) The early sound period of the 1930s. The Italian film industry offers film in the Italian language to a national audience, aided by the trade barriers (1938) set by the fascist government against Hollywood films.

(4) The rebuilding of the Italian film industry after WWII, aided by government laws requiring theaters to screen domestic films a fixed number of days per year.

(5) The late 1950s and 60s with the banner year of 1960 in which, the Italian film industry is second in the world and first in Europe.

(6) Decline in production in the late-1970s to the present due to competition with television and new media, and with other new national cinemas, despite relaxing of censorship.

When was the film made?

Did national/international conditions in the film industry and the larger economic picture condition the film?

Narrative

Rules of narrative regarding action, characters, themes, and mood were first defined by Aristotle who was writing about the theater. Aristotle divided theatrical performances between tragedy where characters end badly and must expiate their pride or hubris, and comedy, which features resolutive marriages between characters and happy endings. Other important theories of narrative from the Russian formalist school have focused on the tendency of basic story lines of equilibrium establishment, disruption, and reestablishment to repeat in fairy tales.

In film, the study of narrative has focused on the idea of **genre** or type of film. Since its earliest days the cinema has followed the divisions in literature in the type of films and the conventions that an audience expects of those genres.[10] Shot selection, soundtracks, and the overall *mise en scène* of a film and its genre are often closely related and defined by conventions. Over the course of film history, audiences have been conditioned to expect certain types of camera work, music, and narrative patterns according to different types of films. The definition of specific genres is often dependent on narrative tendencies and historical settings, which can vary and even overlap. The **documentary** was a pivotal form from the earliest days of newsreels to the copying of documentary style by the postwar neorealists. The **peplum** is a historical drama about the ancient world. Other **historical dramas** have also constituted definite currents in the Italian cinema such as the Medieval/Renaissance drama, the Unification/Risorgimento drama, the Fascist era/WWII drama, and lately the 1970s drama. Comedy in Italy has also gone through various incarnations from the slapstick of the silent period to the *telefono bianco* (white telephone) romantic comedy of the 1930s to the *commedia all'italiana* social comedies mainly of the 1950s and 1960s, and the sexy comedy of the 1970s. Comedies have been a constant in Italian production as exemplified by the careers of comedians such as Ettore Petrolini, Totò, Macario, Alberto Sordi to more recent actor directors such as Roberto Benigni, Massimo Troisi, Nanni Moretti, Carlo Verdone. The Italian cinema has offered musical **biopics** about Italian operatic or historical figures, which were among the most popular Italian films from the 1930s to the 1950s, as well as **musicals** featuring popular performers such as Mario Lanza and Domenico Modugno and even musicals adapted to regional realities such as Robert Torre's *Tano da morire*. The Italian cinema has also produced **beach/vacation movies, buddy films, horror films, military farces,** *poliziesco* **crime film, road movies, spaghetti westerns, the spy films.** The Italian cinema offered **melodramas** on the struggle for social elevation from the earliest silent period and *strappalacrime* weepies into the 1950s and 1960s. The famed style of Italian **neorealism** and the later more fatalistic narrative of the Italian art film grew out of the melodramatic genre in which a family or protagonist tries to raise his or her social status. With neorealism there were currents such as *neorealismo rosa* (pink neorealism), which was attentive to audience tastes or *neorealismo nero* (black neorealism), which approached the crime film or psychologically laced *noir* film. The Italian cinema has also developed the **political film** and its corrollary the *instant movie*, which depict political themes or historical events often with an eye toward conspiracy theories.

Does the film conform to ideas about genre (type of film—musical, melodrama, western, horror, crime/psychological thriller, comedy, mystery, buddy film, costume drama, gangster, road, war, etc.)?

What types of characters does the genre in question rely on?

Is the treatment of the genre different in the context of the Italian cinema than in other examples?

Cinematic narrative, like any art form, is subject to the ideological and political influences of the period in which it was made. Italian films of various periods have an ideological component. Whether it is in Catholicism, Consumer/Capitalism, Fascism, antifascism, Femminism, Hedonism, Marxism (Gramsci), Nationalism, Social Darwinism, Third Worldism (Third Cinema), etc.

Does the film express or reject an identifiable ideology?

How is the ideology related to the period in which the film was made?

What position does the film defend or challenge in terms of politics, religion, gender, class, nation?

Just as a literary narrative depends exclusively upon the written word, a filmic narrative comes through visual and audio images. And yet, there are clear connections between books and films. Just as a book has a title page that gives, besides its title, the author's name and the publisher's, a film uses the printed word in the opening titles, where a good amount of information is given about the title, the director, and several other important people who helped in making the film such as the actors, staff, writers, and the producer.

Sometimes the printed word appears outside the lists of opening or ending credits, and becomes a narrative detail that works toward the development of the story and its understanding on the part of the audience. Relying again on Visconti's *The Leopard*, we find a long written explanation about the historical times in which the story is taking place, presented over the background of the Salina's estate during the opening-credits sequence.

An interesting development in the technical development of narrative and screenwriting is the difference between the traditional **Italian screenplay** in which authors divide the manuscript page with visual elements on the left side of a page and sound elements including dialogue on the right side in contrast to the **American** or **Hollywood screenplay**, which combines visual and aural instructions in the format of a theatrical play script.

Why does the movie start and end as it does? How are the opening credits presented? What are the opening and closing shots of the film? How are they related to the story?

What does the title mean in relation to the story?

How does the film end? Is there closure? What is the concluding image?

How is this film different or similar to recent or older classic narrative mainstream Hollywood films or other traditions (Russian formalism, German expressionism, French poetic realism, art cinema, avant-garde, oppositional cinema/distanciation, documentary etc.)?

Is the narrative objective or subjective? From whose point of view?

Is the narrative continuous/seamless or is it disrupted (flashbacks, dissolves)?

What does close analysis of one of the film's three or four key sequences reveal?

Who are the central characters and what might they represent? Are they stereotypes? How do their actions create meaning in the story?

What importance do certain props have to the story?

How is the film different or similar to its literary or theatrical source?

Is the film linked to the artistic vision of the director as an auteur?

How is the film representative of the work of the screenwriter?

Sound

The preparation of the artificial sound track is one of the key tools at a director's disposal for the creation of filmic style. In the opening credits or even precredits, filmmakers often insert visual and/or sound material with suggestions for the narrative. The most important voice devices are to be found in dialogue and narration, the latter usually referring to the voice of a speaker who comments upon the visual events being presented on the screen. The function of narrative in film is close to the written word, that is, it aims at giving additional information—in this case, through sound to the visual content of the screen. Music is used mostly for emotional reinforcement, usually at moments of crisis or suspense, and as a transitional device intended to be identified with a character or location. It may also create the mood of a certain scene or sequence essential to the narrative, creating, just like characters and backgrounds, important connections for the development of the story. Some sound tracks by Italian composers like Fiorenzo Carpi, Ennio Morricone or Nino Rota are powerful enough to immediately identity a specific film or genre. Music can be **internal,** when it is heard by the film characters as well as by the audience, or **external,** when it is heard only by the audience. **Direct sound** is the actual sound when the film was made, which particularly in the case of the Italian cinema is replaced in the process of **post-synchronous sound,** or the creation of a particular sound track of **sound effects, music,** and **dubbing** of Italian for any foreign language spoken by an actor.

How is sound/music used? Are certain musical themes linked to specific characters or plot sequences?

Does the film rely on the work of a specific composer or type of music?

Appendix 2: Box Office

Italian Top Ten, 1945–2005[11]

Data is given for Italian and co production films only in the year of their first release.

1945

1. *Roma città aperta*	Roberto Rosselini
2. *Partenza ore 7*	Mario Mattoli
3. *La vita ricomincia*	Mario Mattoli
4. *Due lettere anonime*	Mario Camerini
5. *O sole mio*	Giacomo Gentiluomo
6. *Il fabbro del convento*	M. Calandri
7. *Il barbiere di Siviglia*	M. Costa
8. *Torna . . . a Sorrento*	C.L. Bragaglia
9. *Un americano in vacanza*	L. Zampa
10. *Abbasso la miseria*	G. Righelli

1946

1. *Aquila nera*	R. Freda
2. *Il bandito*	A. Lattuada
3. *Avanti a lui tremava tutta Roma*	C. Gallone
4. *Furia*	G. Alessandrini
5. *Abasso la richezza*	G. Righelli
6. *Paisà*	R. Rossellini
7. *Il cavaliere del sogno*	C. Mastrocinque
8. *Il sole sorge ancora*	A. Vergano
9. *Mio figlio professore*	R. Castellani
10. *Addio, mia bella Napoli*	M. Bonnard

1947

1. *Come persi la guerra*	C. Borghesio
2. *O.K. John*	C. L. Bragaglia
3. *La figlia del capitano*	M. Camerini
4. *Rigoletto*	C. Gallone

5. *Genoveffa di Brabante*	P. Zeglio
6. *La monaca di Monza*	R. Pacini
7. *La primula bianca*	C. L. Bragaglia
8. *I due orfanelli*	M. Mattoli
9. *Il passatore*	D. Coletti
10. *Tombolo, paradiso nero*	G. Ferroni

1948

1. *Fifa e arena*	M. Mattoli
2. *Natale aal campo 119*	P. Francisci
3. *L'eroe della strada*	C. Borghesio
4. *Totò al giro d'Italia*	M. Mattoli
5. *Anni difficili*	L. Zampa
6. *Il diavolo bianco*	N. Malasomma
7. *La signora delle camelie*	C. Gallone
8. *Ladri di biciclette*	Vittorio De Sica
9. *L'ebreo errante*	G. Alessandrini
10. *Follie per l'opera*	M. Costa

1949

1. *La sepolta viva*	G. Brignone
2. *Fabiola*	A. Blasetti
3. *In nome della legge*	P. Germi
4. *I pompieri di Viggiù*	M. Mattoli
5. *L'imperatore di Capri*	L. Comencini
6. *Riso amaro*	G. De Santis
7. *Cielo sulla palude*	A. Genina
8. *Il lupo della Sila*	D. Coletti
9. *Totò le Moko*	C. L. Bragaglia
10. *Il bacio di una morta*	G. Brignone

1950

1. *Gli ultimi giorni di Pompei*	P. Moffa/M. L'Herbier
2. *Domani è troppo tardi*	L. Moguy
3. *Il brigante Mussolino*	M. Camerini
4. *Catene*	R. Matarazzo
5. *Il ladro di Venezia*	J. Brahm
6. *Totò sceicco*	M. Mattoli
7. *Il caimano del Piave*	G. Bianchi
8. *I cadetti di Guascogna*	M. Mattoli
9. *47 morto che parla*	C. L. Bragaglia
10. *Napoli milionaria*	E. De Filippo

1951

1. *I figli di nessuno*	R. Matarazzo
2. *Tormento*	R. Matarazzo

3. *Trieste mia*	M. Costa
4. *Guardie e ladri*	Steno/M. Monicelli
5. *Enrico Caruso*	M. Gentilomo
6. *Messalina*	C. Gallone
7. *La portatrice del pane*	M. Cloche
8. *Totò terzo uomo*	M. Mattoli
9. *Io sono il Capataz*	G. C. Simonelli
10. *O.K. Nerone*	M. Soldati

1952

1. *Don Camillo*	J. Duvivier
2. *Anna*	A. Lattuada
3. *Totò a colori*	Steno
4. *Canzoni di mezzo secolo*	D. Paolella
5. *Core 'ngrato*	G. Brignone
6. *La nemica*	G. Bianchi
7. *Sensualità*	C. Fracassi
8. *Altri tempi*	A. Blasetti
9. *La regina di Saba*	C. Francisci
10. *Totò e le donne*	Steno/M. Monicelli

1953

1. *Pane amore e fantasia*	L. Comencini
2. *Giuseppe Verdi*	R. Matarazzo
3. *Il ritorno di Don Camillo*	J. Duvivier
4. *Puccini*	C. Gallone
5. *Perdonami*	M. Costa
6. *Aida*	C. Fracassi
7. *Il turco napoletano*	M. Mattoli
8. *I vitelloni*	F. Fellini
9. *Canzoni canzoni canzoni*	D. Paolella
10. *Lucrezia Borgia*	C. Jacque

1954

1. *Ulisse*	M. Camerini
2. *Pane amore e gelosia*	L. Comencini
3. *Giulietta e Romeo*	R. Castellani
4. *Carosello napoletano*	G. Giannini
5. *L'oro di Napoli*	V. De Sica
6. *Maddalena*	A. Genina
7. *Senso*	L. Visconti
8. *Mambo*	R. Rossen
9. *Casa Ricordi*	C. Gallone
10. *La romana*	L. Zampa

1955

1. *Guerra e pace*	K. Vidor
2. *La donna più bella del mondo*	Z.R. Leonard

3. *Marcellino pane e vino*	L. Vajda
4. *Pane, amore e . . . .*	D. Risi
5. *Don Camillo e l'onorevole Peppone*	C. Gallone
6. *Racconti romani*	G. Franciolini
7. *Siamo uomini o caporali*	C. Mastrocinque
8. *La bella mugnaia*	M. Camerini
9. *Il segno di venere*	D. Risi
10. *La Risaia*	R. Matarazzo

1956

1. *Poveri ma belli*	D. Risi
2. *Il ferroviere*	P. Germi
3. *Michele Strogoff*	C. Gallone
4. *Guaglione*	G. Simonelli
5. *Totò Peppino e la malafemmena*	C. Mastrocinque
6. *Le schiave di Cartagine*	G. Brignone
7. *Donatella*	M. Monicelli
8. *Maruzzella*	L. Capuano
9. *Canzone proibita*	F. Calzavara
10. *Montecarlo*	Sam Taylor

1957

1. *Belle ma povere*	D. Risi
2. *Lazzarella*	C.L. Bragaglia
3. *Arrivederci Roma*	R. Rowland/M. Russo
4. *La diga sul pacifico*	R. Clement
5. *Vacanze a Ischia*	M. Camerini
6. *Souvenire d'Italie*	A. Pietrangeli
7. *La Nonna Sabella*	D. Risi
8. *Mariti in città*	L. Comencini
9. *La Gerusalemme liberata*	C.L. Bragaglia
10. *Orlando e i Paladini di Francia*	P. Francisi

1958

1. *La tempesta*	A. Lattuada
2. *La maja desnuda*	H. Kostner
3. *I soliti ignoti*	M. Monicelli
4. *Le fatiche di Ercole*	P. Francisi
5. *I miserabili*	J. P. Le Chanois
6. *Racconti d'estate*	G. Franciolini
7. *Mogli pericolose*	L. Comencini
8. *Venezia, la luna e tu*	D. Risi
9. *Anna di Brooklyn*	C. Lastricati
10. *La rivolta dei gladiatori*	V. Cottafavi

1959

1. *La grande guerra*	M. Monicelli
2. *Europa di notte*	A. Blasetti
3. *Ercole e la regina di Lidia*	Pietro Francisi
4. *Peccatori in blue jeans*	Marcel Carne
5. *Gli ultimi giorni di Pompeii*	M. Bonnard
6. *Terrore dei barbari*	R. Campogalliani
7. *L'audace colpo dei soliti ignoti*	Nanni Loy
8. *Costa azzurra*	Vittorio Sala
9. *Il Generale della Rovere*	R. Rossellini
10. *Nel segno di Roma*	G. Brignone/Riccardo Freda

1960

1. *La dolce vita*	Federico Fellini
2. *Rocco e i suoi fratelli*	Luchino Visconti
3. *La Ciociara*	Vittorio De Sica
4. *Tutti a casa*	Luigi Comencini
5. *Il mondo di notte*	Luigi Vanzi
6. *Crimen*	Mario Camerini
7. *Il vigile*	Luigi Zampa
8. *Sotto dieci bandiere*	Dulio Coletti
9. *Il gobbo*	Carlo Lizzani
10. *Jovanka e le altre*	Martin Ritt

1961

1. *El Cid*	Anthony Mann
2. *Barabba*	Richard Fleischer
3. *Divorzio all'italiana*	Pietro Germi
4. *Don Camillo Monsignore ma non troppo*	Carmine Gallone
5. *I due nemici*	Guy Hamilton
6. *Una vita difficile*	Dino Risi
7. *Il federale*	Luciano Salce
8. *Madame Sans Gene*	Christian Jacque
9. *Giuseppe venduto dai fratelli*	Irving Rapper
10. *La guerra di Troia*	Giorgio Ferroni

1962

1. *Il sorpasso*	D. Risi
2. *Sodoma e Gomorra*	R. Aldrich/S. Leone
3. *Boccaccio '70*	F. Fellini, L. Visconti, V. De Sica, M. Monicelli
4. *Il figlio di Spartacus*	Sergio Corbucci
5. *Mondo cane*	G. Jacopetti
6. *Il mafioso*	A. Lattuada

7. *Le quattro giornate di Napoli*	N. Loy
8. *Venere imperiale*	Jean Delannoy
9. *La marcia su Roma*	D. Risi
10. *Salvatore Giuliano*	Francesco Rosi

1963

1. *Il gattopardo*	L. Visconti
2. *Ieri, oggi e domani*	V. De Sica
3. *La ragazza di Bube*	L. Comencini
4. *La noia*	Damiano Damiani
5. *Una storia moderna—l'ape regina*	Marco Ferreri
6. *I mostri*	D. Risi
7. *Il successo*	Mauro Morassi
8. *La donna nel mondo—Eva sconosciuta*	Gualtieri Japopetti
9. *Otto e mezzo*	F. Fellini
10. *Il processo di Verona*	Carlo Lizzani

1964

1. *Per un pugno di dollari*	S. Leone
2. *Matrimonio all'italiana*	V. De Sica
3. *Angelica*	Bernard Borderie
4. *Il magnifico cornuto*	A. Pietrangeli
5. *Due mafiosi nel far West*	G. Simonelli
6. *002 Agenti segretissimi*	Lucio Fulci
7. *La congiuntura*	Ettore Scola
8. *Due evasi di Sing Sing*	Lucio Fulci
9. *I due torreri*	G. Simonelli
10. *Sedotta e abbandonata*	P. Germi

1965

1. *Per qualche dollaro in più*	S. Leone
2. *Un dollaro bucato*	G. Ferroni
3. *Adios Gringo*	G. Stregani
4. *Una pistola per Ringo*	Duccio Tessari
5. *Il ritorno di Ringo*	Duccio Tessari
6. *Sette uomini d'oro*	Marco Vicario
7. *Centomila dollari per Ringo*	Alberto De Martino
8. *Due mafiosi contro Goldfinger*	Giorgio Simonelli
9. *I complessi*	D. Risi, F. Rossi, L.F. D'Amico
10. *Per un dollaro a Tucson si muore*	C. Canevari

1966

1. *Il buono, il brutto e il cattivo*	S. Leone
2. *La Bibbia*	John Huston
3. *L'armata Brancaleone*	M. Monicelli
4. *Operazione San Gennaro*	Dino Risi

5. *Africa addio*	G. Jacopetti
6. *Il grande colpo dei sette uomini d'oro*	Marco Vicario
7. *Signore e signori*	Pietro Germi
8. *Per pochi dollari ancora*	Giorgio Ferroni
9. *L'arcidiavolo*	Ettore Scola
10. *Arizona colt*	Michele Lupo

1967

1. *Dio perdona . . . io no!*	Alfio Colizzi
2. *I giorni dell'ira*	Tonino Valerii
3. *Bella di giorno*	Luis Bunuel
4. *La resa dei conti*	S. Sollima
5. *La bisbetica domata*	F. Zeffirelli
6. *Il tigre*	D. Risi
7. *Da uomo a uomo*	G. Petroni
8. *C'era una volta*	Francesco Rosi
9. *Wanted*	G. Ferroni
10. *Faccia a faccia*	S. Sollima

1968

1. *Serafino*	P. Germi
2. *Il medico della mutua*	L. Zampa
3. *C'era una vola il West*	S. Leone
4. *I quattro dell'Ave Maria*	Alfio Colizzi
5. *Straziami ma di baci saziami*	D. Risi
6. *Bora Bora*	Ugo Libertadore
7. *Riusciranno i nostri eroi . . . ?*	E. Scola
8. *La ragazza con la pistola*	M. Monicelli
9. *Banditi a Milano*	C. Lizzani
10. *Il giorno della civetta*	D. Damiani

1969

1. *Nell'anno del signore*	L. Magni
2. *Il Prof. Dott. Guido Tersilli*	L. Salce
3. *Vedo nudo*	D. Risi
4. *La caduta degli Dei*	L. Visconti
5. *Amore mio aiutami*	A. Sordi
6. *La collina degli stivali*	G. Colizzi
7. *Fellini Satyricon*	F. Fellini
8. *La monaca di Monza*	E. Visconti
9. *Metti una sera a cena*	G. Patroni Griffi
10. *Il commissario Pepe*	E. Scola
11. *Queimada*	G. Pontecorvo

1970

1. *Lo chiamavano Trinità*	E. Barboni
2. *La moglie del prete*	D. Risi

3. *Anonimo veneziano*   E.M. Salerno
4. *I girasoli*   V. De Sica
5. *Borsalino*   J. Defray
6. *Il prete sposato*   M. Vicario
7. *Venga a prendere il caffè fa noi*   A. Lattuada
8. *Indagine su un cittadino al di sopra*   E. Petri
9. *Brancaleone alle croiate*   M. Monicelli
10. *Presidente del Borgorosso Football Club*   L.F. D'Amico

1971

1. *Continuavano a chiamarlo Trinità*   E. Barboni
2. *Il Decameron*   P.P. Pasolini
3. *Per grazia ricevuta*   N. Manfredi
4. *Bello onesto emigrato australia sposerebbe*   L. Zampa
5. *Sole rosso*   T. Young
6. *Giù la testa*   S. Leone
7. *Il gatto a nove code*   D. Argento
8. *Er più—storia d'amore e di coltello*   S. Corbucci
9. *Quattro mosche di velluto grigio*   D. Argento
10. *Homo eroticus*   M. Vicario

1972

1. *Ultimo tango a Parigi*   B. Bertolucci
2. *Più forte ragazzi*   A. Colizzi
3. *Mimì metallurgico ferito nell'onore*   L. Wertmüller
4. *E poi lo chiamavano il magnifico*   E. Barboni
5. *La quiete prima della notte*   V. Zurlini
6. *Alfredo, Alfredo*   P. Germi
7. *Joe Valachi—i segreti di cosa nostra*   T. Young
8. *I racconti di Canterbury*   P.P. Pasolini
9. *Lo chiameremo Andrea*   V. De Sica
10. *Una ragione per sopravivere una per morire*   T. Valerii

1973

1. *Malizia*   S. Samperi
2. *Sessomatto*   D. Risi
3. *Il mio nome è nessuno*   T. Valerii
4. *Anche gli angeli mangiano fagioli*   E. Barboni
5. *Amarcord*   F. Fellini
6. *Paolo il caldo*   M. Vicario
7. *Piedone lo sbirro*   Steno
8. *Pane e ciocolata*   F. Brusati
9. *Zanna bianca*   L. Fulci
10. *L'emigrante*   Festa Campanile

1974

1. *Altirmenti ci arrabbiamo*	M. Fondato
2. *Porgi l'altra guancia*	F. Rossi
3. *Peccato veniale*	S. Samperi
4. *Il bestione*	S. Corbucci
5. *Romanzo popolare*	M. Monicelli
6. *Travoli da un insolito destino . . .*	L. Wertmüller
7. *C'eravamo tanto amati*	E. Scola
8. *Serpico*	S. Lumet
9. *Il portiere di notte*	L. Cavani
10. *Ultime grida alla savana*	A. Climati/M. Morra

1975

1. *Amici miei*	M. Monicellı
2. *Fantozzi*	L. Salce
3. *Di che segno sei?*	S. Corbucci
4. *A mezzanotte va la ronda del piacere*	M. Fondato
5. *Paolo Barca mestro elementare praticamente nudista*	F. Mogherini
6. *Yuppi du*	A. Celentano
7. *L'anatra all'arancia*	L. Salce
8. *Piedone a Hong Kong*	Steno
9. *Il padrone e l'operaio*	Steno
10. *Profondo rosso*	D. Argento

1976

1. *Novecento (I, II)*	B. Bertolucci
2. *Bluff storie di truffe e imbroglioni*	S. Corbucci
3. *Sturmtruppen*	S. Sampieri
4. *Cassandra Crossing*	P.G. Cosmatos
5. *Il corsaro nero*	S. Sollima
6. *Il secondo tragico Fantozzi*	L. Salce
7. *Salon Kitty*	T. Brass
8. *Il soldato di ventura*	Festa Camapanile
9. *Quelle strane occasioni*	L. Comencini
10. *L'innocente*	L. Visconti

1977

1. *Due superpiedi quasi piatti*	E. Barboni
2. *La stanza del vescovo*	D. Risi
3. *Ecco noi per esempio*	S. Corbucci
4. *Suspira*	D. Argento
5. *Un borghese piccolo piccolo*	M. Monicelli
6. *L'altra metà del cielo*	F. Rossi
7. *Tre tigri contro tre tigri*	S. Corbucci/Steno

8. *Porci con le ali*	P. Pietrangeli
9. *Marito in collegio*	M. Lucidi
10. *Prefetto di ferro*	P. Squittieri

1978

1. *Il vizietto*	E. Molinaro
2. *Amori miei*	Steno
3. *Pari e dispari*	M. Amendola S. Corbucci
4. *La mezzetta*	S. Corbucci
5. *Dove vai in vacanza?*	A. Sordi/M. Bolognini/L. Salce
6. *Come perdere una moglie . . . e trovare un'amante*	Festa Campanile
7. *L'albero degli zoccoli*	E. Olmi
8. *Eutanasia di un amore*	Enrico Maria Salerno
9. *Coreleone*	Pasquale Squittieri
10. *Geppo il folle*	A. Celentano

1979

1. *Qua la mano*	Pasuale Festa Campanile
2. *Il malato immaginario*	Tonino Cervi
3. *Mani di velluto*	Franceo Castellano, Giuseppe Moccia
4. *Cafè Express*	Nanni Loy
5. *Io sto con gli ippopotami*	Italo Zingarelli
6. *Ratataplan*	Maurizio Nichetti
7. *La patata bollente*	Steno
8. *Il ladrone*	Pasquale Festa Campanile
9. *Inferno*	Dario Argento
10. *La luna*	Bernardo Bertolucci

1980

1. *Il bisbetico domato*	Franco Castellano, Giuseppe Moccia
2. *Ricomincio da tre*	Massimo Troisi
3. *Fantozzi contro tutti*	Luciano Salce
4. *Il pap'occhio*	Renzo Arbore
5. *Mia moglie è una strega*	Franco Castellano, Giuseppe Moccia
6. *Asso*	Franco Castellano, Giuseppe Moccia
7. *Il vizietto II*	Edouard Molinaro
8. *Zucchero e miele e*	Sergio Martino
9. *Mi faccio la barba*	Sergio Corbucci
10. *Io e Caterina*	Alberto Sordi

1981

1. *Innamorato pazzo*	Franco Castellano, Giuseppe Moccia
2. *Il marchese del grillo*	Mario Monicelli
3. *Culo e camicia*	Pasquale Festa Campanile
4. *Nessuno è perfetto*	Pasquale Festa Campanile
5. *Eccezziunale . . . veramente*	Carlo Vanzina
6. *I fichissimi*	Carlo Vanzina
7. *Fracchia e la belva umana*	Neri Parenti

8. *Pierino contro tutti*	Marino Girolami
9. *Il tango della gelosia*	Steno
10. *Borotalco*	Carlo Verdone

1982

1. *Grand Hotel Excelsior*	Franco Castellano Giuseppe Moccia
2. *Amici miei Atto II*	Mario Monicelli
3. *In viaggio con papa*	Alberto Sordi
4. *Scusate il ritardo*	Massimo Troisi
5. *Bingo bongo*	Pasquale Festa Campanile
6. *Testa o croce*	Nanni Loy
7. *Sapore di mare*	Carlo Vanzina
8. *Tenebre*	Dario Argento
9. *Io so che tu sai che io so*	Alberto Sordi
10. *Il conte Tacchia*	Sergio Corbucci

1983

1. *La chiave*	Tinto Brass
2. *Segni particolari bellissimo*	Franco Castellano Giuseppe Moccia
3. *Vacanza di natale*	Carlo Vanzina
4. *Il tassinaro*	Alberto Sordi
5. *Mi manda Piccone*	Nanni Loy
6. *Sing Sing*	Sergio Corbucci
7. *Acqua e sapone*	Carlo Verdone
8. *Fantozzi subisce ancora*	Neri Parenti
9. *Sapore di mare 2 un anno dopo*	Bruno Cortini
10. *Bianca*	Nanni Moretti

1984

1. *Non ci resta che piangere*	Roberto Benigni/Massmio Troisi
2. *I due carabinieri*	Carlo Verdone
3. *Lui è peggio di me*	Enrico Oldoini
4. *C'era una volta l'America*	Sergio Leone
5. *Phenomena*	Daio Argento
6. *Così parlò Bellavista*	Luciano De Crescenzo
7. *Il ragazzo di campagna*	Franco Castellano Giuseppe Moccia
8. *Bertoldo Bertolino e Cacasenno*	Mario Monicelli
9. *Casablanca Casablanca*	Francesco Nuti

1985

1. *Amici miei Atto III*	Nanni Loy
2. *Speriamo che sia femmina*	Mario Monicelli
3. *Tutta colpa del paradiso*	Francesco Nuti
4. *Troppo forte*	Carlo Verdone
5. *Miranda*	Tinto Brass
6. *Yuppies*	Carlo Vanzina

7. *Maccheroni*	Ettore Scola
8. *Joan Lui*	Adriano Celentano
9. *Sotto il vestito niente*	Carlo Vanzina
10. *Un complicato intrigo di . . .*	Lina Wertmüller

1986

1. *In nome della rosa*	Jean Jacques-Annaud
2. *Yuppies 2*	Enrico Oldoini
3. *7 chili in 7 giorni*	Luca Verdone
4. *Ultimo tango a Parigi (reissue)*	Bernardo Bertolucci
5. *La famiglia*	Ettore Scola
6. *Scuola di ladri*	Neri Parenti
7. *Noi uomini duri*	Maurizio Ponti
8. *Grandi magazzini*	Franco Castellano Giuseppe Moccia
9. *Superfantozzi*	Neri Parenti
10. *Stregati*	Francesco Nuti

1987

1. *L'ultimo imperatore*	Bernardo Bertolucci
2. *Le vie del signore sono finite*	Massimo Troisi
3. *Io e mia sorella*	Carlo Verdone
4. *Opera*	Dario Argento
5. *Da grande*	Franco Amurri
6. *I miei primi 40 anni*	Carlo Vanzina
7. *Montecarlo gran casinò*	Carlo Vanzina
8. *Oci ciorne*	Nikita Mikhalkov
9. *I picari*	Mario Monicelli
10. *Roba da ricchi*	Sergio Corbucci

1988

1. *Il piccolo diavolo*	Roberto Benigni
2. *Caruiso Pascosk: di padre polaccoi*	Francesco Nuti
3. *Compagni di scuola*	Carlo Verdone
4. *Fantozzi va in pensione*	Neri Parenti
5. *La leggenda del santo bevitore . . . .*	Ermanno Olmi
6. *Francesco*	Liliana Cavani
7. *La chiesa*	Michele Soavi
8. *Sotto il vestito niente II*	Carlo Vanzina
9. *Mery per sempre*	Marco Risi
10. *Il frullo del passero*	Gianfranco Minigozzi

1989

1. *Willy signorie vengono da lontano*	Francesco Nuti
2. *Ho vinto la lotteria di Capodanno*	Neri Parenti
3. *La voce della luna*	Federico Fellini
4. *Nuovo cinema paradiso*	Giuseppe Tornatore

5. *Che ora è*	Ettore Scola
6. *Il bambino e il poliziotto*	Carlo Verdone
7. *Leviathan*	George P. Cosmatos
8. *L'avaro*	Tonino Cervi
9. *La palombella rossa*	Nanni Moretti
10. *La più bella del reame*	Cesare Ferrario

1990

1. *Le comiche*	Neri Parenti
2. *Il te nel deserto*	Bernardo Bertolucci
3. *Stasera a casa di Alice*	Carlo Verdone
4. *Fantozzi alla riscossa*	Neri Parenti
5. *Nikita*	Luc Besson
6. *Paprika*	Tinto Brass
7. *Ragazzi fuori*	Marco Risi
8. *Volere volare*	Maurizio Nichetti
9. *Il portaborse*	Daniele Luchetti
10. *Ultra*	Ricky Tognazzi

1991

1. *Johnny Stecchino*	Roberto Benigni
2. *Donne con le gonne*	Francesco Nuti
3. *Vacanze di Natale '91*	Enrico Oldoini
4. *Pensavo fosse amore in vece . . . .*	Massimo Troisi
5. *Maledetto il giorno che*	Carlo Verdone
6. *Le comiche 2*	Neri Parenti
7. *Mediterraneo*	Gabriele Salvatores
8. *Il ladro dei bambini*	Gianni Amelio
9. *Piedi piatti*	Carlo Vanzina
10. *Così fan tutti*	Tinto Brass

1992

1. *Anni 90*	Enrico Oldoini
2. *Sognando la California*	Carlo Vanzina
3. *Puerto Escondido*	Gabriele Salvatores
4. *Al lupo al lupo*	Carlo Verdone
5. *Io speriamo che me la cavo*	Lina Wertmüller
6. *La scorta*	Ricky Tognazzi
7. *Il grande cocomero*	Francesco Archbugi
8. *Nel continente nero*	Marco Risi
9. *Infelci e contenti*	Neri Parenti
10. *Trauma*	Dario Argento

1993

1. *Piccolo Buddha*	Bernardo Bertolucci
2. *Anni 90 parte II*	Enrico Oldoini
3. *Perdiamoci di vista*	Carlo Verdone
4. *Caro diario*	Nanni Moretti
5. *Per amore solo per amore*	Giovanni Veronesi

6. *Maniaci sentimentali*	Simona Izzo
7. *Sud*	Gabriele Salvatores
8. *Giovanni Falcone*	Giuseppe Ferrara
9. *L'uomo che guarda*	Tinto Brass
10. *Il silenzio dei prosciutti*	Ezio Greggio

1994

1. *Il mostro*	Roberto Benigni
2. *SPQR 2000 e ½ anni fa*	Carlo Vanzina
3. *Il postino*	Michael Radford
4. *La scuola*	Daniele Luchetti
5. *Uomini, uomini uomini*	Christian De Sica
6. *Belle al bar*	Alessandro Benvenuti
7. *Occhiopinocchio*	Francesco Nuti
8. *Sostiene Periera*	Roberto Faenza
9. *L'amore molesto*	Mario Martone
10. *Con gli occhi chiusi*	Francesca Archibugi

1995

1. *Viaggi di nozze*	Carlo Verdone
2. *Vacanze di natale '95*	Neri Parenti
3. *Io ballo da sola*	Bernardo Bertolucci
4. *I laureati*	Leonardo Pieraccioni
5. *Va' dove ti porta il cuore*	Cristina Comencini
6. *Selvaggi*	Carlo Vanzina
7. *Al di là delle nuovole*	Michelangelo Antonioni/Wim Wenders
8. *L'uomo delle stelle*	Giuseppe Tornatore
9. *La sindrome di Stendhal*	Dario Argento
10. *Io no spik inglish*	Carlo Vanzina

1996

1. *Il ciclone*	Leonardo Pieraccioni
2. *A spasso nel tempo*	Carlo Vanzina
3. *Nirvana*	Gabriele Salvatores
4. *Sono pazzo di Iris Blond*	Carlo Verdone
5. *L'uomo d'acqua dolce*	Antonio Albanese
6. *Il barbiere di Rio*	Giovanni Veronesi
7. *Fantozzi il ritorno*	Neri Parenti
8. *Bambola*	Bigas Luna
9. *La tregua*	Francesco Rosi
10. *La lupa*	Gabriele Lavia

1997

1. *Fuochi d'artificio*	Leonardo Pieraccioni
2. *La vita è bella*	Roberto Benigni

3. *Tre uomini e una gamba*   Aldo, Giovanni, Giacomo
4. *A spasso nel tempo l'avventura continua*   Carlo Vanzina
5. *Ovosodo*   Paolo Virzì
6. *Il testimone dello sposo*   Pupi Avati
7. *Viola bacia tutti*   G. Veronesi
8. *La parola amore esiste*   M. Calopresti
9. *Auguri professore*   R. Milani
10. *Il macellaio*   A. Grimaldi

1998

1. *Così è la vita—una storia vera*   Aldo, Giovanni, Giacomo
2. *Paparazzi*   Neri Parenti
3. *Gallo Cedrone*   Carlo Verdone
4. *La gabbianella e il gatto*   Enzo d'Alò
5. *Il mio West*   Giovanni Veronesi
6. *La fame e la sete*   Antonio Albanese
7. *La leggenda del pianista sull'oceano*   Giuseppe Tornatore
8. *Il Signor Quindipalle*   Francesco Nuti
9. *Bagnomaria*   Giorgio Panariello
10. *L'amico del cuore*   Vincenzo Salemme
11. *Lucignolo*   Massimo Ceccherini

1999

1. *Il pesce innamorato*   Leonardo Pieraccioni
2. *Vacanze di Natale 2000*   Carlo Vanzina
3. *Tifosi*   Neri Parenti
4. *Amore a prima vista*   Vincenzo Salemme
5. *Canone inverso*   Ricky Tognazzi
6. *Io amo Andrea*   Francesco Nuti
7. *Tutti gli uomini del deficente*   Paolo Costella
8. *C'era un cinese in coma*   Carlo Verdone
9. *E allora mambo!*   Lucio Pellegrini
10. *Guardami*   Davide Ferrario

2000

1. *Chiedimi se sono felice*   Aldo, Giovanni, Giacomo
2. *L'ultimo bacio*   Gabriele Muccino
3. *Body Guards*   Neri Parenti
4. *A ruota libera*   Vincenzo Salemme
5. *Malena*   Giuseppe Tornatore
6. *I cento passi*   Marco Tullio Giordana
7. *Faccia di Picasso*   Massimo Ceccherini
8. *Non ho sonno*   Dario Argento
9. *La lingua del santo*   Carlo Mazzacurati
10. *Amici Ahrarara!*   Franco Amurri

2001

1. *Il principe e il pirata* — Leonardo Pieraccioni
2. *Santa Maradona* — Marco Ponti
3. *Il nostro matrimonio è in crisi* — Antonio Albanese
4. *Da zero a dieci* — Luciano Ligabue
5. *Casomai* — Alessandro D'Alatri
6. *Il più bel giorno della mia vita* — Cristina Comencini
7. *Amnesia* — Gabriele Salvatores
8. *L'ora di religione* — Marco Bellocchio
9. *Volesse il cielo* — Vincenzo Salemme
10. *Ravanello pallido* — Gianni Costantino

2002

1. *Natale sul Nilo* — Neri Parenti
2. *Pinocchio* — Roberto Benigni
3. *La leggenda di Al, John e Jack* — Aldo, Giovanni, Giacomo
4. *Ma che colpa abbiamo noi* — Carlo Verdone
5. *Febbre da cavallo—La mandrakata* — Carlo Vanzina
6. *Un viaggio chiamato amore* — Michele Placido
7. *Il cuore altrove* — Pupi Avati
8. *Il più bel giorno della mia vita* — Cristina Comencini
9. *L'ora di religione* — Marco Bellocchio
10. *Brucio nel vento* — Silvio Soldini

2003

1. *Il paradiso all'improviso* — Leonardo Pieraccioni
2. *Natale in India* — Neri Parenti
3. *L'amore è eterno finché dura* — Carlo Verdone
4. *Le barzellette* — Carlo Vanzina
5. *Che ne sarà di noi* — Giovanni Veronesi
6. *Caterina va in città* — Paolo Virzì
7. *Buongiorno notte* — Marco Bellocchio
8. *Il cartaio* — Dario Argento
9. *Ho visto le stelle* — Vincenzo Salemme
10. *A/R Andata + Ritorno* — Marco Ponti

2004

1. *Christmas in Love* — Neri Parenti
2. *Tu conosci la Claudia* — Massimo Venier
3. *Manuale d'amore* — Giovanni Veronesi
4. *Il mercante di Venezia* — Michael Radford
5. *Le chiavi di casa* — Gianni Amelio
6. *Cuore sacro* — Ferznon Ozpetek
7. *La febbre* — Alessandro D'Alatri
8. *Il ritorno del Monnezza* — Carlo Vanzina
9. *Ovunque sei* — Michele Placido
10. *Ma quando arrivano le ragazze* — Pupi Avati

2005

1. *Natale a Miami* — Neri Parenti
2. *Ti amo in tutte le lingue del mondo* — Leonardo Pieraccioni
3. *Il mio miglior nemico* — Carlo Verdone
4. *La tigre e la neve* — Roberto Benigni
5. *La notte prima degli esami* — Fausto Brizzi
6. *Eccezziunale veramente capitolo secondo* — Carlo Verdone
7. *Il Caimano* — Nanni Moretti
8. *Melissa P.* — Luca Guadagnino
9. *La bestia nel cuore* — Cristina Comencini
10. *Romanzo criminale* — Michele Placido

Appendix 3: The Major Directors

This appendix, by no means complete, presents information about select Italian directors with basic information about their lives and selected filmographies.

Antonioni, Michelangelo (1912–)

Born in Ferrara, Michelangelo Antonioni went to Rome to study at the CSC, the Rome film institute in 1940–41. He also became a film critic for the magazine *Cinema* (1940–49) before writing screenplays for Rossellini, Fellini, and others (1942–52). As a director, he made several documentaries before working on a feature film; including *People from the Po Valley* (1947) and *Sanitation Department* (1948). He developed a signature long-take camera style, which has become part of the language of art cinema.

1943	*Gente del Po/People of the Po River*
	Nettezza urbana/ N.U.
	Oltre l'oblio
	Roma-Montevideo
	L'amorosa menzogna/ Loving Lie
	Bomarzo
	Ragazze in bianco
	Sette canne, un vestito
	Superstizione/ Superstition
1950	*La funivia del faloria*
	Uomini in più
	La villa dei mostri/ The Villa of Monsters
	Cronaca di un amore/Story of a Love Affair
1953	*I vinti/The Vanquished*
	La signora senza camelie/ The Lady without Camelias
	L'amore in città/Love in the City "Tentato suicido" episode
	Le amiche/The Girlfriends
1957	*Il grido/The Outcry*
1960	*L'Avventura*
1961	*La notte/The Night*
1962	*L'eclisse/The Eclipse*
1964	*Il deserto rosso/Red Desert*
1965	*I tre volti/Three Faces of a Woman* "il provino" episode
1966	*Blow-Up*
1970	*Zabrinsky Point*
1972	*Chung Kuo*

1975   *Professione: reporter/The Passenger*
1981   *Il mistero di OberwaldThe Oberwald Mystery*
1982   *Identificazione di una donna/Identification of a Woman*
1989   *12 registi per 12 città "Roma" episode*
1995   *Al di là delle nuvole/Beyond the Clouds*
2004   *Lo sguardo di Michelangelo/Michelangelo Eye to Eye*
       Eros "Il filo pericoloso delle cose" episode

Benigni, Roberto (1952–)

Roberto Benigni was born in Misericordia, Tuscany, into a humble family. In his youth he performed with Tuscan improvising poets (*poeti a braccio*). His breakthrough theatrical monologue *Cioni Mario di Gaspare fu Giulia/Mario Cioni son of Gaspare and the late Giulia* (1975)
was adapted to film as *Berlinguer ti voglio bene/Berlinguer I Love You* (1977) directed by
Giuseppe Bertolucci. As a director Benigni has been the most successful of his generation,
attaining recognition through collaborations with important figures in the Italian cinema history such as Cesare Zavattini and Federico Fellini and receiving awards at Cannes and the Oscar
ceremonies for his film *La vita è bella/Life is Beautiful* (1997). He has also appeared on Italian
television reciting and commenting on Dante's *Divine Comedy* to record-setting audiences.

1983   *Tu mi turbi/You Bother Me*
1985   *Non ci resta che piangere/ Nothing Left to Do But Cry*
1988   *Il piccolo diavolo/ Little Devil*
1991   *Johnny Stecchino/Johnny Toothpick*
1995   *Il Mostro/The Monster*
1997   *La vita è bella/Life Is Beautiful*
2002   *Pinocchio/Roberto Benigni's Pinocchio*
2005   *La tigre e la neve/ The Tiger and the Snow*

Bertolucci, Bernardo (1940–)

He was born in Parma in 1940 and was the son of an important poet, Attillio Bertolucci.
Although strongly attracted to literature and poetry, Bernardo, like his brother the director
Giuseppe, felt the need to excel in a field different from his father's. He moved to Rome and
his first cinematic experience was as assistant director for Pier Paolo Pasolini's *Accattone*
(1961). He made his first feature film in 1962, *The Grim Reaper*, and went on from there to
a successes from his early film in the style of the French New Wave, *Before the Revolution*
(1964), to the huge box office success of his sexually explicit film starring Marlon Brando
Last Tango in Paris and his Oscar winning *The Last Emperor* (1987).

1962   *La comare secca/The Grim Reaper*
1964   *Prima della rivoluzione/Before the Revolution*
1965   *Le vie del petrolio Il canale*
1968   *Partner*
1969   *Lo stratagia del ragno/The Spider's Stratagem*
1970   *Ili conformista/The Conformist*
1972   *Ultimo tango a Parigi/Last Tango in Paris*
1976   *Novecento/1900*
1979   *La luna*

1981	*Tragedia di un uomo ridicolo/Tragedy of a Ridiculous Man*
1987	*The Last Emperor*
1989	*Tè nel deserto/Sheltering Sky 12 registi per 12 città* "Bologna" episode
1993	*Little Buddha*
1996	*Io ballo da sola/Stealing Beauty*1998 *Besieged*2003 *The Dreamers*
1998	*Beseiged*
2002	*Ten Minutes Older* "Histoire d'eaux" episode
2003	*The Dreamers*
2007	*Bel canto*

Blasetti, Alessandro (1900–87)

Born in Rome, Blasetti was one of the chief directors of the early sound period. He began in films influenced by the style of Russian silent film and then moved to specialize in historical dramas before WWII. After the war he returned to filmmaking with colossal productions such as *Fabiola* as well as ground-breaking films featuring *maggiorata fisiche* (buxom actresses) such as *Altri tempi/In Olden Days*. He plays himself in Visconti's *Bellissima* (1951) and De Sica's *Una vita difficile/A Difficult Life*.

1916	*La crociata degli innocenti*
1929	*Sole*
1930	*Nerone*
1931	*Terra madre*
	Resurrectio
1932	*La tavola dei poveri*
	Palio
1933	*Impiegata di Papà*
	Il Caso Haller
1934	*1860/Gesuzza the Garibaldian Wife*
1935	*Vecchia guardia/ Old Guard*
	Aldebaran
1937	*La Contessa di Parma/ Duchess of Parma*
1938	*Ettore Fieramosca*
	Un avventura di Salvator Rosa/An Adventure of Salvator Rosa
1939	*Retroscena*
1941	*La corona di ferro/ Iron Crown*
1942	*La cena delle beffe*
	Quattro passi fra le nuvole/Four Steps in the Clouds
1945	*Nessuno torna indietro/Responsibility Comes Back*
1946	*Un giorno nella vita/A Day in the Life*
1947	*Il duomo di Milano*
	La gemma orientale dei papi
	Fabiola
1950	*Prima comunione/Father's Dilemma*
	Ippodromi all'alba
1951	*La Fiammata, Quelli che soffrono per voi/The Flame*
1952	*Altri tempi/In Olden Days*
1953	*Miracolo a Ferrara*
1954	*Tempi nostri/The Anatomy of Love*
1955	*Peccato che sia una canaglia/Too Bad She's Bad*

1956	*La Fortuna di essere donna/ Lucky to Be a Woman*
1958	*Amore e chiacchiere/Love and Chatter*
1959	*Europa di notte/ Europe by Night*
1960	*Io amo, tu ami/ I Love, You Love*
1962	*Three Fables of Love*
1963	*Liolà/Very Handy Man*
1964	*Io, io, io . . . e gli altri/ Me, Me, Me . . . and the Others*
1965	*La ragazza del bersagliere*
1969	*Simón Bolívar*
1978	*Racconti di fantascienza*

Camerini, Mario (1885–1981)

Born in Rome, Mario Camerini was one of the chief directors of the early sound period. Other members of Camerini's family such as his brother Augusto Camerini and his cousin Augusto Genina were also active in the cinema. Camerini began his directing career during the silent period, even making a Maciste film, *Maciste contro lo sceicco/ Maciste in Africa* in 1925. He is best known for his *telefono bianco* romantic comedies of the 1930s, which often starred future director Vittorio De Sica as leading man. After the war, Camerini continued to make films in a variety of genres including remakes of his films from the 1930s.

1923	*Jolly clown da circo/Jolly the Circus Clown*
	Walli
1924	*La casa dei pulcini/House of Pulcini*
1925	*Voglio tradire mio marito/I Want to Betray My Husband*
	Saetta, principe per un giorno
	Maciste contro lo sceicco/ Maciste in Africa
1928	*Kiff Tebbi/Come vuoi*
1929	*Rotaie/Rails*
1931	*La riva dei bruti*
	Figaro e la sua gran giornata/Figaro and His Great Day
1932	*Gli uomini, che mascalzoni!/What Scoundrels Men Are!*
	L'ultima avventura/The Last Adventure
1933	*T'amerò sempre/ I Will Love You Always*
	Cento di questi giorni
1934	*Giallo*
	Come le foglie/ Like the Leaves
	Il cappello a tre punte/ Three Cornered Hat
1936	*Ma non è una cosa seria/But It's Nothing Serious*
	Il grande appello/The Last Roll-Call
	Darò un milione/I'll Give a Million
1937	*Il Signor Max/Mister Max*
1938	*Il documento*
	I grandi magazzini/Department Store
1939	*Batticuore/Heartbeat*
1940	*Centomila dollari*
1941	*I promessi sposi*
1942	*Una storia d'amore/Love Story*
1943	*T'amerò sempre*

1944	*Due lettere anonime/Two Anonymous Letters*
1946	*L' angelo e il diavolo/Angel and the Devil*
1947	*La figlia del capitano/The Captain's Daughter*
1948	*Molti sogni per le strade/ Woman Trouble*
1950	*Due mogli sono troppe/Honeymoon Deferred*
	Il brigante Musolino/Outlaw Girl
1952	*Moglie per una notte/Wife for a Night*
1953	*Gli eroi della domenica/ Sunday Heroes*
1955	*Ulisse/Ulysses*
	La bella mugnaia/The Miller's Beautiful Wife
1957	*Suor Letizia/The Awakening*
	Vacanze a Ischia/Holiday Island
1958	*Primo amore/First Love*
1960	*Crimen/Killing in Monte Carlo*
1961	*I briganti italiani/The Italian Brigands*
1963	*Via Margutta/Run with the Devil*
	Kali Yug, la dea della vendetta/Goddess of Vengeance
	Il mistero del tempio indiano
1966	*Delitto quasi perfetto/ Almost Perfect Crime*
1971	*Io non vedo, tu non parli, lui non sente*
1972	*Don Camillo e i giovani d'oggi*

De Santis, Giuseppe (1917–97)

Born in Fondi outside Rome, De Santis studied at the CSC, the Rome film institute, of which he became the director in the 1970s. He contributed to *Cinema* (1941–43) and started his cinematic career as assistant to Visconti for *Obsession* (1942). He made his first feature film in 1947, *Tragic Hunt*, which was the first of his land trilogy, the other two being *Bitter Rice* and *Under the Olive Tree*. His neorealist-era films were amongst the most commercially successful of the period.

1947	*Caccia tragica/Tragic Hunt*
1948	*Riso amaro/Bitter Rice*
1949	*Non c'è pace tra gli ulivi/No Peace under the Olive Tree*
1952	*Roma ore 11/Rome 11:00*
1953	*Un marito per Anna Zaccheo/A Husband for Anna*
1954	*Days of Love*
1956	*Uomini e lupi/Men and Wolves*
1958	*La strada lunga un anno/The Year Long Road*
1960	*La Garçonnière*
1964	*Italiani, brava gente/Attack and Retreat*
1972	*Un apprezzato professionista di sicuro avvenire*

De Sica, Vittorio (1902–74)

Born outside Rome, De Sica started his career as a theater actor in 1923 working his way into film as a leading man including apperences in the comedies of the 1930s directed by Mario Camerini. De Sica continued his acting career after World War II becoming a consummate showman, eventually appearing in over 150 films. His career as a director in collaboration with screenwriter Cesare Zavattini began in the early 1940s resulting in outstanding examples of neorealist cinema, especially *The Bicycle Thief* in 1948, *Umberto D.* (1952) as well as films with a lighter more magical touch such as *Miracle in Milan* (1952) and *The Gold of Naples* (1954). His later directing career features adaptations of literary works such as *Two Women* (1960), and *The Garden of the Finzi-Contini* (1970) as well as films featuring the romantic pair Marcello Mastroianni and Sophia Loren including *Marriage Italian Style* (1964).

1940	*Rose scarlatte/Red roses*
	Maddalena . . . .zero in condotta/Maddalena . . . zero for conduct
1941	*Teresa Venerdì/Doctor Beware*
1942	*Un garibaldino in convento/ A Garibaldian in the Convent*
1943	*I bambini ci guardano/The Children are Watching Us*
1945	*La porta del cielo/The Gate of Heaven*
1946	*Sciuscia'/Shoeshine*
1948	*Ladri di biciclette/The Bicycle Thief*
	Cuore/ Heart and Soul (children's scenes)
1950	*Miracolo a Milano/Miracle in Milan*
1952	*Umberto D.*
1953	*Stazione termini/Indiscretion of an American Wife*
	Villa Borghese/It Happened in the Park
1954	*L'oro di Napoli/Gold of Naples*
1956	*Il tetto/The Roof*
1958	*Anna di Brooklyn/Fast and Sexy*
1960	*La ciociara/Two Women*
1961	*Il giudizio Universale/The Last Judgement*
1962	*Boccaccio '70 "la riffa" episode*
	I sequestrati di Altona/The Condemned of Altona
1963	*Il Boom*
	Ieri, Oggi e domain/Yesterday, Today, and Tomorrow
	The Condemned of Altoona
1964	*Matrimonio all'italiana/Marriage Italian Style*
1965	*Un nuovo mondo/A Young World*
1966	*Caccia alla volpe/After the Fox*
1967	*Woman Times Seven*
	Le streghe "Una sera come le altre" episode
1968	*Amanti/A Place for Lovers*
1970	*I girasoli/Sunflower*
	Il giardino dei Finzi-Contini/The Garden of the Finzi Contini
	Le coppie/The Couple "Il leone," episode
1972	*Lo chiameremo Andrea/We Will Call Him Andrew*
1973	*Una breve vacanza/A Brief Vacation*
1974	*Il viaggio/The Voyage*

Fellini, Federico (1920–93)

Born in Rimini, Fellini moved to Rome in 1939 where he worked as a cartoonist and journalist. There he met Giulietta Masina whom he married in 1943 and who became one of the main actresses in his films. He helped Rossellini and Amidei write the script for *Open City* and in 1946 he became Rossellini's assistant director for *Paisà*. In 1950 he codirected *Variety Lights* with Alberto Lattuada and in 1952 he made his first feature film, *The White Sheik,* and eventually became one of the most important art cinema directors in film history. Fellini has accumulated a long list of awards that culminated in the Oscar Career Award in 1993.

1950   *Le luci del varietà/Variety Lights*
1951   *Lo sceicco bianco/The White Sheik*
1953   *L'amore in città/ Love in the City* "Un'agenzia matrimoniale" episode
        I vitelloni/The Young and the Passionate
1954   *La Strada*
1955   *Il bidone/The Swindle*
1956   *Le notti di Cabiria/The Nights of Cabiria*
1960   *La dolce vita*
1962   *Boccaccio '70* "Le tentazioni del dottor Antonio" episode
1963   *8 1/2*
1965   *Giulietta degli spiriti/Juliet of the Spirits*
1968   *Tre passi nel delirio* "Toby Dammit" episode
1969   *Block-notes di un regista/Fellini: A Director's Notebook*
        Satyricon/Fellini Satyricon
1970   *The Clowns*
1972   *Roma/Fellini Roma*
1974   *Amarcord*
1976   *Il Casanova di Federico Fellini/ Fellini's Casanova*
1978   *Prova d'orchestra/Orchestra Rehearsal*
1980   *La città delle donne/City of Women*
1983   *E la nave va/And the Ship Sails on*
1986   *Ginger and Fred*
1987   *L'intervista/Fellini's Interview*
1990   *La voce della luna/The Voice of the Moon*

Germi, Pietro (1914–74)

Born in Genoa, Pietro Germi was a student at the CSC, the Rome film institute, and started his career as assistant to Alessandro Blasetti in the late 1930s-early 1940s. As a director, Germi made films that adapt the formats of genres like the noir, the melodrama, the western and the road movie to Italian themes with politically and socially relevant examinations of immigration, way ward youth and the mafia. His later films combine political and social criticism of southern and rural Italy with the genre of comedy Italian style.

1946   *Il testimone/The Witness*
1947   *Gioventù perduta/Lost Youth*
1949   *In nome della legge/In the Name of the Law*
1950   *Il camino della speranza/Path of Hope*
1951   *La città si difende/ Four Ways out*
1952   *La presidentessa/Mademoiselle Gobette*
        Il brigante di Tacca del Lupo/The Bandit of Tacca del lupo
1953   *Gelosia/Jealousy*
1954   *Amori di mezzo secolo* "Guerra 1915/18" episode
1956   *Il ferroviere/The Railman Man*

1957   *L'uomo di paglia/A Man of Straw*
1959   *Un maledetto imbroglio/The Facts of Murder*
1961   *Divorzio all'italiana/Divorce Italian Style*
1964   *Sedotta e abbandonata/Seduced and Abandoned*
1965   *Signore e signori/The Birds, the Bees, and the Italians*
1967   *L'immorale/ The Climax*
1968   *Serafino*
1970   *Le castagne sono buone/A Pocketful of Chestnuts*
1972   *Alfredo, Alfredo*

Leone, Sergio (1929–89)

Born in Rome into a family that worked in the film industry. Leone began as an assistant director on De Sica's *The Bicycle Thief* and then gained experience as an assistant on films such as *Fabiola* (1949), *Quo Vadis* (1951) and *Ben-Hur* (1959). He finished the peplum *Ultimi giorni di Pompei/ Last Days of Pompeii* for an ailing Mario Bonnard and then worked as a director in his own right in the peplum genre then popular in Italy and around the world. His greatest contribution was in the so-called spaghetti western, with three films starring Clint Eastwood: *A Fistful of Dollars* (1964), *For a Few Dollars More* (1965), and *The Good, the Bad and the Ugly* (1966). Leone offered a new approach to the western, hugely influential in Italy and in Hollywood. In his later years he produced the films of Roman comedian Carlo Verdone such as *Un sacco bello/Fun is Beautiful* (1980).

1959   *Ultimi giorni di Pompei/Last Days of Pompeii* (uncredited)
1961   *Il colosso di Rodi,/Colossus of Rhodes*
1964   *Per un pugno di dollari/For a Fistful of Dollars*
1965   *Per qualche dollaro in più/For a Few Dollars More*
1966   *Il buono, il brutto, il cattivo/The Good, the Bad and the Ugly*
1968   *C'era una volta il West/Once Upon a Time in the West*
1971   *Giù la testa/A Fistful of Dynamite*
1973   *Il mio nome è Nessuno/My Name Is Nobody* (uncredited)
1975   *Un genio, due compari, un pollo/The Genius*
1984   *C'era una volta in America/Once Upon a Time in America*

Moretti, Nanni (1953–)

Born in Brunico in Trentino-Alto Adige, Moretti grew up and was educated in Rome influenced by the climate of the 1960s and early 1970s. He often casts himself in an alter ego character in films that examine larger social and political themes through a personal lens. His films have been critically well received, particularly in France where he has won the prestigious Palm d'Or at the Cannes film festival. Besides starring in his own films, Moretti has appeared as an actor in *Il Portaborse/The Yes Man* (1991) and *La Seconda volta* (1996).

1973	*La sconfitta*
1973	*Paté de bourgeois*
1974	*Come parli, frate?*
1976	*Io sono un autarchico/I Am Self Sufficient*
1978	*Ecce Bombo*
1981	*Sogni d'oro/Sweet Dreams*
1983	*Bianca/Sweet Body of Bianca*
1984	*La messa è finita/The Mass Is Ended*
1989	*Palombella rossa/Red Wood Pigeon*
1990	*La Cosa/The Thing*
1994	*Caro diario/Dear Diary*
	L'unico paese al mondo
1996	*Il giorno della prima di Close Up/Opening Day of Close-Up*
1998	*Aprile/April*
2001	*La stanza del figlio/The Son's Room*
2003	*L'ultimo cliente/The Last Customer*
2006	*Il caimano/The Caiman*

Monicelli, Mario (1915–)

Born at Viareggio in Tuscany, Monicelli began as an assistant director on Pietro Germi's *Gioventù perduta/Lost Youth* (1947) as well as a number of productions during the 1930s and early 1940s. He is known as the prime exponent of the *commedia all'italiana* (Italian comedy) style, which gained popularity in the 1950s and 1960s with actors such as Alberto Sordi, Nino Manfredi, Ugo Tognazzi, Marcello Mastroanni, and Vitttorio Gassman. Monicelli has been one of the most prolific directors in Italian film history.

1949	*Totò cerca casa/Totò Looks for an Apartment*
	Al diavolo la celebrità/Fame and the Devil
1950	*Vita da cani/It's a Dog's Life*
	È arrivato il cavaliere!
1951	*Totò e i re di Roma/Toto and the King of Rome*
	Guardie e ladri/Cops and Robbers
1952	*Totò e le donne/Toto and the Women*
1953	*Le infedeli/Unfaithfuls*
1954	*Proibito/Forbidden*
	Totò e Carolina/Toto and Carolina
1955	*Un eroe dei nostri tempi/A Hero of Our Times*
1956	*Donatella*
1957	*Il medico e lo stregone/Doctor and the Healer*
1958	*Padri e figli/Like Father, Like Son*
	I soliti ignoti/Big Deal on Madonna Street
1959	*Lettere dei condannati a morte*
1959	*La grande guerra/The Great War*
1960	*Risate di gioia/Joyful Laughter*
1962	*Boccaccio '70*—"Renzo e Luciana" episode
1963	*I compagni/The Organiser*
1964	*Alta infedeltà/ High Infidelity*—"Gente Moderna" episode

1965   *Casanova '70*
1966   *Le Fate/The Queens* "Fata Armenia" episode
        L' armata Brancaleone/For Love and Gold
1968   *Capriccio all'italiana/Caprice Italian Style*—"La Bambinaia" episode
        La ragazza con la pistola/Girl with a Pistol
1969   *Toh, è morta la nonna!/Oh, Grandmother's Dead*
1970   *Le coppie/Couples* "Il Frigorifero" episode
        Brancaleone alle crociate/Brancaleone at the Crusades
1971   *La mortadella/The Sausage*
1973   *Vogliamo i colonnelli/We Want the Colonels*
1974   *Romanzo popolare/Come Home and Meet My Wife*
1975   *Amici miei/My Friends*
1976   *Signore e signori, buonanotte/Goodnight, Ladies and Gentlemen*
        Caro Michele/Dear Michael
1977   *Un borghese piccolo piccolo/An Average Little Man*
        I nuovi mostri/The New Monsters
1979   *Viaggio con Anita/Lovers and Liars*
        Temporale Rosy/Hurricane Rosie
        Camera d'albergo
1981   *Il marchese del Grillo*
1982   *Amici miei atto II/All My Friends Part 2*
1984   *Bertoldo, Bertoldino e . . . Cacasenno*
1985   *Le due vite di Mattia Pascal/The Two Lives of Mattia Pascal*
1986   *Speriamo che sia femmina/Let's Hope It's a Girl*
1988   *I picari/The Rogues*
1989   *La moglie ingenua e il marito malato*
        12 registi per 12 città "Verona" episode
1990   *Il male oscuro/ Dark Illness*
1991   *Rossini! Rossini!*
1992   *Parenti serpenti/Dearest Relatives, Poisonous Relations*
1994   *Cari fottutissimi amici/Dear Goddamned Friends*
1995   *Facciamo paradiso/Looking for Paradise*
1996   *Esercizi di stile*—"Idillio edile"
1997   *I corti italiani* "Topi di appartamento" episode
1999   *Panni sporchi/Dirty Linen*
1999   *Un amico magico: il maestro Nino Rota*
2003   *Firenze, il nostro domani*

Pasolini, Pier Paolo (1922–75)

Born in Bologna, before starting a cinematic career, Pasolini was a poet and novelist. As a director he adapted cannonical texts to films such as Sophocles's *Oedipus Rex*, Aeschilus's *Medea*, Boccaccio's *Decameron*, Chaucer's *The Canterbury Tale* and *the Gospel of Mathew*. He moved to Rome in 1949 where he earned his living as a teacher in the city suburbs and where he collected material for his first book *Ragazzi di vita* eventually making his first feature film, *Accattone*, in 1961. Pasolini faced periodic bouts with censorship as the contents of some his films and declarations revealed uncomfortable hypocricies at times threatening the status quo on both the political right and left. He died a violent death in Ostia in 1975.

1961   *Accattone*
1962   *Mamma Roma*
1963   *Ro.Go.Pa.G.* "La ricotta" episode
1964   *Il vangelo secondo Matteo/The Gospel according to St Matthew*
1965   *Comizi d'amore/Assembly of Love*
1966   *Uccellacci e uccellini/ The Hawks and the Sparrows*
1967   *Edipo re/Oedipus Rex*
        Le streghe "La terra vista dalla luna" episode
1968   *Teorema*
1969   *Il porcile/Pigpen*
        Medea
1970   *Appunti per un'Orestiade Africana/Notes for an African Orestes*
1971   *Il decamerone/The Decameron*
1972   *I racconti di Canterbury/The Canterbury Tales*
1974   *Il fiore delle mille e una notte/A Thousand and One Night*
1975   *Salò o le 120 giornate di Sodoma/Salò, The 120 Days of Sodom*

Rosi, Francesco (1922–)

Born in Naples, Rosi worked as a radio journalist in the early 1940s. Before getting involved with cinema, he worked in the theater as an actor, a stage designer, and assistant director in Rome. After 1946, he started writing scripts for film directors and made his first film, *The Challenge*, in 1958. He is one of the most important directors of political films.

1952   *Camicie rosse/ Anita Garibaldi*
1956   *Kean*
1958   *La sfida/The Challenge*
1959   *I magliari/The Magliari*
1961   *Salvatore Giuliano*
1963   *Le mani sulla città/Hands over the City*
1965   *Il momento della verità/The Moment of Truth*
1967   *C'era una volta/More than a Miracle*
1970   *Uomini contro/Many Wars Ago*
1972   *Il caso Mattei/The Mattei Affair*
1973   *Lucky Luciano*
1976   *Cadaveri eccellenti/Illutrious Corpses*
1979   *Cristo si è fermato a Eboli/Christ Stopped at Eboli*
1981   *Tre fratelli/Three Brothers*
1984   *Carmen/Bizet's Carmen*
1988   *Cronaca di una morte annunciata/Chronicle of a Death Foretold*
1989   *12 registi per 12 città* "Napoli" episode
1990   *Dimenticare Palermo/To Forget Palermo*
1992   *Diario napoletano*
1997   *La tregua/The Truce*

Rossellini, Roberto (1906–77)

Born in Rome, Rossellini was involved with scriptwriting and filmmaking in the Italian cinema of the 1930s, working on several war dramas before WWII. In the 1940s he worked with Antonioni and Fellini and produced the neorealist war trilogy *Open City, Paisan, Germany Year Zero*. Rossellini's films in the 1950s including *Stromboli, Europe '51, Voyage to Italy* were important for the development of art cinema. In the later years of his career, Rossellini favored documentary or historical films, based on historical or religious characters, such as, *The Rise of Louis XIV, Socrates, Augustine of Hippo, Blaise Pascal, The Messiah*.

1941	*La nave bianca/The White Ship*
1942	*Un pilota ritorna/A pilot returns*
	La nave bianca/The White Ship
1943	*Uomo dalla croce/Man of the Cross*
1945	*Roma città aperta/Open City*
1946	*Paisà/Paisan*
1947	*Germania anno zero/Germany, Year Zero*
1948	*L'amore/Ways of Love* "Il miracolo" episode
1949	*Stromboli*
1950	*Francesco giullare di dio/Flowers of St. Francis*
1952	*Europe '51*
	La macchina ammazzacattivi/The Machine that Kills Bad People
	Les Sept péchés capitaux/The Seven Deadly Sins "Envie, L'/Envy" episode
1953	*Siamo donne/ We, the Women* "Ingrid Bergman" episode
	Viaggio in Italia/Voyage to Italy
1954	*Amori di mezzo secolo* "Naples" episode
	Giovanna d'Arco al rogo/Joan of Arc at the Stake
	Paura/Fear
1958	*India*
1959	*Il generale della R overe/General Della Rovere*
	Era notta a Roma/It was night in Rome
1961	*Viva l'Italia/Garibaldi*
	Vanina Vanini/The Berayer
	Blood on the Balcony
1962	*Anima nera*
1963	*Ro.Go.Pa.G.* "Illibatezza" episode
1964	*L'età di ferro/ The Iron Age*
1966	*The Rise of Louis XIV*
1967	*Idea di un'isola*
1968	*Atti degli apostolic/Acts of the Apostles*
1970	*Socrate/Socrates*
1971	*Blaise Pascal*
1972	*Agostino d'Ippona/Augustine of Hippo*
1973	*L'età di Cosimo de Medici/The Age of the Medici*
1974	*Cartesius*
	Anno uno/Year One
1976	*Il messia/The Messiah*

Scola, Ettore (1931–)

Scola was born in Trevico, Avellino, in southern Italy. He started as a scriptwriter in the early 50s and then moved on to making films in the early 1960s. He is one of the strongest representatives of comedy Italian style genre and one of the most innovative directors of the post-neorealism generation.

1964   *Se permettete parliamo di donne/Let's Talk about Women*
1966   *L'Arcidiavolo/The Devil in Love*
1968   *Il Commissario Pepe/ Police Chief Pepe*
         Riusciranno i nostri eroi a trovare il loro amico misteriosamente scomparso in Africa?/ Will Our Friends Succeed in Finding Their Friend Who Disappeared in Africa?
1970   *Dramma della gelosia—tutti i particolari in cronaca/The Pizza Triangle: A Drama of Jealousy*
1971   *Permette? Rocco Papaleo/Rocco Papaleo*
1972   *La più bella serata della mia vita/ The Most Wonderful Evening of My Life*
1973   *Trevico-Torino: Viaggio nel Fiatnam*
1974   *C'eravamo tanto amati/We All Loved Each Other So Much*
1976   *Brutti sporchi e cattivi /Down and Dirty*
1977   *Una giornata particolare/A Special Day*
         I nuovi mostri/The New Monsters
1980   *La terrazza/The Terrace*
1981   *Passione d'amore/Passion of Love*
1982   *La nuit de Varennes/Il mondo nuovo*
1984   *Le bal/Ballando, ballando*
1985   *Maccheroni/Macaroni*
1987   *La famiglia/The Family*
1989   *Splendor*
1990   *Che ora è?/What Time is it?*
1991   *Il viaggio di Capitan Fracassa /The Travels of Captain Fracassa*
1993   *Mario, Maria e Mario*
1995   *Il romanzo di un giovane povero*
1998   *La cena*
2001   *Concorrenza sleale/Unfair Competition*
2003   *Gente di Roma*

Visconti, Luchino (1906–76)

Born in 1906, Visconti started his career on the stage as an actor and stage designer (1928–29). Later on, he went to Paris and worked as an assistant to Jean Renoir. His first film *Obsession* (1943) is considered one of the forerunners of neorealism. Visconti later adapted his abilities in directing opera and stage production to art cinema with lavish productions such as *The Leopard* and *Ludwig*.

1943   *Ossessione/Obsession*
1945   *Giorni di gloria*
1947   *La terra trema: episodio di mare/The Earth Trembles*
1951   *Bellissima*
         Appunti di un fatto di cronaca
1953   *Siamo donne/We, the Women* "Anna Magnani" episode
1954   *Senso/Livia*
1957   *Le notti bianche/White Nights*

1960   *Rocco e I suoi fratelli/Rocco and His Brothers*
1962   *Boccaccio '70* "Il lavoro" episode
1963   *Il gattopardo/The Leopard*
1965   *Vaghe stelle dell'Orsa/ Sandra of a Thousand Delights*
1967   *Lo straniero/The Stranger*
        Le streghe "La strega bruciata viva" episode
1969   *La caduta degli dei-Gotterdammerung / The Damned*
1970   *Alla ricerca di Tadzio*
1971   *Morte a Venezia/Death in Venice*
1972   *Ludwig*
1974   *Gruppo di famiglia in un interno/ Conversation Piece*
1976   *L'innocente/The Innocent*

Wertmüller, Lina (1928—)

Born in Rome, Wertmüller studied at the Theatre Academy in Rome in 1947–51. She started her career in theater as an actress, stage manager, and set designer. She also wrote for the theater, radio, and television before becoming an assistant to Fellini on *8 1/2* in 1962. Soon after she made her first feature film, *The Lizards* (1963). Her second film *Now Let's Talk about Men* (1965) is a take-off from Scola's 1964 *Let's Talk about Women*. As a woman director she enjoyed dealing with highly controversial topics and became internationally famous in the 1970s. The titles of her films are particularly lengthy (another Scola's influence!) in their attempts at describing their contents from a singular point of view, which mixes irony and sentimentality.

1963   *I basilischi/The Lizards*
1964   *Il giornalino di Gian Burrasca/Gian Burrasca's Diary*
1965   *Questa volta parliamo di uomini/Now, Let's Talk about Men*
1967   *Non stuzzicate la zanzara/Don't Tease the Mosquito*
1972   *Mimì metallurgico ferito nell'onore/The Seduction of Mimi*
1973   *Film d'amore e d'anarchia/Love and Anarchy*
1974   *Tutto a posto e niente in ordine/All Screwed up*
        Travolti da un insolito destino . . ./Swept Away
1975   *Pasqualino Settebellezze/Seven Beauties*
1978   *Fine del mondo nel nostro solito letto/A Night Full of Rain*
1979   *Fatto di sangue fra due uomini . . . /Blood Feud*
1981   *E una domenica sera di novembre*
1984   *Scherzo di destino in agguato . . ./A Joke of Destiny*
1984   *Sotto . . . sotto . . . / Softly . . . Softly*
1985   *Un complicato intrigo di donne, vicoli e delitti/Camorra*
1987   *Notte d'estate con profile greco . . . ./Summer Night with a Greek Profile . . . ,*
1989   *In una notte di chiaro di luna/As Long as It's Love*
1990   *Sabato, domenica e lunedì/Saturday, Sunday, Monday*
1992   *Io, speriamo che me la cavo/Ciao Professore!*
1996   *Ninfa plebea/The Nymph*
1996   *Metalmeccanico e parruchiera in un turbine di sesso e politica/The Worker and the Hairdresser*
1999   *Ferdinando e Carolina*
2001   *Francesca e Nunziata/Francesca and Nunziata*
2004   *Peperoni ripieni e pesci in faccia/ Too Much Romance . . . It's Time for Stuffed Peppers*

Appendix 4: Italian Political Parties

Following the postwar elections of 1946 and 1948, the Italian political system developed parties (from Left to Right) whose philosophy may be identified as below.

1946–1990

Left						Right
PCI	PSI	PSDI	PRI	DC	PLI	MSI

Following the fall of the Berlin Wall (1989), symbolically marking the end of the Cold War, some Italian political parties changed their names (the PCI, the Italian Communist Party, became the DS, (Democratici della Sinistra or the Democrats of the Left) and others ceased to exist such as the DC (Christian Democrats). The members of extinct parties came under the control of newly established parties (such as Forza Italia or the Northern League) or the UDC (Unione Democratica Cristiana) or the DS. These parties have organized themselves into two coalitions/alliances—the Liberty House and the Olive Alliance with membership and placement subject to change and negotiation within the parliamentary system.

1991–2006

Left					Right
	Olive Coalition		**Liberty Coalition**		
Rifondazione	Comunisti Italiani	Nuovo PSI	Forza Italia		MSI-FT
comunista	Verdi	Radicali	Allenaza Nazionale		
	Democratici di Sinistra		Lega Nord		
	Socialisti Democratici italiani		UDC		
	Margherita				
	UDEUR				
	Lista Di Pietro				

Notes

Remote History

* Dates adapted from a number of sources including: Valerio Lintner, "A Traveler's History of Italy" (New York: Interlink Books, 1995), 236–246. Bruce Wetterau, *World History* (New York: Henry Holt, 1994), 564–572; Giuseppe Vottari, *Storia d'Italia (1861–2001) un sommario ragionato* (Milan: Alpha Test, 2004), *World Literature and Its Times: Italian Literature and Its Times*, ed. Joyce Moss (Los Angeles: Moss Publishing Group, 2005), xvii–xxix.

1. Sources for an introduction to film theory include Pam Cook, *The Cinema Book* (London: British Film Institute Publishing, 1999); Leo Braudy and Marshall Cohen, eds., *Film Theory and Criticism: Introductory Readings* (New York: Oxford University Press, 1999); Robert Stam and Toby Miller, eds., *Film and Theory: An Anthology* (Malden, Mass.: Blackwell Publishers, 2000); Francesco Casetti, *Teorie del cinema 1945–1990* (Milan: Bompiani, 1994).
2. Roy Armes, *Patterns of Realism* (South Brunswick: A.S. Barnes, 1971), 18.

1   Italy from Unification to World War I

1. Denis Mack Smith, *Italy A Modern History* (Ann Arbor: University of Michigan Press, 1969), 1.
2. Christopher Hibbert, *Garibaldi and His Enemies: The Clash of Arms and Personalities in the Making of Italy* (Boston: Little, Brown, 1966), 331.
3. Vottari, *Storia d'Italia*.
4. H. Stuart Hughes, *The United States and Italy* (Cambridge, Mass.: Harvard University Press, 1979), 81.
5. Joseph LaPalombara, *Democracy Italian Style* (New Haven: Yale University Press, 1987), 23.
6. Bego de la Serna-Lopez, "Europe: The Creation of a Nation? A Comparative Analysis of Nation-Building," in J. Andrew, M. Crook, M. Waller, eds., *Why Europe? Problems of Culture and Identity* (New York: MacMillan, 2000), 159.
7. LaPalombara, *Democracy Italian Style*.
8. See Mary Gibson, *Born to Crime: Cesare Lombroso and the Origins of Biological Criminology* (Westport, Conn.: Praeger, 2002).
9. Christopher Duggan, *A Concise History of Italy* (Cambridge University Press, 1994), 183.
10. See Jared M. Becker, *Nationalism and Culture Gabriele D'Annunzio and Italy after the Risorgimento* (New York: Peter Lang, 1994); Francesco Piga, *Il mito del superuonmo in Nietzsche e D'Annunzio* (Florence: Vallecchi, 1979).
11. Gian Piero Brunetta, *Cent'anni di cinema italiano 1905–2003* (Bari: Einaudi, 1991), 65.

12. Paolo Cerchi Usai and Livio Iacob, eds., *I comici del muto italiano* (Genova: Cineteca D.W. Griffith, 1985).

13. Gian Piero Brunetta, *Guida alla storia del cinema italiano: 1905–2003* (Turin: G. Einaudi, 2003), 427.

14. Vittorio Martinelli, "Il cinema muto italiano," *Bianco e Nero* Numero Speciale, 1993, 75.

15. These include *La Gioconda* (1910), *Il Sogno di un tramonto d'autunno* (1911), *Francesca da Rimini* (1911), *La Nave* (1912), *The Devil's Daughter* (1915), *Giovanni Episcopo* (1916), *La Gioconda* (1916), *Forse che sì forse che no* (1916), *La Figlia di Jorio* (1917), *Forse che sì forse che no* (1920), *La Nave* (1920), *Il Paradiso nell'ombre delle spade* (1920). See Renzo Rizzi, *Sperduto nel buio il cinema italiano e il suo tempo (1905–1930)* (Bologna: Capelli, 1991); Mario Verdone, *Bianco e Nero*, August 25, 1963, 2; Tom Antongini, *Vita segreta di Gabriele D'Annunzio* (Mondadori, Milan), 171–191; Gianni Rodolino, *Gabriele D'Annunzio grandezza e delirio nell'industria dello spettacolo* (Turin: Costa & Nolan, 1988).

16. Martinelli, "Il cinema muto italiano," 76.

17. See Becker, *Nationalism and Culture*.

18. Barbara Spackman, *Decadent Geneologies: The Rhetoric of Sickness from Baudelaire to D'Annunzio* (Ithaca: Cornell University Press, 1989), 27; E. Michael Jones, *Dionysious Rising. The Birth of Cultural Revolution out of the Spirit of Music* (San Francisco: Ignatius, 1994); Eileen Romano, *Album di D'Annunzio* (Milan: Mondadori, 1990), 305; "D'Annunzio blu," *Playmen*, March 1975, which refers to D'Annunzio's blue movie entitled *Saffo e priapo* (1921, 22). See *Annuario cinema autunno*, 1978, 73.

19. Mario Verdone, "Pastrone ultimo incontro," *Bianco e Nero*, January 1961.

20. Valentina Ruffin, "La lingua del fascismo nel cinema," in R. Renzi, G.L. Farinelli, and N. Mazzanti, eds., *Il cinema dei dittatori Mussolini, Stalin, Hitler* (Roma: Grafis, 1992), 44. *Cinema dei dittatori*. James Hay, *Popular Film Culture in Fascist Italy* (Bloomington: Indiana University Press, 1987); Renzo de Felice and Luigi Coglia, *Storia fotografica del fascismo* (Rome: Laterza, 1982) ; Massimo Cardillo, *Il Duce in moviola Politica e divismo nei cinegiornali e documentari Luce* (Bari: Dedalo, 1982).

21. Paolo Cerchi Usai in Rodolino, *Gabriele D'Annunzio grandezza*, 232. Adrian Lyttelton, *The Seizure of Power: Fascism in Italy, 1919–1929* (New York: Routledge, 2004).

22. Renzo De Felice, *Storia degli ebrei italiani sotto il fascismo* (Torino: Einaudi 1961).

23. Brunetta, *Guida alla storia del cinema italiano*, 428. Gianni Rondolino, *I giorni di Cabiria* (Turin: Linsdrau, 1993), 118.

24. Brunetta, *Guida alla storia del cinema italiano*, 429.

2   The Fascist Years (1922–1943)

1. Italy (1922), Spain and Turkey (1923), Albania (1925), Poland, Portugal, Lithuania (1926), Yugoslavia (1929), Romania (1930), Germany, Austria (1933), Greece and Spain again (1936), and Vichy France in 1940.

2. Emilio Lussu, *Marcia su Roma e Dintorni* (Italy: Mondadori, 1976), 3.

3. Ernst Nolte, *Three Faces of Fascism* (New York: Signet, 1963).

4. Ibid.

5. Norberto Bobbio, "Lungo viaggio nel Novecento," *Corriere della sera*, May 15, 1997, 23.

6. Hughes, *The United States and Italy*, 83.

7. Denis Mack Smith, *Cavour* (New York: Knopf, 1985).

8. Dennis Mack Smith, *Mussolini* (New York: Knopf, 1982); *Mussolini's Roman Empire* (New York: Viking Press, 1976).

9. Brunetta, *Cent'anni di cinema italiano*, 431.

10. Ruffin, "La lingua del fascismo nel cinema," 116. For studies of the linguistic policies during Fascism see the work of Mino Argentieri, Erasmo Leso, Sergio Raffaelli, and Gabriella Klein.

11. Brunetta, *Cent'anni di cinema italiano*, 431.

12. Marcia Landy, *Cinematic Uses of the Past* (Minneapolis: Minnesota University Press, 1996), 78.

13. Ruffin, "La lingua del fascismo nel cinema," 118.

14. Angelo Cammarosano, *Lezioni di cultura fascista* (Ancona: Nacci, 1934).

15. Gianfranco Casadio, *Il grigio e il nero. Spettacolo e propaganda nel cinema italiano degli anni trenta (1931–1943)*, (Ravenna: Longo, 1989), 10.

16. Brunetta, *Cent'anni di cinema italiano*, 429.

17. Ibid., 430.

18. Ibid., 431.

19. Ibid., 433.

20. Ibid., 434.

21. Ibid., 265.

22. Carlo Celli, "Alessandro Blasetti and Representations of Italian Fascism in the 1930s," *Italian Culture*, 16, 2 (1998), 99–109.

23. Pierre Sorlin, "Il Risorgimento italiano: 1860," in Gianfranco Miro Gori, ed., *La storia al cinema Ricostruzione del passato interpretazione del presente* (Rome: Bulzoni, 1994), 416.

24. Fernaldo Di Giammateo, *Dizionario del cinema italiano. Dall'inizio del secolo a oggi i film che hanno segnato la storia del nostro cinema* (Roma: Riuniti, 1995), 317.

25. Casadio, *Il grigio e il nero*, 55.

26. Carlo Celli, "The Legacy of Mario Camerini in Vittorio De Sica's The Bicycle Thief (1948)," *Cinema Journal* 40, 4 (2001), 3–17. Copyright ©2001 by the University of Texas Press. All rights reserved.

27. Gianfranco Casadio, Ernesto G. Laura, and Filippo Cristiano, *Telefoni bianchi : realtà e finzione nella società e nel cinema italiano degli anni trenta* (Ravenna: Longo, 1991).

28. Celli, "The Legacy of Mario Camerini," 3–17.

29. Mario Camerini, "Comment realise-t-on un film (How to Make a Film)," in Alberto Farassino, ed., *Mario Camerini* (Locarno: Editions Yellow Now, 1992), 159. Originally in Italian in *Il dramma* 9, 170 (September 9, 1933) and *La gazzetta del popolo*, May 12, 1933.

30. Ibid., 160.

31. Francesco Savio, "Mario Camerini," in Tullio Kezich, ed., *Cinecittà anni trenta: parlano 116 protagonisti del secondo cinema italiano (1930–1943)* (Rome: Bulzoni, 1979), 225.

32. Steven Ricci, "Camerini et Hollywood Questions d'identité (nationale)," in Alberto Farassino, ed., Jaqueline Fumigalli, trans., *Mario Camerini* (Locarno: Editions Yellow, 1992), 37.

33. Celli, "The Legacy of Mario Camerini," 3–17. Camerini's *Darò un milione* (1935) became Walter Lang's *I'll Give a Million* (1938), *Batticuore* (1939) became Sam Woods's *Heartbeat* (1946). Camerini's relations with Hollywood continued after the war with his direction of Kurt Douglas in *Ulysses* (1954), and his screenplay of *War and Peace* (1956) directed by King Vidor. Eugene Levy remade Camerini's *Crimen/And Suddenly It's Murder* (1960) as *Criminals* (1992).

34. Di Giammateo, *Dizionario del cinema italiano*, 62.

35. Paolo Nuzzi and O. Iemma, *De Sica & Zavattini Parliamo tanto di noi* (Rome: Editori riuniti, 1997), 34.

36. Marga Cottino Jones, *A Student's Guide to Italian Film* (Dubuque, Iowa: Kendall/Hunt Publishing, 1993), 22.

37. Peter Bondanella, "Three Neorealist Classics by Vittorio De Sica," *Cineaste*, 23, 1 (1997), 52–53.

38. Brunetta, *Guida alla storia del cinema italiano*, 434.

39. Paolo Mereghetti, *Il Mereghetti Dizionario dei Film 2004* (Milan: Baldini Castoldi, 2003), 2366.

40. Di Giammateo, *Dizionario del cinema italiano*, 237.

41. See Siegfried Kracauer, *The Mass Ornament: Weimar Essays* (Cambridge, Mass.: Harvard University Press, 1995).

3   World War II

1. Limuti Emanuele and Bruno Aurelio, *Spie a Palermo. Dall'Ovra allo sbarco in Sicilia. Da Lucky Luciano ai missili di Cuba* (Italy: Lussografica, 2004). The relationship between the regime and the mafia is depicted in Pasquale Squittieri's *Il prefetto di ferro/The Iron Prefect* (1977).

2. "Interview with Marcello Pezzetti," *Critical Inquiry*, 27 (Autumn 2000), 149–157.

3. Filippini Massimo, *La tragedia di Cefalonia. Una verità scomoda* (Italia: IBN, 2004).

4. Oliva Gianni, *Profughi. Dalle foibe all'esodo: la tragedia degli italiani d'Istria, Fiume e Dalmazia* (Milan: Mondadori, 2005).

5. Giampaolo Pansa, *Sconosciuto 1945* (Milan: Sperling & Kupfer, 2005).

6. See Guido Aristarco, "Come si perpetua l'equivoco sul neorealismo di Zavattini," *Cinema Nuovo*, 29, 9–10 June (1980); Peter Bondanella, "Neorealist Aesthetics and the Fantastic: The Machine to Kill People and Miracle in Milan," *Film Criticism*, 3, 24–29 (1979); Bert Cardullo, *What Is Neorealism? A Critical English-Language Bibliography of Italian Cinematic Neorealism* (Lanham: University Press of America, 1991); Millicent Marcus, *Italian Film in the Light of Neorealism* (Princeton: Princeton University Press, 1986); Cesare Zavattini, *Neorealismo, ecc.* (Milano: Bompiani 1979); Zavattini, *C. Zavattini: Sequences from a Cinematic Life* (Englewood Cliffs: Prentice Hall, 1970).

7. Jones, *A Student's Guide to Italian Film*, 27.

8. Pierre Lephron, *The Italian Cinema* (New York: Praeger, 1971), 98.

9. A. Canziani and G. Bragaglia, *La stagione neorealistica* (Bologna: Cooperativa Libraria Universitaria Editrice, 1976).

10. P. Hovald, *Le Néoréalisme Italien et ses créateurs* (Paris: Cerf, 1959), 201.

11. For Rossellini, see especially P. Brunette, *Roberto Rossellini* (Oxford: Oxford University Press, 1987); Peter Bondanella, *The Films of Roberto Rossellini* (Cambridge and New York: Cambridge University Press, 1993); R. Rossellini, *Il mio metodo: scritti e interviste* (Venezia: Marsilio, 1987); R. Rossellini, *Quasi un'autobiografia* (Milano: Mondadori, 1987); R. Rossellini, *My Method Writings and Interviews Roberto Rossellini*, ed. Adriano Aprà, trans. Annapaola Cagnogni (New York: Marsilio, 1995).

12. R. Chitti and E. Lancia, *Dizionario del cinema italiano I film vol. 1 dal 1930 al 1944* (Roma: Gremese Editore, 1993), 259.

13. Carlo Celli, "Italian Neorealism's Wartime Legacy: Roberto Rossellini's *Open City* and *Man of the Cross*," *Romance Languages Annual*, 10 (1998), 225–228.

14. Mary P. Wood, *Italian Cinema* (New York: Berg, 2005), 101.

15. Vittorio De Sica, *La porta del cielo Memorie 1901–1952* (Rome: Avagliano Editore, 2004). "A Lost De Sica Film—*La porta del cielo/The Gate of Heaven* (1945)," *Quarterly Review of Film & Video*, 18, 4 (2001), 361–370. Emilio Lonero and Aldo Anziano, *La storia della Orbis—Universalia* (Turin: Effata' Editrice, 2004).

16. Maurizio Baroni, *Platea in piedi 1945–1958* (Sasso Marconi, Bologna: Bolelli, 1995), 5.
17. Gianni Rondolino, *Catalogo Bolaffi del cinema italiano, 1966–1975: Tutti i film italiani degli ultimi dieci anni* (Torino: Bolaffi, 1975).
18. André Bazin, *What Is Cinema? II* (Berkeley: University of California Press, 1971), 60.

4   Reconstruction and the Late '40s

1. Paul Ginsborg, *A History of Contemporary Italy: Society and Politics 1943–1998* (New York: Penguin, 1990), 98.
2. Smith, *Italy A Modern History*, 487–524.
3. Baroni, *Platea in piedi 1945–1958.*
4. Antonio Vitti, *Giuseppe De Santis and Postwar Italian Cinema* (Toronto: University of Toronto Press, 1996).
5. Gregory D. Black, *The Catholic Crusade against the Movies, 1940–1975* (New York: Cambridge University Press, 1998).
6. Carlo Celli, "The Legacy of Mario Camerini in Vittorio De Sica's The Bicycle Thief (1948)," *Cinema Journal* 40, 4 (2001), 3–17. ©2001 by the University of Texas Press. All rights reserved.
7. Nuzzi and Iemma, *De Sica*, 34.
8. Savio, "Mario Camerini," 209–221.
9. P. Adams Sitney, *Vital Crisis in Italian Cinema* (Texas UP, 1995), 93.
10. Tomasulo, "*The Bicycle Thief*: A Re-Reading," 13.
11. Mary Ann Doane, *The Desire to Desire the Woman's Film of the 1940's* (Bloomington: Indiana University Press, 1987), 39.
12. Marcus, *Italian Film in the Light of Neorealism*, 69.
13. P. Adams Sitney, *Vital Crisis in Italian Cinema* (Texas University Press, 1995), 2.
14. This and other instances in which the protagonist of *The Bicycle Thief* Antonio Ricci lack pragmatism are noted by Sitney, Ibid., 94.
15. Camerini did direct a film version of Alessandro Manzoni's Catholic novel *I promessi sposi/The Betrothed* (1941) but has claimed that it was due to a contractual obligation rather than ideological mission on his part. When presented with the choice of making an air force film for minister Pavolini or a film version of the classic Italian novel, Camerini chose the latter. Savio, "Mario Camerini," 221.
16. Tomasulo, "*The Bicycle Thief*: A Re-Reading," *Cinema Journal*, 21, 2 (Spring 1982), 8. See also Wilhelm Reich, *The Mass Psychology of Fascism*, ed. Mary Higgins and C.M. Raphael, trans. V.R. Carfagno (London: Souvenir, 1972). Vincent Rocchio, *Cinema of Anxiety: A psychoanalysis of Italian Neorealism* (Austin: University of Texas Press, 1999), 77.
17. Cecilia Dau Novelli, "La famiglia come soggetto della ricostruzione sociale (1942–1949)," in G. De Rosa, ed., *Cattolici, chiesa, resistenza* (Bologna: Il Mulino, 1997), 469–490.
18. Tomasulo, "*The Bicycle Thief*: A Re-Reading," 12.
19. Nuzzi and Iemma, *De Sica*, 119. The columns by Piero Regnoli under the pen name *Vice* appeared in *L'avvenire d'Italia* and *L'osservatore romano*. The excerpt from the film is "Io voglio uscire da questo luogo santo sentendomi purificato nell'anima e rasserenato nello spirito. (I want to exit this holy place feeling purified in soul and reassured in spirit)."
20. Tomasulo, "*The Bicycle Thief*: A Re-Reading," 11. These observations are credited to Andre Bazin.
21. Franco Fortini, "*Ladri di biciclette* (1949)," in *Dieci inverni, 1947–1959: Contributi a un discorso socialista* (Milan: Feltrinelli, 1958), 128–131. Also Sitney, *Vital Crisis in Italian Cinema*, 96.

22. Peter Bondanella, *Italian Cinema from Neorealism to the Present* (New York: Continuum, 1995), 61. Also Tomasulo, "*The Bicycle Thief: A Re-Reading*," 4, 11–12.

23. Franco Pecori, *De Sica. Il castoro cinema* (Florence: La nuova Italia, 1980), 21.

24. Jacqueline Reich, "Reading, Writing, and Rebellion: Collectivity, Specularity, and Sexuality in the Italian Schoolgirl Comedy, 1934–43," in Robin Pickering-Iazzi, ed., *Mothers of Invention Women, Italian Fascism and Culture* (Minneapolis: Minnesota University Press, 1995), 220–251.

25. Marcus, *Italian Film in the Light of Neorealism*, 75.

26. Tomasulo, "The Bicycle Thief: A Re-Reading," 9.

27. Ruffin, "La lingua del fascismo nel cinema," 118.

28. Bondanella, *Italian Cinema from Neorealism to the Present*, 60.

29. Duggan, *A Concise History of Italy*, 252.

30. Tomasulo, "*The Bicycle Thief:* A Re-Reading," 13.

31. Marcus, *Italian Film in the Light of Neorealism*, 70. Also Franco La Polla "La citta' e lo spazio," *Bianco e nero*, 36 (September–December 1975), 69.

5   The 1950s

1. Irene Bignardi, *Memorie Estorte a uno smemorato Vita di Gillo Pontecorvo* (Milan: Feltrinelli, 1999), 74.

2. Mereghetti, *Il Mereghetti Dizionario dei Film 2004*, 2594.

3. See Cook, *The Cinema Book*.

4. Casadio, *Il grigio e il nero*, 16.

5. Ibid.

6. Marga Cottino-Jones, *A Student's Guide to Italian Film* (Dubuque, Iowa: Kendall/Hunt Publishing, 1993), 51.

7. Brunetta, *Cent'anni di cinema italiano*, 436. Mario Sesti, *Tutto il cinema di Pietro Germi* (Milan: Baldini&Castoldi, 1997).

8. Carlo Salinari, "Il neorealismo," in Giampaolo Borghello, ed., *Letteratura e marxismo* (Milano: Zanichelli, 1978).

9. Carlo Celli, "Critical and Philosophical discussions regarding Italian Neo-Realism," *Romance Languages Annual*, VII, 1995, 222–226. Bazin, *What Is Cinema?* 37.

10. Antonio Gramsci, *Letters from Prison*, ed., Frank Rosengarten, trans. Raymond Rosenthal (New York: Columbia University Press, 1994).

11. Borghello, *Letteratura e marxismo*, 152.

12. E. Mancini, *Luchino Visconti: A Guide to References and Resources* (Boston: G.K. Hall, 1986); G. Nowell-Smith, *Luchino Visconti* (London, Secker & Warburg in association with the British Film Institute, 1967).

13. See P. Bondanella, *Federico Fellini, Essays in criticism* (New York: Oxford University Press, 1978); F. Fellini, *Fellini on Fellini* (New York : Delacorte Press/S. Lawrence, 1976); F. Fellini, *Fellini on Fellini*. trans. Isabel Quigley (Great Britain: Delacorte Press, 1976), 154. Guido Aristarco, *Cinema italiano romanzo e antiromanzo* (Milan: Il Seggiatore, 1961). Siegfried Kracauer, *Theory of Film* (New York: Oxford University Press, 1960), 270. Pier Paolo Pasolini in Peter Bondanella and Cristina degli Espositi, eds., *Perspectives on Fellini* (New York: MacMillan, 1993), 105.

14. See *La Strada, Federico Fellini, Director*, ed. P. Bondanella and M. Gieri (New Brunswick: Rutgers University Press, 1987). Peter Bondanella, *The Cinema of Federico Fellini* (Princeton, N.J.: Princeton University Press, 1992).

15. A. Banti, "Neo-realismo nel cinema italiano," *Paragone*, 1, 8 (August 1950), 22–32. Guido Aristarco, "*Ladri di biciclette*," *Cinema*, n.s., 7 (January 30, 1949), 220–222.

Guido Aristarco saw a decline in De Sica's film production after *Umberto D.* in 1952. See Guido Aristarco, "Zavattini e l'iternerario di Vittorio De Sica," *Cinema nuovo*, 23, 232 (November–December, 1974), 443–445. Fellini, *Fellini on Fellini*, 59.

16. Guido Aristarco, *Cinema italiano romanzo e antiromanzo* (Milan: Il Seggiatore, 1961). Siegfried Kracauer, *Theory of Film* (New York: Oxford University Press, 1960), 270.

17. Celli, "A Master Narrative in Italian Cinema?", 73–83.

18. See Fellini, *Fellini on Fellini*, 151.

19. "Federico Fellini's Anti-Intellectualism," *Romance Languages Annual*, 8 (1996), 168–171.

20. The origin of the term *maggiorata fisica* is from a line delivered by De Sica in *Altri tempi* (1951), an episodic film directed by Alessandro Blasetti. In the *Il processo di Frine* episode, Gina Lollobrigida portrays a woman who killed her mother-in-law and is absolved when the lawyer placed by De Sica convinces a jury of her worth and trustworthiness by using the term *maggiorata fisica* (physically buxom). Mereghetti, *Il Mereghetti Dizionario dei Film 2004*, 56.

21. Jon Stratton, *The Desirable Body: Cultural Fetishism and the Erotics of Consumption* (Urbana: University of Illinois Press, 2001), 49. This change was actually a wider phenomenon in Western cinema. After the war the Hollywood film industry featured such actresses as Marilyn Monroe and the corpulent Jane Russell in the *Outlaw* (begun in 1943 by Howard Hawks and completed by Howard Hughes for release in 1950 after passing censorship barriers).

22. William Arrowsmith, *Antonioni The Poet of Images*, edited and introduction by Ted Perry (New York: Oxford University Press, 1995). Michelangelo Antonioni, *The Architecture of Vision: Writings and Interviews on Cinema*, ed. Marga Cottino-Jones (New York: Marsilio, 1996).

23. See Arrowsmith, *Antonioni*.

6   The Early 1960s

1. Christopher Wagstaff, *Popular European Cinema*, ed., R. Dyer and G. Vincendeau (New York: Routledge, 1992), 250.

2. Emilio Cecchi, *America amara* (Florence: Sansoni, 1946).

3. These statistics and others are taken from the *Garzanti atlante storico* (Italy: Garzanti, 1982). See also Ginsborg, *A History of Contemporary Italy*.

4. See Ginsborg, *A History of Contemporary Italy*.

5. See Pierre Sorlin, *Italian National Cinema 1896–1996* (New York: Routeledge, 1996).

6. Wood, *Italian Cinema*, 150.

7. Renato Barilli and Angelo Guglielmi, *Gruppo 63: critica e teoria* (Torino: Testo & immagine, 2003).

8. Paola Agostini Del Sorbo, "1948–1998 I cinquant'anni di un eroe senza tempo," *Storia e dossier*, 21, 127 (May 1998), 65. Christopher Frayling, *Spaghetti Westerns: Cowboys and Europeans from Karl May to Sergio Leone* (London and New York: I.B. Tauris, 1998).

9. Landy, *Cinematic Uses of the Past*, 81.

10. "Cold War Subtexts in Sergio Leone's *Per un pugno di dollari/ Fistful of Dollars* (1964)," *Rivista di studi italiani*, June 2003, 412–420. Carlo Verdone, whose first feature *Un sacco bello* (1980) was produced by Leone, has stated that the villains in Leone's westerns, such as Mario Braga, actually portray the materialistic cynicism typical of the Roman character as it appears in the poetry of Belli.

11. Christopher Frayling, *Spaghetti Westerns: Cowboys and Europeans from Karl May to Sergio Leone* (London and New York: I.B. Tauris, 1998).

12. Ibid.

7 The Later 1960s

1. Bernardo Bertolucci, *Segnocinema*, Mag Giu 1994, 20.
2. See T. De Lauretis, "Fellini's 9½" in *Technologies of Gender: Essays on Theory, Film, and Fiction* (Bloomington: University of Indiana Press, 1987), 95–106; as well as T. De Lauretis, *Alice Doesn't: Feminism, Semiotics, Cinema* (Bloomington: University of Indiana Press, 1984), 138. The seminal work on this subject is Laura Mulvey, "Visual Pleasure in Narrative Cinema," in *Visual and Other Pleasures* (Bloomington: Indiana University Press, 1989).
3. Carlo Celli, "Federico Fellini's Anti-Intellectualism," *Romance Languages Annual*, VIII, 1996, 168–171.
4. See Arrowsmith, *Antonioni. Poet of Images.*
5. *Vittorio De Sica Contemporary Perspectives*, ed., Howard Curle and Stephen Snyder, (Toronto: University of Toronto Press, 2000), 49.
6. Carlo Celli, "Review of Curle and Snyder, *Vittorio De Sica Contemporary Perspectives*," *Italica*, 79, 2 (Summer 2002), 283–285.
7. Bazin, *What Is Cinema?*
8. See the following studies on Pasolini: Beverly Allen, ed., *Pier Paolo Pasolini: The Poestics of Heresy* (Saratoga: Anma Libri, 1982); N. Green, *Pier Paolo Pasolini: Cinema as Heresy* (Princeton: Princeton University Press, 1990); L. Martellini, *Introduzione a Pasolini* (Roma: Laterza, 1989).
9. This article appeared in the magazine *Espresso*, June 16, 1968. See Pier Paolo Pasolini, *Scritti corsari* (Milan: Garzanti Editore, 1975).
10. Ibid.
11. See T.G. Kline, *Bertolucci's Dream Loom: A Psychoanalytic study of Cinema* (Amhert, Massachusetts, 1987); E. Ungari ed., *Bertolucci by Bertolucci* (London: Plexus, 1987); R. Burgoyne, *Bertolucci's 1900: A Narrative and Historical Analysis* (Detroit: Wayne State University Press, 1991); F. Casetti, *Bernardo Bertolucci* (Firenze: La Nuova Italia, 1976).
12. Pauline Kael, "Last Tango in Paris," in Roger Ebert, ed., *Roger Ebert's Book of Film* (New York: W.W. Norton, 1997), 307–313.
13. Mereghetti, *Il Mereghetti Dizionario dei Film 2004*, 2462.

8 The 1970s

1. Ginsborg, *A History of Contemporary Italy*, 333.
2. Ibid., 361, 362.
3. Berlinguer published a series of articles in *Rinascita* in October 5, 9, 1973 entitled "Riflessioni sull'Italia dopo i fatti di Cile," which has been defined as the beginning of the *Compromesso storico* for their invitation to seek common ground with the DC and prevent a further slide toward authoritarianism by the liberal pro-American parties.
4. See Aldo Grasso, *Storia della televisione* (Rome: Garzanti 1992).
5. "Sono incazzato, perché non lo so, Per fatti mia, Sono incazzato con i parenti, sono incazzato coi conoscenti, Sono incazzato, sono aggressivo, sono incazzato, se trovo il prete lo mangio vivo. *I'm pissed off I don't know why, it suits me, I'm pissed off at my relatives, I'm pissed off at everyone I know, I'm pissed off I want to fight I'm pissed off if I find a priest I'll eat him alive*"; Roberto Benigni, *Quando Benigni ruppe il video* (Torino: Nuova ERI), 22.

6. Geoffrey Nowell-Smith, *The Companion to Italian Cinema* (London: BFI, 1996), 162–163.

7. Massimo Martinelli, *Benigni Roberto di Luigi fu Remigio* (Milan: Leonardo Arte, 1997), 59; Carlo Celli, *The Divine Comic: The Cinema of Roberto Benigni* (Maryland: Scarecrow, 2001).

8. The immediate relevance of recent history was also a factor in the development of neo-realism. *Open City* (1945) has been mentioned as an early example of the *instant movie* since it offers a version of events of the Nazi occupation of Rome from 1943 to 1944 with references to the *fosse ardeatine* massacre.

9. Stuart Klawans, "Lessons of the Pentagon's Favorite Training Film," *The New York Times*, January 4, 2004, 26.

10. See Carlo Celli, *Gillo Pontecorvo: From Resistance to Terrorism* (Lanham, Maryland: Scarecrow Press, 2005).

11. Ibid., vii.

12. Gianfranco Casadio, *Col cuore in gola: assassini, ladri e poliziotti nel cinema italiano dal 1930 ad oggi* (Ravenna: A. Longo, 2002).

13. Mauro Manicotti, *La resistenza nel cinema italiano 1945/1995* (Torino: Istituto Storico della Resistenza in Liguria, 1995), 322.

14. Fellini has a tendency to mythologize about his past as demonstrated in Tullio Kezich's biography, *Fellini* (Milan: Camunia, 1987.) Nevertheless Fellini received a typical education in the Fascist school system in Rimini. He also maintains that he attended an *asilo* run by the nuns of San Vincenzo, who gave him a start in Catholic education. See also Federico Fellini, *Fare un film* (Turin: Einaudi, 1980), 16.

15. Celli, "Federico Fellini's Anti-Intellectualism," 168–171.

9   1980s and 1990s: A Changing Society

1. Wood, *Italian Cinema*, 150.

2. Bondanella, *The Cinema of Federico Fellini*, 327–333.

3. Ibid.

4. For an Anglo-American perspective on the southern Italian question see Robert Putnam, *Making Democracy Work: Civic Traditions in Modern Italy* (Princeton: Princeton University Press, 1997).

5. Carlo Celli, "The Nostalgia Current in the Italian Cinema," in Antonio Vitti, ed., *Incontri con il cinema italiano* (Caltanisetta: Salvatore Sciascia Editore, 2003), 277–288.

6. See Celli, *The Divine Cornic: The Cinema of Roberto Benigni.*

7. Colin McCabe, "*Life Is Beautiful* (review)," *Sight & Sound*, 9, 2 (February 1999), 46.

8. See Alain Kinkielkraut, *Une voix vient de l'autre rive* (Paris: Gallimard, 1999).

9. See Jean Michel Frodon, *La projection nationale: cinema et nation* (Paris: O. Jacob, 1998). See also Elio Girlanda "Il cinema delle nazioni," in *Gillo Pontecorvo. La dittatura della verità* (Assisi: ANNCI, 1998). See Gary Wills, *John Wayne's America* (New York: Simon and Schuster, 1993). Marcia Landy, *Italian Film* (Cambridge: Cambridge UP, 2000), 120. Carlo Celli, *The Divine Comic: The Cinema of Roberto Benigni* (Lantham, Md.: Scarecrow, 2001).

10. Roberto Benigni and Vincenzo Cerami, *La vita è bella* (Milano: Einaudi, 1998), 172.

11. Vincenzo Cerami, *Consigli a un giovane autore* (Torino: Einaudi, 1996), 15.

12. Andrea Cosentino, *La scena dell'osceno alle radici della drammaturgia di Roberto Benigni* (Rome: Oradek, 1998).

13. Carlo Celli, "Preface," in Grace Russo Bullaro, ed., *Beyond Life is Beautiful: Comedy and Tragedy in the Cinema of Roberto Benigni* (Leicester, England: Troubadour Publishing Ltd., 2004), 11–13.

10   The Next Millennium

1. Paul Ginsborg, *Italy and Its Discontents: Family, Civil Society, State, 1980–2001* (New York: Palgrave Macmillan, 2003).
2. Ibid. Regarding the recent tendency to delay adulthood in Italy see Paolo Bianchi, *Avere 30 anni e vivere con la mamma* (Milano: Bietti Società, 1997). Francesco M. Cataluccio, *Immaturità. La malattia del nostro tempo* (Torino: Einaudi, 2005).
3. Bianchi, *Avere 30 anni e vivere con la mamma.* Cataluccio, *Immaturità. La malattia del nostro tempo.*
4. Silvio Soldini and Doriana Leondeff, *Pane e tulipani La sceneggiatura e protagonisti, le immagini del film dell'anno,* ed. Roberto Ferrucci (Venice: Marsilio, 2000).

Appendices

1. Timothy Corrigan, *A short guide to writing about film* (New York : Pearson/Longman, 2004).
2. David Bordwell, Kristin Thompson, *Film art: an introduction* (Boston : McGraw-Hill, 2004); Louis D. Giannetti, *Understanding movies* (Upper Saddle River, NJ : Prentice Hall, 2002).
3. Vijay Mishra, "Towards a Theoretical Critique of Bombay Cinema. 133–144, Mishra, Vijay *Bollywood cinema : temples of desire* (New York :Routledge, 2002).
4. Carlo Celli, "A Master Narrative in Italian Cinema?" *Italica,* vol. 81:1, 2004, 73–83.
5. See for example, Arthur Pontynen, *For the Love of Beauty Art History and the Moral Foundation of Aesthetic Judgement.* (New Jersey: Transaction, 2005).
6. Giorgio Vasari, *The great masters : Giotto, Botticelli, Leonardo, Raphael, Michelangelo, Titian.* Trans. Gaston Du C. de Vere; Ed. Michael Sonino, (New York : Macmillan Pub. Co., 1986).
7. André Bazin, *What is Cinema? II* (Berkeley: University of California Press, 1971)
8. Pam Cook, *The Cinema Book* (London: British Film Institute Publishing, 1999); Leo Braudy, Marshall Cohen Ed. *Film theory and criticism: introductory readings* (New York: Oxford University Press, 1999); Robert Stam, Toby Miller Ed. *Film and theory: an anthology* (Malden, Mass.: Blackwell Publishers, 2000); Francesco Casetti, *Teorie del cinema 1945–1990* (Milan: Bompiani, 1994); Peter Wollen, *Paris Hollywood Writings on Film* (New York: Verso, 2002).
9. Laura Mulvey, *Visual and other pleasures* (Bloomington: Indiana University Press, 1989).
10. Gian Piero Brunetta, *Guida alla storia del cinema italiano*: 1905–2003 (Turin: Einaudi, 2003). Rick Altman, *Film/Genre* London: BFI Publishing, 1999.
11. Data is given for Italian and co production films only in the year of their first release. Data was compiled from several often conflicting sources: Gianni Rondolino Ed. *Catalogo Bolaffi del cinema italiano tutti i film dal 1945 al 1955,* 3 vols. (Torino: Giulio Bolaffi Editore, 1979); Casadio, Gianfranco *Adultere, fedifraghe, innocenti: la donna del "neorealismo popolare" nel cinema italiano degli anni Cinquanta.* Ravenna: Longo, 1990. Maurizio Baroni, *Platea in piedi 1945–1978,* Sasso Marconi (Bologna): Bolelli, 1995);

A.G.I.S Associazione Generale Italiana dello Spettacolo, *Catalogo generale dei film italiani dal 1956 al 1965* (Rome: AGIS, 1965). A.G.I.S Associazione Generale Italiana dello Spettacolo, *Catalogo generale dei film italiani dal 1965 al 1978* (Rome: AGIS, 1978). The *Borsa Film* lists in the *Giornale dello spettacolo* and the Italian yearly box office in the August issues of *Ciak* (1985–2005). The authors can provide no assurance for the reliability of these data, particularly for the years 1945–1955. When available, data from AGIS was given precedence over other lists and films are listed only for the years in which they are released. Data from the *Catagolo Bolaffi del cinema italiano* provide receipts until 1952 and data from 1951–54 including receipts to 1965, figures also reproduced in Gianfranco Casadio, *Adultere, fedifraghe, innocenti: la donna del "neorealismo popolare" nel cinema italiano degli anni Cinquanta* (Ravenna: Longo, 1990), 24–27.

Data from 1978 to 2005 was compiled from several (at times contradictory) sources: the trade weekly *Il Giornale dello spettacolo Borsa film*; *Annuario del cinema italiano & audiovisivi. 1994–2005* (Roma: Centro di studi di cultura, promozione e difusione del cinema); ANICA, Associazione Nazionale Industrie Cinematografiche Audiovisive e Multimediali data for the years 2000–2005 from the internet site http://www.anica.it/rassegna/dati.htm. The authors can provide no assurance for the absolute scientific reliability of these data. Sources for this information include the Internet Movie Database, www.imdb.com.

Selected Bibliography

Altman, Rick. *Film/Genre*. London: BFI Publishing, 1999.

Antongini, Tom. *Vita segreta di Gabriele D'Annunzio*. Milan: Mondadori, 1938.

Aristarco, Guido. "Come si perpetua l'equivoco sul neorealismo di Zavattini," *Cinema Nuovo*, 29 (June 9–10, 1980).

——. *Cinema italiano romanzo e antiromanzo*. Milan: Il Seggiatore, 1961.

——. "*Ladri di biciclette*." *Cinema*, n.s., 7 (January 30, 1949), 220–222.

——. "Zavattini e l'iternerario di Vittorio De Sica." *Cinema Nuovo*, 23, 232 (November–December, 1974), 443–445.

Armes, Roy. *Patterns of Realism*. South Brunswick: A.S. Barnes, 1971.

Arrowsmith, William. *Antonioni: The Poet of Images*. Edited and introduction by Ted Perry. New York: Oxford University Press, 1995.

Baldelli, Pio. *Roberto Rossellini. I film 1936–72 e la filmografia nella completa analisi del cinema del grande regista*. Rome: La nuova sinistra, 1972.

——. *Cinema dell'ambiguità: Rossellini, De Sica, Zavattini, Fellini*. Rome: Samonà e Savelli, 1969.

——. *I Film di Luchino Visconti*. Manduria: Lacaitra, 1965.

Banti, A. "Neo-realismo nel cinema italiano." *Paragone* 1, 8 (August 1950), 22–32.

Barilli, Renato and Angelo Guglielmi. *Gruppo 63: critica e teoria*. Torino: Testo & immagine, 2003.

Baroni, Maurizio *Platea in piedi 1945–1958*. Sasso Marconi, Bologna: Bolelli, 1995.

Bazin, André. *What Is Cinema? II*. Berkeley: University of California Press, 1971.

Becker, Jared M. *Nationalism and Culture: Gabriele D'Annunzio and Italy after the Risorgimento*. New York: Peter Lang, 1994.

Benigni, Roberto and Vincenzo Cerami. *La vita è bella*. Milano: Einaudi, 1998.

Berlinguer, Enrico. "Riflessioni sull'Italia dopo i fatti di Cile." *Rinascita*, 5, 9 (October 1973).

Bertolucci, Bernardo. *Segnocinema*. Mag. Giu. 1994, 20.

Bianchi, Paolo. *Avere 30 anni e vivere con la mamma*. Milano: Bietti Società, 1997.

Black, Gregory D. *The Catholic Crusade against the Movies, 1940–1975*. New York: Cambridge University Press, 1998.

Bobbio, Norberto. "Lungo viaggio nel Novecento." *Corriere della sera* (May 15, 1997), 23.

Bondanella, Peter. "Three Neorealist Classics by Vittorio De Sica." *Cineaste*, 23, 1 (1997), 52–53.

——. *Italian Cinema from Neorealism to the Present*. New York: Continuum, 1995.

——. *The Films of Roberto Rossellini*. New York: Cambridge University Press, 1993.

——. *Perspectives on Fellini*. Ed. Peter Bondanella and Cristina degli Esposti. New York: MacMillan, 1993.

——. *The Cinema of Federico Fellini*. Princeton, N.J.: Princeton University Press, 1992.

——. "Neorealist Aesthetics and the Fantastic: The Machine to Kill People and Miracle in Milan." *Film Criticism*, 3, 24–29 (1979).

Bondanella, Peter. *Federico Fellini, Essays in Criticism*. New York: Oxford University Press, 1978.
——. *La Strada, Federico Fellini, Director*. Ed. P. Bondanella and M. Gieri. New Brunswick: Rutgers University Press, 1987.
Bordwell, David and Kristin Thompson. *Film Art: An Introduction*. Boston: McGraw-Hill, 2004.
Borghello, Giampaolo. *Letteratura e marxismo*. Bologna: Zanichelli, 1974.
Bragaglia, C. and A. Canziani. *La stagione neorealistica*. Bologna: Cooperativa libraria universitaria editrice, 1976.
Braudy, Leo and Marshall Cohen, eds. *Film Theory and Criticism: Introductory Readings*. New York: Oxford University Press, 1999.
Brunetta, Gian Piero *Cent'anni di cinema italiano 1905–2003*. Bari: Einaudi, 1991.
Brunette, P. *Roberto Rossellini*. Oxford: Oxford University Press, 1987.
Bruno, E. *R.R. Roberto Rossellini*. Roma: Bulzoni, 1979.
Burke, F. *Fellini: From Variety Lights to* La dolce vita. Boston: Twayne, 1984.
Camerini, Mario "Comment realise-t-on un film How to Make a Film." In Alberto Farassino, ed. *Mario Camerini*. Locarno: Editions Yellow Now, 1992.
Cammarosano, Angelo. *Lezioni di cultura fascista*. Ancona: Nacci, 1934.
Canziani, A. *Gli anni del neorealismo*. Florence: La nuova Italia, 1977.
Canziani, A. and G. Bragaglia. *La stagione neorealistica*. Bologna: Cooperativa Libraria Universitaria Editrice, 1976.
Cardillo, Massimo. *Il Duce in moviola Politica e divismo nei cinegiornali e documentari Luce*. Bari: Dedalo, 1982.
Cardullo, B. *What Is Neorealism? A Critical English-Language Bibliography of Italian Cinematic Neorealism*. Lanham, Md.: University Press of America, 1991.
Casadio, Gianfranco. *Col cuore in gola: assassini, ladri e poliziotti nel cinema italiano dal 1930 ad oggi*. Ravenna: A. Longo, 2002.
——. *Il grigio e il nero. Spettacolo e propaganda nel cinema italiano degli anni trenta 1931–1943*. Ravenna: Longo, 1989.
——. *Telefoni bianchi: realtà e finzione nella società e nel cinema italiano degli anni*. Ravenna: Longo, 1991.
Casetti, Francesco. *Teorie del cinema 1945–1990*. Milan: Bompiani, 1994.
Cataluccio, Francesco M. *Immaturità. La malattia del nostro tempo*. Torino: Einaudi, 2005.
Celli, Carlo. *Gillo Pontecorvo: From Resistance to Terrorism*. Lanham, Maryland: Scarecrow Press, 2005.
——. "A Master Narrative in Italian Cinema?" *Italica*, 81, 1 (2004), 73–83.
——. "Preface." *Beyond Life Is Beautiful: Comedy and Tragedy in the Cinema of Roberto Benigni*. Ed. Grace Russo Bullaro. Leicester, England: Troubadour Publishing Ltd, 2004.
——. "Cold War Subtexts in Sergio Leone's *Per un pugno di dollari/ Fistful of Dollars* 1964." *Rivista di studi italiani* (June 2003), 412–420.
——. "The Nostalgia Current in the Italian Cinema." In Antonio Vitti, ed. *Incontri con il cinema italiano*. Caltanisetta: Salvatore Sciascia Editore, 2003.
——. "Review of Howard Curle and S. Snyder, eds. *Vittorio De Sica Contemporary Perspectives*. University of Toronto Press, 2000." *Italica*, 79, 2 (Summer 2002), 283–285.
——. *The Divine Comic: The Cinema of Roberto Benigni*. Maryland: Scarecrow, 2001.
——. "The Legacy of Mario Camerini in Vittorio De Sica's *The Bicycle Thief* 1948." *Cinema Journal*, 40, 4 (2001), 3–17.
——. "A Lost De Sica Film—*La porta del cielo/ The Gate of Heaven* 1945." *Quarterly Review of Film & Video*, 18, 4 (2001), 361–370.
——. "Interview with Marcello Pezzetti." *Critical Inquiry*, 27 (Autumn 2000), 149–157.

——. "Alessandro Blasetti and Representations of Italian Fascism in the 1930s." *Italian Culture*, 16, 2 (1998), 99 –109.

——. "Italian Neorealism's Wartime Legacy: Roberto Rossellini's *Open City* and *Man of the Cross*." *Romance Languages Annual*, 10 (1998), 225–228.

——. "Federico Fellini's Anti-Intellectualism." *Romance Languages Annual*, 8 (1996), 168–171.

Cerami, Vincenzo. *Consigli a un giovane autore*. Torino: Einaudi, 1996.

Cerchi Usai, Paolo. In Gianni Rodolino. *Gabriele D'Annunzio grandezza e delirio nell'industria dello spettacolo*. Turin: Costa & Nolan, 1988.

Cerchi Usai, Paolo and Livio Iacob, eds. *I comici del muto italiano*. Genova: Cineteca D. W. Griffith, 1985.

Chitti, R.E. Lancia. *Dizionario del cinema italiano I film vol. 1 dal 1930 al 1944*. Rome; Gremese Editore, 1993.

Cook, Pam. *The Cinema Book*. New York: Pantheon Books, 1985.

Corrigan, Timothy. *A Short Guide to Writing about Film*. New York: Pearson/Longman, 2004.

Cosentino, Andrea. *La scena dell'osceno Alle radici della drammaturgia di Roberto Benigni*. Rome: Oradek, 1998.

Cottino Jones, Marga. *Michelangelo Antonioni, The Architecture of Vision: Writings and Interviews on Cinema*. New York: Marsilio, 1996.

——. *A Student's Guide to Italian Film*. Dubuque, Iowa: Kendall/Hunt Publishing, 1993.

Curle, Howard and Stephen Snyder, eds. *Vittorio De Sica Contemporary Perspectives*. Toronto: University of Toronto Press, 2000.

De Felice, Renzo. *Storia degli ebrei italiani sotto il fascismo*. Torino: Einaudi, 1961.

De Felice, Renzo and Luigi Coglia. *Storia fotografica del fascismo*. Rome: Laterza, 1982.

De Giusti, L. *I Film di Luchino Visconti*. Rome: Gremese, 1985.

De Lauretis, T. "Fellini's 9½." In *Technologies of Gender: Essays on Theory, Film, and Fiction*. Bloomington: University of Indiana Press, 1987.

——. *Alice Doesn't: Feminism, Semiotics, Cinema*. Bloomington: University of Indiana Press, 1984.

De la Serna-Lopez, Bego. "Europe the Creation of a Nation? A Comparative Analysis of Nation-Building." In J. Andrew, M. Crook, M. Waller, eds. *Why Europe? Problems of Culture and Identity*. New York: MacMillan, 2000.

De Sica, Vittorio. *La porta del cielo Memorie 19901–1952*. Rome: Avagliano Editore, 2004.

Del Sorbo, Paola Agostini. "1948–1998 I cinquant'anni di un eroe senza tempo." *Storia e dossier*, 21, 127 (May 1998), 65.

Di Giammateo, Fernaldo. *Dizionario del cinema italiano. Dall'inizio del secolo a oggi i film che hanno segnato la storia del nostro cinema*. Rome: Riuniti, 1995.

Doane, Mary Ann. *The Desire to Desire: The Woman's Film of the 1940's*. Bloomington: Indiana University Press, 1987.

Duggan, Christopher. *A Concise History of Italy*. Cambridge: Cambridge University Press, 1994.

Farassino, A. *Neorealismo. Cinema Italiano 1945–49*. Torino: EDT, 1989.

Fellini, Federico. *Fellini on Fellini*. Trans. Elizabeth Quigley. Great Britain: Delacorte Press, 1976.

Filippini, Massimo. *La tragedia di Cefalonia. Una verità scomoda*. Rome: IBN, 2004.

Fortini, Franco. "*Ladri di biciclette* 1949." In *Dieci inverni, 1947–1959: Contributi a un discorso socialista*. Milan: Feltrinelli, 1958.

Frayling, Christopher. *Spaghetti Westerns: Cowboys and Europeans from Karl May to Sergio Leone*. London and New York: I.B. Tauris, 1998.

Frodon, Jean Michel. *La projection nationale: cinema et nation*. Paris: O. Jacob, 1998.

Giannetti, Louis D. *Understanding Movies*. Upper Saddle River, N.J.: Prentice Hall, 2002.

Gibson, Mary. *Born to Crime: Cesare Lombroso and the Origins of Biological Criminology*. Westport, Conn.: Praeger, 2002.

——. *Garzanti atlante storico*. Milan: Garzanti, 1982.

Ginsborg, Paul. *A History of Contemporary Italy Society and Politics 1943–1998*. New York: Penguin, 1990.

Girlanda, Elio. *Italy and Its Discontents: Family, Civil Society, State, 1980–2001*. New York: Palgrave Macmillan, 2003.

——. "Il cinema delle nazioni." *Gillo Pontecorvo. La dittatura della verità*. Assisi: ANNCI, 1998.

Gramsci, Antonio. *Letters from Prison*. Ed. Frank Rosengarten. Trans. Raymond Rosenthal. New York: Columbia University Press, 1994.

Grasso, Aldo. *Storia della televisione*. Rome: Garzanti, 1992.

Guarner, J. *Roberto Rossellini*. New York: Praeger, 1981.

Hay, James. *Popular Film Culture in Fascist Italy*. Bloomington, Ind.: Indiana University Press, 1987.

Hibbert, Christopher. *Garibaldi and His Enemies: The Clash of Arms and Personalities in the Making of Italy*. Boston: Little, Brown, 1966.

Hovald, P. *Le Néoréalisme Italien et ses créateurs*. Paris: Cerf, 1959.

Hughes, H. Stuart. *The United States and Italy*. Cambridge, Mass.: Harvard University Press, 1979.

Jones, E. Michael. *Dionysious Rising. The Birth of Cultural Revolution out of the Spirit of Music*. San Francsico: Ignatius, 1994.

Kael, Pauline. "Last Tango in Paris." In Roger Ebert, ed. *Roger Ebert's Book of Film* New York: W.W. Norton, 1997.

Kezich, Tullio. *Fellini*. Milan: Camunia, 1987.

Kinkielkraut, Alain. *Une voix vient de l'autre rive*. Paris: Gallimard. 1999.

Klawans, Stuart. "Lessons of the Pentagon's Favorite Training Film." *The New York Times* (January 4, 2004), 26.

Kline, T.G. *Bertolucci's Dream Loom: A Psychoanalytic Study of Cinema*. Amherst: University of Massachusetts Press, 1987.

Kracauer, Siegfried. *The Mass Ornament: Weimer Essays*. Cambridge, Mass.: Harvard University Press, 1995.

——. *Theory of Film*. New York: Oxford University Press, 1960.

Landy, Marcia. *Italian Film*. Cambridge: Cambridge University Press, 2000.

——. *Cinematic Uses of the Past*. Minneapolis: Minnesota University Press, 1996.

La Polla, Franco. "La citta' e lo spazio." *Bianco e nero*, 36 (September–December), 1975.

LaPalombara, Joseph. *Democracy Italian Style*. New Haven: Yale University Press, 1987.

Laura, Ernesto G. and Filippo Cristiano. *Se sei vivo spara!: storie di pistoleri, banditi e bounty killers nel western all'italiana, 1942–1998*. Ravenna: Longo, 2004.

——. *Opera e cinema: la musica lirica nel cinema italiano dall'avvento del sonoro ad oggi*. Ravenna: Longo, 1995.

——. *Adultere, fedifraghe, innocenti: la donna del "neorealismo popolare" nel cinema italiano degli anni Cinquanta*. Ravenna: Longo, 1990.

Lephron, Pierre. *The Italian Cinema*. New York: Praeger, 1971.

Liehm, M. *Passion and Defiance: Film in Italy from 1942 to the Present*. Berkeley: University of California Press, 1984.

Limuti Emanuele and Bruno Aurelio. *Spie a Palermo. Dall'Ovra allo sbarco in Sicilia. Da Lucky Luciano ai missili di Cuba*. Italy: Lussografica, 2004.

Lintner, Valerio. "A Traveler's History of Italy." New York: Interlink Books, 1995.

Lonero, Emilio and Aldo Anziano. *La storia della Orbis- Universalia*. Turin: Effata' Editrice, 2004.

Lussu, Emilio. *Marcia su Roma e Dintorni*. Milan: Mondadori, 1976.

Lyttelton, Adrian. *The Seizure of Power: Fascism in Italy, 1919–1929*. New York: Routledge, 2004.

Mancini, Elaine. *Luchino Visconti: A Guide to References and Resources*. Boston: G.K. Hall, 1986.

Manicotti, Mauro. *La resistenza nel cinema italiano 1945/1995*. Torino: Istituto Storico della Resistenza in Liguria, 1995.

Marcus, Millicent. *Italian Film in the Light of Neorealism*. Princeton: Princeton University Press, 1986.

Martinelli, Massimo. *Benigni Roberto di Luigi fu Remigio*. Milan: Leonardo Arte, 1997.

Martinelli, Vittorio. *Il cinema muto italiano Bianco e Nero*. Numero Speciale, 1993.

McCabe, Colin. "*Life Is Beautiful* review." *Sight & Sound*, 9, 2 (February 1999), 46.

Mereghetti, Paolo. *Il Mereghetti Dizionario dei Film 2004*. Milan: Baldini Castoldi, 2003.

Michalczyk, John. *The Italian Political Filmmakers*. Rutherford: Fairleigh Dickinson Press, 1986.

Milanini, C. *Neorealismo, poetiche e polemiche*. Milano: Saggiatore, 1980.

Mishra, Vijay. "Towards a Theoretical Critique of Bombay Cinema." *Screen* 26, 3/4 (1985), 133–144.

Mulvey, Laura. *Visual and Other Pleasures*. Bloomington: Indiana University Press, 1989.

Nolte, Ernst. *Three Faces of Fascism*. New York: Signet, 1963.

Novelli, Cecilia Dau. "La famiglia come soggetto della ricostruzione sociale 1942–1949." In G. De Rosa, ed. *Cattolici, chiesa, resistenza*. Bologna: Il Mulino, 1997.

Nowell-Smith, G. *The Companion the Italian Cinema*. London: BFI, 1996.

———. *Luchino Visconti*. New York: London: Secker & Warburg in association with the British Film Institute, 1967.

Nuzzi, Paolo O. Iemma. *De Sica & Zavattini Parliamo tanto di noi De Sica and Zavattini Let's Talk about Us*. Rome: Editori riuniti, 1997.

Oliva, Gianni. *Profughi. Dalle foibe all'esodo: la tragedia degli italiani d'Istria, Fiume e Dalmazia*. Milan: Mondadori, 2005.

Pansa, Giampaolo. *Sconosciuto 1945*. Milan: Sperling & Kupfer, 2005.

Pasolini, Pier Paolo. *Scritti corsari*. Milan: Garzanti Editore, 1975.

Pecori, Franco. *De Sica. Il castoro cinema*. Florence: La nuova Italia, 1980.

Perry, T. "Roots of Neorealism." *Film Criticism*, 3, 3–7 (1979).

———. *Michelangelo Antonioni: A Guide to References and Resources*. Boston: G.K. Hall, 1986.

Piga, Francesco. *Il mito del superuomo in Nietzsche e D'Annunzio*. Florence; Vallecchi 1979.

Pontynen, Arthur. *For the Love of Beauty Art History and the Moral Foundation of Aesthetic Judgement*. New Jersey: Transaction, 2005.

Putnam, Robert. *Making Democracy Work: Civic Traditions in Modern Italy*. Princeton: Princeton University Press, 1997.

Reich, Wilhelm. *The Mass Psychology of Fascism*. Ed. Mary Higgins and C.M. Raphael. Trans. V.R. Carfagno. London: Souvenir, 1972.

Ricci, Steven. "Camerini et Hollywood Questions d'identité nationale." In Alberto Farassino, ed. Jacqueline Fumagalli, trans. *Mario Camerini*. Locarno: Editions Yellow Now, 1992.

Rizzi, Renzo. *Sperduto nel buio il cinema italiano e il suo tempo 1905–1930*. Bologna: Capelli, 1991.

Rocchio, Vincent. *Cinema of Anxiety: A Psychoanalysis of Italian Neorealism.* Austin: University of Texas Press, 1999.

Romano, Eileen. *Album di D'Annunzio.* Milan: Mondadori, 1990.

Rondolino, Gianni. *I giorni di Cabiria.* Turin: Linsdrau, 1993.

——. *Gabriele D'Annunzio grandezza e delirio nell'industria dello spettacolo.* Turin: Costa & Nolan, 1988.

——. *Roberto Rosselini.* Torino, UTET, 1985.

——. *Catalogo Bolaffi Catalogo Bolaffi del cinema italiano, 1945–65:* Torino: Bolaffi, 1965.

——. *Catalogo Bolaffi Catalogo Bolaffi del cinema italiano, 1966–1975:Tutti i film italiani degli ultimi dieci anni.* Torino: Bolaffi, 1975.

Rossellini, R. *Il mio metodo: scritti e interviste.* Venezia: Marsilio, 1987.

——. *My Method Writings and Interviews Roberto Rossellini.* Ed. Adriano Aprà. Trans. Annapaola Cagnogni. New York: Marsilio, 1995.

Ruffin, Valentina. "La lingua del fascismo nel cinema." In R. Renzi, G.L. Farinelli, and N. Mazzanti, eds. *Il cinema dei dittatori Mussolini, Stalin, Hitler.* Roma: Grafis, 1992.

Salinari' Carlo. "Il neorealismo." Giampaolo Borghello, ed. *Letteratura e marxismo.* Milano: Zanichelli, 1978.

Savio, Francesco. "Mario Camerini." Ullio Kezich, ed. *Cinecittà anni trenta: parlano 116 protagonisti del secondo cinema italiano 1930–1943.* Rome: Bulzoni, 1979.

Sesti, Mario. *Tutto il cinema di Pietro Germi.* Milan: Baldini & Castoldi, 1997.

Sitney, P. Adams. *Vital Crisis in Italian Cinema.* Austin: University of Texas Press, 1995.

Smith, Denis Mack. *Cavour.* New York: Knopf, 1985.

——. *Mussolini.* New York: Knopf, 1982.

——. *Mussolini's Roman Empire.* New York: Viking Press, 1976.

——. *Italy A Modern History.* Ann Arbor: University of Michigan Press, 1969.

Soldini, Silvio and Doriana Leondeff. *Pane e tulipani La sceneggiatura e protagonisti, le immagini del film dell'anno.* Ed. Roberto Ferrucci. Venice: Marsilio, 2000.

Sorlin, Pierre. *Italian National Cinema 1896–1996.* New York: Routeledge, 1996.

——. "Il Risorgimento italiano: 1860." In Gianfranco Miro Gori, ed. *La storia al cinema Ricostruzione del passato interpretazione del presente.* Rome: Bulzoni, 1994.

Spackman, Barbara. *Decadent Geneologies: The Rhetoric of Sickness from Baudelaire to D'Annunzio.* Ithaca: Cornell University Press, 1989.

Stam, Robert and Toby Miller, eds. *Film and Theory: An Anthology.* Malden, Mass.: Blackwell Publishers, 2000.

Stratton, Jon. *The Desirable Body: Cultural Fetishism and the Erotics of Consumption.* Urbana: University of Illinois Press, 2001.

Tinazzi, G. "L'Italia di Zavattini." *Bianco & Nero,* 44, 6–20 (April/June 1983).

Tomasulo, Frank P. "*The Bicycle Thief:* A Re-Reading." *Cinema Journal,* 21, 2 (Spring 1982).

Ungari, E. *Bertolucci by Bertolucci.* London: Plexus, 1987.

Vasari, Giorgio. *The Great Masters: Giotto, Botticelli, Leonardo, Raphael, Michelangelo, Titian.* Trans. Gaston Du C. de Vere. Ed. Michael Sonino. New York: Macmillan Pub. Co., 1986.

Verdone, Mario. "A Discussion of Neorealism." *Screen,* 14, 69–77 (1973/74).

——. *Bianco e Nero.* Anno 25 Luglio (August 1963).

——. "Pastrone ultimo incontro." *Bianco e Nero* (January 1961).

Vitti, Antonio. *Giuseppe De Santis and Postwar Italian cinema.* Toronto: University of Toronto Press, 1996.

Vottari, Giuseppe. *Storia d'Italia 1861–2001. Un sommario ragionato.* Milan: Alpha Test, 2004.

Wagstaff, Christopher. *Popular European Cinema*. Ed. R. Dyer and G. Vincendeau. New York: Routledge, 1992.

Wetterau, Bruce. *World History*. New York: Henry Holt, 1994.

Wills, Gary. *John Wayne's America*. New York: Simon and Schuster, 1993.

Wollen, Peter. *Paris Hollywood Writings on Film*. New York: Verso, 2002.

Wood, Mary P. *Italian Cinema*. New York: Berg, 2005.

Zavattini, Cesare. *Neorealismo, ecc.* Milano: Bompiani, 1979.

———. *Zavattini: Sequences from a Cinematic Life*. Englewood Cliffs: Prentice Hall, 1970.

Index